Shakespeare and Costume

Shakespeare and Costume

*Edited by Patricia Lennox
and Bella Mirabella*

Bloomsbury Arden Shakespeare
An imprint of Bloomsbury Publishing Plc

B L O O M S B U R Y
LONDON • OXFORD • NEW YORK • NEW DELHI • SYDNEY

Bloomsbury Arden Shakespeare

An imprint of Bloomsbury Publishing Plc

50 Bedford Square
London
WC1B 3DP
UK

1385 Broadway
New York
NY 10018
USA

www.bloomsbury.com

BLOOMSBURY, ARDEN SHAKESPEARE and the Diana logo are trademarks of Bloomsbury Publishing Plc

First published 2015
Paperback edition first published 2016

Editorial matter and selection © Patricia Lennox and Bella Mirabella, 2015

Lin, Erika T. "Popular Festivity and the Early Modern Stage: The Case of George a Greene." *Theatre Journal* 61:2 (2009), 271–297. © 2009 The John Hopkins University Press. Revised and reprinted with permission of John Hopkins University Press.

All rights reserved. No part of this publication may be reproduced or transmitted in any form or by any means, electronic or mechanical, including photocopying, recording, or any information storage or retrieval system, without prior permission in writing from the publishers.

No responsibility for loss caused to any individual or organization acting on or refraining from action as a result of the material in this publication can be accepted by Bloomsbury or the authors.

British Library Cataloguing-in-Publication Data
A catalogue record for this book is available from the British Library.

ISBN: HB: 978-1-472-52507-9
PB: 978-1-350-00447-4
ePDF: 978-1-472-53245-9
ePUb: 978-1-472-53250-3

Library of Congress Cataloging-in-Publication Data
A catalog record for this book is available from the Library of Congress

Typeset by RefineCatch Limited, Bungay, Suffolk

For Aaron, Rell and Quinn, and the memory of Theoni V. Aldredge, my first real costume designer.
Patricia Lennox

For my dear sister, Joyce.
Bella Mirabella

CONTENTS

Abbreviations ix
List of illustrations x
Acknowledgements xiii
List of contributors xiv

Introduction 1
Patricia Lennox and Bella Mirabella

Brief Overview: A Stage History of Shakespeare and Costume 9
Russell Jackson

PART I Dressing Shakespeare in His Own Time – Theatre, Fashion and Social Practice 21

'The Compass of a Lie'? Royal Clothing at Court and in the Plays of Shakespeare, 1598–1613 23
Maria Hayward

Suits of Green: Festive Livery on Shakespeare's Stage 47
Erika T. Lin

'Honest Clothes' in *The Merry Wives of Windsor* 63
Catherine Richardson

How to Do Things with Shoes   85
Natasha Korda

'Apparel oft Proclaims the Man': Dressing Othello on the English Renaissance Stage   105
Bella Mirabella

PART II Designing Shakespeare: Theatrical Practice and Costume   129

The Stylish Shepherd, or, What to Wear in *As You Like It*'s Forest of Arden   131
Russell Jackson

How Designers Helped Juliet's Nurse Reclaim Her Bawdy   157
Patricia Lennox

Shakespeare Stripped: Costuming Prisoner-of-war Entertainments and Cabaret   185
Kate Dorney

PART III Interviews with Contemporary Designers   205

The Designers   207
Jane Greenwood and Robert Morgan

Notes   225
Index   277

ILLUSTRATIONS

1 George Gower. The Plimpton 'Sieve' portrait of
   Queen Elizabeth I. Oil on panel, 1579. By
   permission of the Folger Shakespeare Library.   25

2 James in his robes and regalia from *James I. The
   workes of the most high and mightie prince, James by
   the grace of God, King of Great Britaine, France and
   Ireland, defender of the faith, etc*. London, 1616.
   By permission of the Folger Shakespeare Library.   32

3 Couple in fashionable clothing from *Royal, military
   and court costumes of the time of James I*. By
   permission of the Folger Shakespeare Library.   34

4a and b   Linen coif and forehead cloth, embroidered
   with linen thread, coif edged with bobbin lace,
   T.57-1947, © Victoria and Albert Museum,
   London.   75

5 Hans Holbein, Mrs Jane Small, formerly Mrs
   Pemberton, P.40&A-1935, © Victoria and Albert
   Museum, London.   82

6 Left slip-on shoe, with zigzag slashes across
   vamp and pinked patterning on heel, found in
   Museum of London Archaeology excavation of
   Rose Theatre. Length 20.5 cm. Photograph:
   Andy Chopping. By permission of Museum of
   London Archaeology.   86

7	Bottom view of Rose shoe, with double-soled, welted construction (treadsole missing) Photograph: Andy Chopping. By permission of Museum of London Archaeology.	87
8	Abd el-Ouahed ben Messaoud ben Mohammed Anoun, Moorish ambassador to Queen Elizabeth I, 1600, © The University of Birmingham Research and Cultural Collections. Artist: unknown.	107
9	Robert Dudley, First Earl of Leicester, © National Portrait Gallery, London. Artist: unknown.	113
10	Sir Walter Ralegh, © National Portrait Gallery, London. Artist unknown.	114
11	The Peacham Drawing, by permission of Marquess of Bath, Longleat House, Warminster, Wiltshire. Artist: Henry Peacham.	121
12	Mrs Stirling as a genteel Nurse in Henry Irving's production. *Illustrated Sporting and Dramatic News*, 15 April 1882. Courtesy of Patricia Lennox.	162
13	Isabel Thornton as Nurse with Gwen Ffrangcon-Davies as Juliet. Birmingham Repertory Company, design by Paul Shelving, 1922. By permission of the Sir Barry Jackson and Birmingham Repertory Theatre Archive, Library of Birmingham.	168
14	Edith Evans as Nurse, costume design by Motley. Hignett's cigarette card, *c.*1933–9, by permission of George Arendts Collection, the New York Public Library, Aston, Lenox and Tilden Foundation.	175

15 Edna May Oliver as Nurse looking for Romeo.
    MGM film, design by Oliver Messel, 1936, screen
    capture.   179

16 Design by Ronald Cobb for Macbeth showgirl in
    Bibliotheque floorshow at the Eve club (1960–70),
    S.716-1996, Theatre & Performance Department,
    Victoria & Albert Museum. © V&A Images.   199

17 Design by Ronald Cobb for Hamlet showgirl in
    Bibliotheque floorshow at the Eve club (1960–70),
    S.713-1996, Theatre & Performance Department,
    Victoria & Albert Museum. © V&A Images.   201

18 Jane Greenwood dresses Jan Miner for *The Merry
    Wives of Windsor* (1971) at the American
    Shakespeare Festival, Stratford, CT. Courtesy of
    Jane Greenwood.   213

19 Sketch by Jane Greenwood for *The Merry Wives of
    Windsor* (1971), Stratford, CT. Courtesy of Jane
    Greenwood.   214

20 Robert Morgan sketch for Maria in *Twelfth Night*.
    Courtesy of Robert Morgan.   219

ACKNOWLEDGEMENTS

This book began life as a Shakespeare Association of America conference seminar on Shakespeare and clothes; we wish to thank Lena Cowen Orlin and Bailey Yaeger of SAA for their help and encouragement at its inception. We would also like to thank Dean Susanne Wofford and New York University's Gallatin School as well as Gary Slapper, Director, New York University London, for their generous support. There are colleagues who have offered invaluable support and knowledge such as Nancy Selleck, Bianca Calabrese, Julie Crawford, Pamela Brown, Tanya Pollard, Natasha Korda, Barbara Hodgdon and Patricia Tatspaugh. Katherine Leech generously put us in contact with designers. Our splendid editor Margaret Bartley was patient and supportive throughout. Emily Hockley at Bloomsbury helped to speed things along. We would both like to thank our contributors for their wonderful work, and finally, Bella Mirabella wishes to thank her husband, Lennard Davis, for his enduring creativity, interest and support, and his ingenious way of getting right to the heart of the matter.

ABBREVIATIONS

AC	*Antony and Cleopatra*	MND	*A Midsummer Night's Dream*
AW	*All's Well That Ends Well*	MV	*The Merchant of Venice*
AYL	*As You Like It*	MW	*The Merry Wives of Windsor*
CE	*The Comedy of Errors*	Oth	*Othello*
Cor	*Coriolanus*	Per	*Pericles*
Cym	*Cymbeline*	PP	*The Passionate Pilgrim*
E3	*King Edward III*	PT	*The Phoenix and Turtle*
Ham	*Hamlet*	R2	*King Richard II*
1H4	*King Henry IV, Part 1*	R3	*King Richard III*
2H4	*King Henry IV, Part 2*	RJ	*Romeo and Juliet*
H5	*King Henry V*	Son	*Sonnets*
1H6	*King Henry VI, Part 1*	STM	*Sir Thomas More*
2H6	*King Henry VI, Part 2*	TC	*Troilus and Cressida*
3H6	*King Henry VI, Part 3*	Tem	*The Tempest*
H8	*King Henry VIII*	TGV	*The Two Gentlemen of Verona*
JC	*Julius Caesar*	Tim	*Timon of Athens*
KJ	*King John*	Tit	*Titus Andronicus*
KL	*King Lear*	TN	*Twelfth Night*
LC	*A Lover's Complaint*	TNK	*The Two Noble Kinsmen*
LLL	*Love's Labour's Lost*	TS	*The Taming of the Shrew*
Luc	*The Rape of Lucrece*	VA	*Venus and Adonis*
MA	*Much Ado about Nothing*	WT	*The Winter's Tale*
Mac	*Macbeth*		
MM	*Measure for Measure*		

CONTRIBUTORS

Kate Dorney is senior curator of Modern & Contemporary Performance at the Victoria & Albert Museum. She is a theatre historian with a particular interest in the role of institutions, including museums, libraries and archives, in shaping theatre practice and history. She has contributed to *Shakespeare Bulletin* and the *Cambridge World Shakespeare Encyclopedia*, and written on a number of areas of post-1945 theatre practice. She is also joint editor of the journal *Studies in Theatre & Performance* and the forthcoming journal *Studies in Costume and Performance*.

Jane Greenwood has been designing on Broadway for more than fifty years. She has designed over a dozen Shakespeare productions at the American Shakespeare Festival Theater in Stratford, CT, and in 2014 worked on her fifth Shakespeare in the Park for the Public Theater. Her awards include the 2014 Special Tony Award for Lifetime Achievement in the Theater, eighteen Tony nominations, the Irene Sharaff Lifetime Achievement Award, the Maharam Award for *Tartuffe*, the Lortel Awards for *Sylvia* and *Old Money*, and the Helen Hayes Life Achievement Award. Ms. Greenwood was inducted into the Theatre Hall of Fame in 2003. She has also taught at the Yale School of Drama since 1976.

Maria Hayward is Professor of Early Modern History at the University of Southampton. She works on material culture at the Tudor and Stuart courts with a special emphasis on textiles and clothing. Her books include *Dress at the Court of King Henry VIII* (2007), *Rich Apparel: Clothing and the Law in Henry VIII's England* (2009) and, edited with Philip Ward,

The Inventory of King Henry VIII: Vol. 2: Textiles and Dress (2012).

Russell Jackson is Allardyce Nicoll Professor of Drama at the University of Birmingham. He has worked as text adviser for film, theatre and radio productions of Shakespeare by Kenneth Branagh and Michael Grandage. Recent publications include *Shakespeare and the English Speaking Cinema* (2014), *Theatres on Film: how the Cinema Imagines the Stage* (2013), *Great Shakespeareans 16: Gielgud, Olivier, Ashcroft, Dench* (Bloomsbury Arden Shakespeare, 2013) (of which he is editor), *The Cambridge Companion to Shakespeare on Film* (2000; 2nd edition 2007) (of which he is editor) and *Shakespeare Films in the Making: Vision, Production and Reception* (2007).

Natasha Korda is Professor of English at Wesleyan University. Her research interests include early modern English dramatic literature and culture, theatre history, women's social, economic and legal history, and material and visual culture studies. She is author of *Labors Lost: Women's Work and the Early Modern English Stage* (2011) and *Shakespeare's Domestic Economies: Gender and Property in Early Modern England* (2002), and co-editor of two anthologies, *Working Subjects in Early Modern English Drama* (2011) and *Staged Properties in Early Modern English Drama* (2002).

Patricia Lennox is Global Lecturer at New York University and is the editor of *As You Like It* for the New Kittredge Shakespeare Series (2009). Her articles are included in *Shakespeare on Screen: Hamlet* (2011), *Shakespeare's Roman Plays on Screen* (2009), *Shakespeare Survey* (2008), *The Routledge Companion to Directors' Shakespeare* (2008), *North American Players of Shakespeare* (2007) and *Multicultural Shakespeare: Translations, Appropriations and Performance* (2007). Her reviews have appeared in *Shakespeare Bulletin* and the *Shakespeare Newsletter*.

Erika T. Lin is an Associate Professor of English at George Mason University. She is the author of *Shakespeare and the Materiality of Performance*, which won the 2013 David Bevington Award for Best New Book in Early Drama Studies. Her essays have appeared in *Theatre Journal, New Theatre Quarterly* and various edited collections. She is currently writing a book on seasonal festivities and commercial theatre, a project supported by an Andrew W. Mellon Long-Term Fellowship at the Folger Shakespeare Library.

Bella Mirabella, Associate Professor of Literature and Humanities at the Gallatin School, NYU, specializes in Renaissance studies, with a focus on drama, theatre, performance, fashion and gender. Some of her articles include 'Mute Rhetorics: Women, Dance, and the Gaze in Renaissance England', '"Quacking Delilahs": Female Mountebanks in Early Modern England and Italy', '"A Wording Poet": *Othello* among the Mountebanks' and '"In the Sight of all": Queen Elizabeth and the Dance of Diplomacy'. She is the editor of *Ornamentalism: the Art of Renaissance Accessories*, contributing the article '"Embellishing Herself with a Cloth": The Contradictory Life of the Handkerchief'.

Robert Morgan is Associate Artist at San Diego's Old Globe Theater. He has designed for Broadway and regional theatres throughout the United States, including the American Players Theater, the American Conservatory, the McCarter and the Kennedy Center. He has received two New York Drama Desk nominations for Best Costumes and twelve West Coast DramaLogue Awards.

Catherine Richardson is Reader in Renaissance Studies at the University of Kent. Her research focuses on the material experience of daily life in early modern England both onstage and offstage: on houses and furniture, and on the social, moral and personal significance of clothing. She is author of *Shakespeare and Material Culture* (2011) and *Domestic Life* *and Domestic Tragedy: The Material Life of the Household* (2006) and editor of *Clothing Culture 1350–1650* (2004), (with Chris Dyer) *William Dugdale, Historian, 1605–86: His Life, His Writings and His County* (2009) and *Everyday Objects: Medieval and Early Modern Material Culture and its Meanings* (2009) with Tara Hamling, with whom she is writing *A Day at Home in Early Modern England. The Materiality of Domestic Life, 1500–1700* (Yale: 2015).

Introduction

Patricia Lennox and Bella Mirabella

Shakespeare and Costume explores the ways in which costumes have been a feature in the long history of Shakespearean performance. The assumptions that underlie the chapters in this volume include: the fact that costumes have been and still are an integral part of any stage production, that costumes reflect theatrical practices of their time, that costumes are influenced – though in varying degrees – by contemporary clothing; that the choice of costume is shaped by the play but also by the preferences of the players and by practical considerations of the production; and that an analysis of the meaning of costume deepens an understanding of the play and the performance. Performance is a process of simulation, of make-believe, of storytelling and impersonation. And performance is always costumed. The costume is an integral element that helps the actor cross the liminal space between 'real life' and impersonation. As Aoife Monks points out, 'Costumes contain the power to clothe, to shape identity and form bodies'; they 'reconfigure what the actor is made of'.[1]

From the Ancient Greek theatre (possibly even before) until contemporary times, the audience sees on stage performers who are specifically apparelled for the occasion. When performers 'dress for the part', they engage in an essential element of the ritual of performance. Whether the dress is simple black trousers and white tee shirt or an elaborate reproduction of an Elizabethan gown, it is still a costume. Costume is a disguise which transforms the actor, as it did on Shakespeare's stage when men cross-dressed and changed into women. Costume is a visualization of someone other than the actor who wears it, and the clothing is chosen or designed for this particular theatrical moment. The history of Shakespeare and costume is a palimpsest of these moments.

In everyday life, clothing serves many purposes: it provides protection, satisfies a need for adornment, communicates identity and has the potential to be transformative. Stage costume does the same for the play's characters – and for the actor. Actors say they never fully get the character until they see themselves in the costume and make-up. For some actors even a single detail – the right boots, for example – is enough to make a character click. In Michael Blakemore's novel *Next Season*, based on his own acting experience with the Royal Shakespeare Company, a young actor in his first important role obsesses about creating his character's 'look' that includes a false nose, a wig, the right pair of spectacles and a costume pieced together from 'rags of the past' in the theatre's storeroom. The first time he sees himself made up and costumed there is a revelation, an aspect of the character's personality 'that would otherwise have remained captive and mute' was being 'granted freedom'.[2] Like Blakemore's protagonist, this is a common experience actors have with their costumes. In the documentary *Rehearsing Hamlet*, the first time the actor Kathleen Widdoes tries on her costume for Gertrude, she exclaims with delight: 'Now my work is done'.[3]

It has taken a long time for costumes and the way they work in Shakespeare productions to finally receive the attention given to other areas of Shakespeare studies. It is only in the past thirty years that studies of performance history have begun to consider the importance of costumes as an interpretative element that includes but goes beyond the production's design aesthetic. Compared to current publications, earlier works on the topic can be disappointing. For example, although its title is promising, M. Channing Linthicum's 1963 *Costume in the Drama of Shakespeare and his Contemporaries*[4] looks at the physical elements of costumes such as dyeing or use of leather, without considering the significance of the garments and how they would have been used in performance. The first step toward giving currency to the role costumes play within the production was in 1992, with Jean MacIntyre's *Costumes and Scripts in the Elizabethan Theatres*, which addressed the fact that critical and historical studies, even those dealing with acting companies and performance, still did 'not concern themselves as often as they should with how the actors were to look in performance'. MacIntyre points out that even when meticulous attention is paid to the imagery of clothing in Shakespeare texts, it 'rarely recognizes that clothing language may refer to the actor's costumes'.[5] More than twenty years later, spurred by new approaches in performance studies, theatre history, research in material culture and dress history, a rich discussion and exploration of the many aspects of costume in Shakespeare performance has begun through the writings of, among others, Barbara Hodgdon, Carol Chillington Rutter, Bridget Escolme, Jenny Tiramani, Farah Karim-Cooper, Aoife Monks and the contributors to this volume.[6]

This conversation has been particularly inspired by recent explorations in the importance of material culture, especially dress and fashion within early modern studies. For example, Ann Rosalind Jones and Peter Stallybrass's *Renaissance Clothing in the Materials of Memory* (2000), which in many ways initiated the current interest, argues that the construction and exchange of clothing is central to the very construction of Renaissance culture; Jones and Stallybrass analyse clothing from a multidisciplinary perspective, including its role in

English theatre. Other books on Renaissance clothing from an international perspective have followed such as Ann Rosalind Jones and Margaret F. Rosenthal's 2008 translation of Cesare Vecellio's 1590s *Habiti Antichi et Moderni, The Clothing of the Renaissance World*, which offers written and visual portrayals of attire for all of Europe, as well as Asia, Africa and America in the 1590s. Susan Vincent's 2003 *Dressing the Elite* examines the clothing practices of the English aristocracy, and Catherine Richardson's *Shakespeare and Material Culture* and Natasha Korda's *Labor's Lost: Women's Work and the Early Modern English Stage* apply a knowledge of material culture and attire to an analysis of theatre. These are only the smallest sample of the many texts that have contributed to an understanding of the cultural and social practices embedded in attire and costume.[7] Such perspectives have granted scholars and historians, as well as theatre and design practitioners, a deeper understanding of the plays themselves and, as Jean McIntyre has observed, 'how clothing language may refer to the actor's costumes'. *Shakespeare and Costume* combines these two major strains of scholarship – theatre, performance, and costume history with material culture studies applied to Shakespeare's plays – all within an interdisciplinary conversation.

Although all of the chapters here are linked in various ways, the volume is divided into four parts. The introductory material includes Russell Jackson's 'Overview', which offers readers a map of the key sites in the history of costumes in Shakespeare productions. The contributors' chapters are grouped in three parts: early modern material culture and English theatre with a focus on Shakespeare in Part I; performance history in Part II; and first-hand experience designing Shakespeare productions in Part III.

In Part I, 'Dressing Shakespeare in His Own Time – Theatre, Fashion, and Social Practice', the writers' starting point is that, although little is known about the costumes worn on Shakespeare's stage, we do know they functioned to convey social and economic class, power and status, age, possibly geographic connections and definitely gender. Focusing on the historical realities and the social practices of dress and attire, these chapters work with the internal evidence of clothing in the plays, current studies in material culture with a focus on dress, as well as early-modern non-theatrical documents that add to the information available in, for example, Henry Peacham's drawing and Philip Henslowe's *Diary*. The writers explore the connections between Shakespeare's plays and royal robes, middle-class linens, livery, doublet and hose, and the evidence provided by a single shoe.

The section begins with Maria Hayward's '"The Compass of a Lie"? Royal Clothing at Court and in the Plays of Shakespeare, 1598–1613', which looks at how Elizabeth I and James I fashioned their royal selves through their clothing and deportment, cognizant that they were on a political stage. Drawing on material from Henslowe's *Diary*, the revels' accounts and actors' wills, Hayward gives an account of what the monarchs wore, while considering how Shakespeare used language to create an image of royalty for his audiences in comparison with Elizabeth's and James' royal wardrobes. Hayward asserts that all displays of royal power, whether at court or in the theatre, were 'counterfeit', a lie, at some level, as the Puritan writer Stephen Gosson claimed.

Erika Lin's 'Suits of Green: Festive Livery on Shakespeare's Stage' considers festive livery practices within aristocratic homes, the familiarity with this practice among audiences as well as the influence of these festivities in the construction of dramatic narratives in the professional playhouses. Focusing on Shakespeare's *The Merchant of Venice*, Lin examines the significance of livery within the play as a sign of identity and affiliation. Lin also examines livery as a means of payment, for example, with regard to the clothes the servant Lancelot receives when he switches his affiliation from Shylock to Bassanio's household.

Catherine Richardson's '"Honest Clothes" in *The Merry Wives of Windsor*' focuses on the clothing of the gentry and argues that dress signifies reputation, shame, honest, and dishonest behaviour in the play by focusing on two types of clothing – head coverings and linens – around which male and female reputations are negotiated. Richardson explores the ways that clothing constructs gender and establishes morality in the play, through an examination of the significance of kerchiefs and starched and pinned linens, as opposed to dirty, disorderly linen.

In 'How to Do Things with Shoes', Natasha Korda reminds us how deeply early modern English theatre physically encountered and interacted with the material necessities of the stage through the costume accessory of shoes. The focus of this chapter is legs, the feet that trod that stage and the shoes that covered those feet. Korda traces the footsteps of actors through early modern play-texts and other documents of theatre history in an effort to bring to life the shoe, not only as a historical and material object of attire, but as an object of performance.

In '"Apparel oft Proclaims the Man": Dressing Othello on the English Renaissance Stage', Bella Mirabella speculates on how Othello might have been dressed on stage and what this might tell us about his character and his tragic choices. Focusing on the idea of the hard clothing of constraint, embodied in the English doublet and hose in comparison to the soft clothing of concealment captured in the 1600 painting of the Moorish Ambassador, Mirabella examines three possible ways of dressing Othello based on conflicting concepts of masculinity.

The chapters in Part II, 'Designing Shakespeare: Theatrical Practice and Costume', move forward in time to discuss aspects of costumes in Shakespeare productions from the re-opening of the London theatres in 1660 to the twenty-first century. Drawing on documentary evidence in designers' renderings, illustrations in periodicals, paintings, photographs, newspaper reviews and actors' memoirs, the writers explore costume designs in specific Shakespeare productions. Rosalind's cross-dressed disguise as Ganymede is the focus of Russell Jackson's 'The Stylish Shepherd, or, What to Wear in *As You Like It*'s Forest of Arden'. Jackson discusses the challenges faced by both male and female actors in the role with an emphasis on productions from the late nineteenth century to the present and on the numerous factors that affect costuming the role.

In 'How Designers Helped Juliet's Nurse Reclaim Her Bawdy', Patricia Lennox examines five productions of *Romeo and Juliet* between 1922 and 1936, and the designers who invented the now iconic image of the Nurse dressed in a medieval wimple and starched headdress. These productions reinstated the Nurse's earthy lines and were instrumental in rescuing her from the nineteenth-century stage tradition that dressed the Nurse as a genteel elderly lady. Very different types of entertainment presenting Shakespeare's works are the focus of Kate Dorney's 'Shakespeare Stripped: Costuming Prisoner-of-war Entertainments and Cabaret', a discussion of two sets of costume designs in the Victoria & Albert Museum's Theatre and Performance collection: Ronald Searle's sketches for a 1944 revue, *Hamlet Goes Hollywood* (staged when Searle was a prisoner of war in Shanghai) and Ronald Cobb's design renderings for showgirls' skimpy costumes in a Shakespeare-themed cabaret number in London (1960–70).

In Part III, 'Interviews with Contemporary Designers', veteran costume designers Jane Greenwood and Robert Morgan discuss their involvement with Shakespeare productions in England, Canada and the United States. Over the decades they have dressed Shakespeare's characters in a panoply of historical and ahistorical periods, worked with large and small budgets, and coped with various directors' interpretations and requirements, as well as fluctuating theatrical fashions. Their interviews illuminate how costumes come to the stage and the wide range of theatrical interpretations revealed in the choice and construction of the costumes.

Although the volume is divided into separate parts, the chapters are not meant to be read as units distinct from each other, but as a conversation in which many voices speak, talking about clothes, theatre and performance in everyday life and on the stage. The connection among all the pieces is the arc of 400 years of theatrical production, a layering where tradition and invention speak to each other backstage, onstage, to the actors and to the audience. Readers are encouraged to think about the links that run through all the chapters. For example, in trying to imagine how actors were dressed during Shakespeare's time, we see that costume choices, such as a handkerchief, starched linens, headgear, shoes, royal robes or livery, were equally important to the meaning and production of a play then as now. Costumes in modern stagings of Shakespeare embrace an infinite variety that includes at one end of the spectrum the reconstruction of Elizabethan dress in Original Practice productions at the reconstructed Globe in London and at the other end the scraps of clothing used for *Hamlet* in a prisoner-of-war camp in Singapore. Underlying the history of Shakespeare costumes are all the choices made by the playwright, designers, directors and actors. A part of those choices is a knowledge of other productions that can be copied, adapted, emulated or rejected but remain as prompts, just as Rosalinds, decade after decade, have drawn on previous costume traditions, tweaked them and strode forth onto the stage in Ganymede's boots.

Brief Overview: A Stage History of Shakespeare and Costume

Russell Jackson

In an overview of the history of Shakespearean costume on the English-speaking stage, a threefold pattern can be said to emerge. The journey leads from eclecticism, through a period of historically 'authentic' sets and costumes corresponding to the place and time represented in the plays, and back into a freer, happier world of choosing your period for interpretative reasons – though with an understanding of the theatre culture of Shakespeare's own time.[1] With what might be described as 'regional variations', the same might be said of costuming for the plays in North America, Australasia and Continental Europe. The influence and sometimes participation of designers from Germany, France and Russia makes itself felt in the early twentieth century, both by direct exposure to such productions as those of Diaghilev's *Ballets Russes* and the many publications that disseminated the practices of what was often referred to as 'The New Movement in the Theatre' in the years between

1900 and 1930.[2] Theorists and practitioners such as Adolphe Appia and Edward Gordon Craig moved towards various kinds of stylization, inspired by the example of non-representational theatrical traditions in earlier periods and outside Europe. With this came a move towards greater freedom in costume design, away from 'realistic' recreations of historical periods and allowing for symbolism and the simplification of detail. The two volumes of *Twentieth Century Stage Decoration* by Walter René Fuerst and Samuel J. Hume, published by Knopf in London and New York in 1923, give a comprehensive and influential account, with many illustrations, of the new ideas and practices. Collections of production photos published by *The Studio*, and handbooks like Doris Zinkeisen's *Designing for the Stage* (1938) disseminated the 'new theatre's' principles widely to amateur as well as professional theatre-makers on both sides of the Atlantic.

Underlying this series of shifts over three centuries, towards and then away from historical realism, are some basic principles with regard to costume as a vital and dynamic element of the sign-systems of the theatre, notably by virtue of its multivalence. This is a quality that costume shares with other factors, such as the doors in Shakespeare's theatres that can sometimes be doors, or at others merely ways onto the stage, and the pillars that can be trees, columns in an imagined building in another time and place, or simply what they are: parts of the structure sustaining those (real/metaphorical) heavens.

Costumes, in one scheme of the semiotics of the theatre, constitute a medial term: in Keir Elam's representation of the pattern, they participate in theatrical codes ('rules for theatrical costume and its connotations'), cultural codes ('vestimentary codes') and dramatic subcodes ('rules for interpreting costume in terms of status, character, etc.').[3] The traffic between these codes is obvious, and the last can be read only by reference on the part of the audience to the other two. At the same time, costume should be regarded not as a decoration but as an essential part of what Bertolt Brecht describes as the *gestus*, defined succinctly by David Edgar as 'an emblem around and through which the action of the scene unfolds'.[4] Roland Barthes, profoundly influenced by Brecht, insisted in an article published in 1955 that costume's primary function is intellectual rather than pictorial or emotional. Even without this emphasis the vitality and active nature of stage costume should be acknowledged.[5] Costume is a major influence in the audience's negotiation between the 'near' and the 'distant'; it is an important binary that can also be invoked to embrace the nearness to a particular kind of theatrical experience (near to us) that comes from the frequency with which we are exposed to it.[6] Costume sits on the bodies of living, sentient beings whose animation of the fiction is more vivid than the surroundings in which we see and hear them. Costume makes them like and, at the same time, unlike us. Part of this negotiation is that both the concepts of 'clothing' (what gets worn) and 'costume' (what is put on for a purpose), are shadowed by the influence of 'fashion'. The last of these can be both theatrical fashion (how plays usually get performed in a given era) and fashion as a conscious pursuit of aesthetic goals in clothing, both in our own time and in that represented.

'Modern dress', although often invoked, is too vague a concept to be useful, though in some early cases of the transposition of Shakespeare to the modern day the element of surprise at familiarly distant plays being brought closer was both disturbing and exhilarating: in England the Birmingham Repertory Theatre company's 'Hamlet in plus-fours' (in America, knickerbockers) in 1925 was not the first of its director's ventures into this mode, but the canonical significance of the play gave it more impact than the less controversial *Cymbeline* that had preceded it two years earlier. The effect here, and with other productions directed by H.K. Ayliff and designed by Paul Shelving, was not merely to demonstrate that (in Ayliff's words) 'Shakespeare was a modern author', but to create new and unfamiliar worlds that, partly because the language remained that of Shakespeare, were and were not the audience's own.[7] In fact the clothes of no given period can be regarded simply as an unmediated and identifiable constant.

In 1999 I was involved in the filming of *Love's Labour's Lost*, directed by Kenneth Branagh. Our film was set in the late 1930s, as was Neil Jordan's production of Graham Greene's *The End of the Affair*, with which our costume department shared a building at Shepperton Studios. Both costume departments used the walls of their respective sides of the corridor between them to post up the references for their work: facing each other were two distinct versions of the same period, authentic in important respects, but selective according to the overall design concept of each film. There never was and, in retrospect, never can be one '1930s', and this was a visual demonstration of the fact. The costumes for Branagh's musical comedy had a festive, in some cases gently parodic aesthetic, although based on meticulous historical research, while those across the way were sombre, as fitted the theme of novel and film. So many signifiers, so many codings, so much pleasure. The history of costuming in general, and for Shakespeare's plays in particular, is that of a series of different kinds of pleasure, both of recognition and surprise.

In Shakespeare's own theatres, costuming was broadly contemporary, but with significant conventional adjustments for some specific historical periods (notably ancient Rome), places (such as the Middle East) and national stereotypes (such as Dutch, French and Spanish). The first two of these seem to be represented by the figures in the 'Peacham drawing' attached to an excerpt from *Titus Andronicus*, although the specifics of this are open to question.[8] Some indications of the use of contemporary dress in the plays are specific – would Claudius in *Hamlet* have guards who were recognizable as 'Switzers'? (4.5.95) – and intelligible distinctions are suggested by such stage directions as that at the opening of *Cymbeline*, 1.4, which specifies guests at Philario's house in Rome as 'a Dutchman, a Frenchman and a Spaniard' as well as the Italian Iachimo and the perhaps identifiably Roman host. In some cases, where modern designers and directors may choose to mark such distinctions as those between Trojans and Greeks in *Troilus and Cressida*, there is no evidence (or requirement) in the text for such costuming decisions. In *A Midsummer Night's Dream*, when Oberon tells Puck that he should be able to identify Demetrius 'by the Athenian garments he hath on' (2.1.264), the only requirement is that the mortals do not dress like the fairies.

Inigo Jones's costume designs for court masques and other entertainments, together with other pictorial evidence not connected with the public theatres, suggest available conventions for such figures as the Greco-Roman deities (Hymen in *As You like It*, Juno, Ceres and Iris in *The Tempest* and Jupiter in *Cymbeline*, for example) or the 'Worthies' presented in *Love's Labour's Lost*. Within these parameters and with such identifiable exceptional cases, the theatre was responsive to current fashions, and vestimentary conventions distinguishing such factors as social rank, age and trade.[9]

After the re-opening of the playhouses in 1660, and well into the eighteenth century, comparable costuming practices prevailed, with due allowance for changes in contemporary fashion. We find David Garrick and his contemporaries 'playing tragic heroes in contemporary eighteenth-century dress, regardless of the setting or time of the action in the play', but also (in Garrick's case) making significant attempts in the summer of 1757 to refurbish the stock of 'Roman shapes' for a revival of *Antony and Cleopatra* at Drury Lane.[10] This reflects another important and persistent aspect of theatrical custom: the use of a stock of costumes as well as of scenery appropriate for a number of plays of broadly similar periods and locations.

When exceptions are made, they are of considerable note. For example, while Garrick famously adopted a modern suit of mourning clothes in the French style for his Hamlet, the dressing of Macbeth by his older rival Charles Macklin, in an approximation of 'authentic' Scottish attire, was a major departure at a time when Garrick was still playing the role in a contemporary, eighteenth-century scarlet uniform.[11] There was also a generically 'old English manner' of costume announced with pride in playbills for *Every Man in his Humour* (Drury Lane, 1751) and characters 'dress'd in the

Habit of those days' in a production of *Edward, the Black Prince* (1750).[12] To cite one famous example of pictorial evidence for stage practice, William Hogarth's painting of Garrick as Richard III, now in the Walker Art Gallery, Liverpool, depicts the actor in the 'tent scene' (5.5) in the 'Holbein' costume of slashed doublet, silk hose and cloak; this is certainly 'Old English' but hardly Plantagenet. (Images of his successors Edmund Kean and George Frederick Cooke show the same pleasingly antique but inaccurate outfit.)[13]

We can identify this as the beginning of the second phase in costuming for plays set in other periods and places, with increased (or novel) attention to the places and times represented in them but also of attention to the period of their composition; the latter is a factor more applicable to Jonson's city comedies than to most of Shakespeare's plays. The fact that Garrick was aware of the possibilities of 'the Habit of [whatever] days' and that Macklin was striking out for new ground in his Scottish dress suggests a compromise between growing antiquarian interests. Garrick, for example, possessed books of historical costume and this interest was accompanied by an appetite for authenticity in scenic design as well. John Philip Kemble (1757–1823) commissioned period-specific sets and costumes for several plays from William Capon, who shared the actor's enthusiasm for picturesque and accurate landscape paintings, and took pains 'to reproduce the remains of actual buildings "with all the zeal of an antiquary" '.[14] For Kemble's younger brother Charles, the expert on costume history and heraldry, James Robinson Planché supervised a historically accurate costuming of *King John* in 1823. But despite such efforts, and the corresponding quest for authenticity in costume, some conventions remained strong. It was to be many years before most actors playing Hamlet ceased to wear at least some of the traditional 'tragic' black plumes that made the actors' headwear resemble decorations on undertakers' horses dressed for a funeral.

By the time Henry Irving became actor-manager of the Lyceum – where he appeared in principal roles under his own artistic direction from 1878 to 1901 – historical authenticity had long been the governing principle in productions at theatres with any artistic pretensions. William Charles Macready (particularly in *As You Like It* and *King John* under his own management at Drury Lane in 1842–3) and Charles Kean (in a series of elaborately researched 'revivals' at the Princess's Theatre in the 1850s) had set standards that ambitious managers ignored at their peril. Although antiquarian enthusiasm could lead to pedantic absurdities such as Charles Kean's assuring his audience that the tools in Peter Quince's workshop were modelled on evidence from excavations at Herculaneum – not Athens but at least ancient – the tendency was towards artistically unified productions in which settings and costumes harmonised with each other and satisfied the criteria applied to the other visual arts. As on the contemporary operatic stage, these productions resembled convincing historical paintings, now gifted with the adjuncts of music, motion and speech. Compromises might still be made, not merely with tradition (Hamlet's feathers) but also with modern fashion and standards of decency. In the midnineteenth century, in an engraving after a daguerreotype, Isabella Glyn appears as she was seen as Cleopatra in a full skirt of the 1840s that may lack a supporting crinoline but still has the outline corresponding to one; and actors in the Roman lorica and kilt or (as Macbeth) in the Highland kilt still wore 'fleshings' (tights) rather than show bare flesh below the knee. (As well as rendering the legs smooth and complementing the overall effect of the costume, the tights also had a secondary cosmetic purpose, as padding could be added to the calves under the stockings to suggest more warrior-like musculature.)

The idea of the authentic production continues with place as well. In the comedies, for example, with the exception of the uniquely and inescapably English *Merry Wives of Windsor*, Athens would be rendered as 'ancient Greek', Messina, Verona, Padua and their inhabitants would be convincingly 'Renaissance Italian'. Such more or less positively identifiable locations as Illyria and the Forest of Arden would be fanciful but more or less appropriately Balkan or Ardennes-like, though here the compromise was allowed for such vividly Elizabethan and un-Illyrian characters as Sir Toby Belch and Sir Andrew Aguecheek. Irving's 1888–9 production of *Macbeth* at the Lyceum represents a high-water mark of the unified production, in the grand historical-pictorial style, with Ellen Terry's costume as Lady Macbeth, depicted in John Singer Sargent's striking painting of her in character, as one of the most exotic achievements of the costumier's art – although it did prompt Oscar Wilde to observe that 'judging from the banquet, Lady Macbeth evidently patronises local industries for her husband's clothes and the servants' liveries, but she takes care to do all her own shopping in Byzantium'.[15]

The third phase in the development of Shakespearean costuming might be associated with the 'watershed' of the 1914–18 war, but its origins lie in the movement towards the reconstruction of Shakespeare's staging methods by the Elizabethan Stage Society, under the direction of William Poel, and the productions of *Twelfth Night, A Midsummer Night's Dream* and *The Winter's Tale* by Harley Granville Barker at London's Savoy Theatre in 1912–14. Poel's stagings may have approximated to those of the Elizabethan originals, but his costuming could be eclectic, mixing periods and styles. In his *Coriolanus* the eponymous hero wore a leopard skin, Volumnia a Gainsborough dress with a plumed hat, Virgilia a Pre-Raphaelite smock and the citizens 'an attire similar to that of French railway porters'.[16] This, however, was arguably authentic in the sense of corresponding to the eclecticism inherent in the practice of Shakespeare's time. Barker's stagings were closer to the commercial theatre in production values (professional actors in all roles, a longer run in an established theatre, etc.). They also blended authenticity in the use of an apron stage and stylized settings with an adoption of Elizabethan costume that was qualified by a degree of exoticism: his Viola is in doublet and knee breeches, as are Malvolio, Sebastian, Sir Toby and Sir Andrew, but Orsino's court is that of a (vaguely) Eastern potentate.[17] The 'authentic' costumes are themselves stylized, redolent of the work of designers for Sergei Diaghilev's *Ballets Russes* – such as Leon Bakst and Alexander Benois – the colours and patterns of fabrics are distinctively of the new movements in the visual arts, an effect even more evident in those for *The Winter's Tale* and *A Midsummer Night's Dream*. *Dream* was the most influential of the three, marking a decisive break with a tradition of picturesque realistic woodland and ancient Athenian garb whose apogee had been reached by the staging by Sir Herbert Beerbohm Tree, first seen at Her Majesty's Theatre in 1900. Another notable break with tradition came at Stratford-upon-Avon in 1919, the immediate postwar festival season, with Claud Lovat Fraser's bold designs for Nigel Playfair's production of *As You like It*. These used 'period' outlines derived from fourteenth-century missals, with vibrant colours not usually seen on that dustily conservative stage.

The 'Shakespeare Revolution' in critical as well as theatrical treatment of the plays identified by J.L. Styan as a seismic shift in the early twentieth century, is as open to qualification as any historiographical construct.[18] However, it does usefully focus attention on the confirmation for designers and directors of a new freedom to range across historical periods in setting and costume, explored enthusiastically by directors such as Tyrone Guthrie, who indulged a tendency to radically 'update' the plays, moving *Troilus and Cressida* (Old Vic, 1956) into the period immediately before the First World War, and *All's Well That Ends Well* (Stratford Ontario, 1953; Stratford-upon-Avon, 1959), into that of the Second. Guthrie was also capable of moving from one scenic and costume tradition to another, exemplified by his picturesquely 'Victorian' *Midsummer Night's Dream* (Old Vic, 1937), which would not have surprised a time-traveller from a century earlier. Other even more iconoclastic productions, such as those by Terence Gray at the Festival Theatre in Cambridge or the Russian exile Theodore Komisarjevsky at Stratford-upon-Avon in the 1930s, brought with them correspondingly radical costume designs. Nevertheless, the freedom to subordinate realism to other artistic priorities – giving a frankly stylized version of 'period' costume – had a more lasting effect in the work of such designers as the team known as Motley (the sisters Margaret and Sophia Harris, and Elizabeth Montgomery), who by example and teaching influenced several generations of designers from early in the 1930s.[19]

The simplicity, attention to the line and broad patterns of clothing, and the use of cheap fabrics enriched by painted and applied decoration, exemplified by such designers as Motley, lent themselves to the limited resources and the aesthetic of repertory theatres as well as larger commercial enterprises. In the late 1940s and early 1950s there was also a parallel trend towards a more lavish decorative and romantic pictorial approach, identifiable in such designers as Leslie Hurry, Oliver Messel and Roger Furse, the last of whom designed Olivier's three Shakespeare films, *Henry V* (1944), *Hamlet* (1948) and *Richard III* (1951). But Motley's practicality as well as attention to detail subordinated to overall effect can be found in the work of such designers as Tanya Moiseiwitsch, active over five decades in Ireland, England, Canada and the USA, and Desmond Heeley.[20] A distinct but related, Brecht-inspired strain of design can be found in the work of Jocelyn Herbert, who made her reputation in work for the English Stage Company at the Royal Court in the 1950s and 1960s, and John Bury, whose career took him from the defiantly left-wing Theatre Royal in London's Stratford-Atte-Bow to Stratford-upon-Avon, where his designs for *The Wars of the Roses*, first seen in the theatre in 1963 and subsequently adapted for the BBC's television broadcast of the cycle, moved decisively away from the more decorative effect of many excellent designs by Motley or Tanya Moiseiwitsch. (The latter had designed the permanent set for the Theatre's 1951 cycle of history plays.) The 'hard' materials of the sets – distressed timber, steel – were reflected in the costumes' metallic armour and the coarse woven fabrics, often encrusted with a thick impasto of paint and 'gunk' (a rubber solution) to represent richer materials.

Like the Histories, productions of *A Midsummer Night's Dream* offer a helpful set of co-ordinates for a history of Shakespearean costuming and stage design since the nineteenth century.[21] The romantic theatre's preoccupation with realistic woodlands, ancient Athenians and gossamer, balletic fairies gives way to the hieratic, automaton-like attendants on Granville Barker's Oberon (their faces painted gold) and his folkloric, shock-haired Puck. Another change of direction can be identified in Peter Brook's 1970 RSC production, with the soft, loose white trousers and shirts of its fairies, tie-dyed outfits of the lovers and stylized but recognizably practical clothes of the 'ordinary' workmen who inhabited the set's white box. But even there, the sense of a compromise between the near and the distant made itself felt. With the opening of Shakespeare's Globe in Southwark in 1997, the wheel might be thought to have come full circle. Jenny Tiramani, head of costume at a time when the theatre, under the artistic directorship of Mark Rylance, was exploring 'original practices', wrote in the journal *Costume*: 'As designers and costume makers about to work within this new Globe theatre we were faced with the question – what would be the nature of the actors' clothes if we embarked on a similar approach of authentic reconstruction to that of the building itself?'[22] She would go on to reconstruct the period clothing using 'authentic' dyeing methods, hand woven fabric when possible, stitching, recreating fastenings, and including all the layers of (what she calls) 'undress'.

Advice of this kind can be found in such handbooks as Zinkeisen's *Designing for the Stage*, where the contents page identifies 'Chapter 7. Period Costume' with the brief summary: 'Inaccuracy of so-called period costumes. Importance of mastering the silhouettes and bodice-lines of all periods [. . . .] Improvisation of materials.' (The last includes the use of a paper doily to represent a cravat!)[23] Nevertheless, even the Globe has not held to this principle of authenticity for all its productions, and (leaving the question of dyestuffs aside) the notion of finding the right shape and appropriate undergarments is not far removed from common practice where 'authenticity' is not so scrupulously pursued.

Perhaps the most important aspect of the development of costume for these plays is the return to that quality in the texts and their own theatres. 'What country, friends, is this?' asks Viola. 'This is, and is not Illyria, lady' would be the correct answer: one accepted in matters of decor and costume until the end of the eighteenth century, and more likely, after a century dominated by the quest for authenticity, to be confirmed and celebrated since the turn of the nineteenth to the twentieth centuries.

PART ONE

Dressing Shakespeare in His Own Time – Theatre, Fashion and Social Practice

'The Compass of a Lie'? Royal Clothing at Court and in the Plays of Shakespeare, 1598–1613

Maria Hayward

Introduction

In 1582 Stephen Gosson, satirist, complained that an actor or 'a meane person' could 'take vpon him the title of a Prince with counterfeit porte, and traine' and 'by outwarde signes to shewe them selues otherwise then they are, and so with in the compasse of a lye'.[1] In turn Thomas Dekker's comment that an actor could be 'stript out of [their] borrowed Majestie' emphasized how important clothes were in creating the fictive sense of a royal persona in the theatre.[2] Elizabeth I and James VI and I also fashioned their regal image with clothing. Equally, both monarchs knew their public lives were a performance and that their words, deportment and behaviour were central in creating a monarchical identity, and they drew parallels between their own lives and the theatre. Elizabeth I stated that 'We princes, I tell you, are set on stages, in sight and view of all the world'.[3] James echoed this view, observing that 'A King is as one set on a stage, whose smallest actions and gestures, all people gazingly doe behold'.[4] While neither Elizabeth nor James mentioned clothes specifically, the public gaze would have focused upon their physical appearance or, more specifically, their clothed body.

Clothing was essential for Elizabeth and James to fabricate a visual self, just as a costume was for an actor playing a part in one of Shakespeare's History plays.[5] While no costumes have survived and there is very little evidence of what actors wore when performing specific roles in Shakespeare's plays, snippets can be gleaned from sources such as the papers of the theatrical entrepreneur Philip Henslowe, the revels' accounts and actor's wills.[6] In spite of this, written sources reveal that royal power, real and imagined, was often expressed visually in London. It was frequently criticized there too, both at court and in the theatre, with a lack of magnificence being as bad as extravagant conspicuous consumption. With these thoughts in mind, this chapter considers how Shakespeare used language to create an image of royalty for his audiences in comparison with how Elizabeth I and James I dressed in reality. It asserts that all displays of royal power, whether at court or in the theatre, were 'counterfeit' at some level, as Gosson claimed. Shakespeare's presentation of 'This new and gorgeous garment, majesty' (*2H4*, 5.3.44) is discussed under five headings: conspicuous consumption, magnificence, symbols of power, kingship and female rule, and disguisings and disguise.

Conspicuous consumption

The appropriate use of conspicuous consumption was essential for a monarch, and this started with their clothes. Most of Elizabeth's and James' clothing needs were supplied by the Great Wardrobe, which was a sub-section of the royal

FIGURE 1 *George Gower. The Plimpton 'Sieve' portrait of Queen Elizabeth I. Oil on panel, 1579. By permission of the Folger Shakespeare Library.*

household. The monarchs wore bespoke clothing, the product of the royal tailor and a group of craftsmen and women, who worked predominantly but not exclusively for the crown.[7] This was expensive, as reflected by James' first warrant for the wardrobe of the robes dating from September 1603, which came to £15,255 3s 9¼d.[8] Including items for Anne of Denmark, Prince Henry and others participating in the coronation, the cost was considerably more than under Elizabeth I. Her annual expenditure averaged at £2,418 with her spending ranging between £1,030 16s 10½d in 1566–7 and £4,130 3s 9½d in 1578–9.[9] Even so, both monarchs aimed to outspend the nobility, thus making the clothed royal body unique in the richness of its apparel.

The result was substantial royal wardrobes. When Elizabeth's clothing was inventoried in 1600 she owned 102 French gowns, sixty-seven round gowns, 100 loose gowns, 125 kirtles, 136 foreparts, ninety-nine mantles and ninety-nine cloaks.[10] Even so, this was just a percentage of the clothes made for her during her lifetime. While there are no comparable inventories for James I, he ordered sixty-five suits in 1603–4 and fifty-one in 1613–14.[11] In contrast, Elizabeth's accounts for the period 1598–1603 reflect a very different pattern. While ordered on a biannual pattern, her tailor, William Jones, made very few new outer garments for her – just four doublets, one high-bodied gown, one kirtle and three round kirtles.[12] However, these were accompanied by vast numbers of new underpinnings and linen items including seventy-two petticoats, forty-two stomachers and forty-three pairs of flannel sleeves.[13] Jones also undertook numerous repairs and alterations, as well as relining and refashioning gowns, doublets, mantles, sleeves and kirtles.[14]

Elizabeth ordered less from her tailor because gift-giving shaped the queen's wardrobe by the end of her reign. The four extant New Year's gift rolls for 1598–1603 reveal that she received twenty-one doublets, four gowns, twenty loose gowns, thirty-seven round kirtles and twenty-two mantles.[15] A sense of the quality can be gleaned from the 'gowne with a Trayne of pynke Colored taffeta florished all over with lawne Cutworke lyke roses and leaves florished with venys sylver' from the earl of Northumberland in 1599.[16] In contrast, James received fewer items of clothing as gifts. The 1606 roll recorded eighteen pairs of gloves, a handkerchief, a pair of mittens, a nightcap, a pair of pantofles (high-heeled slippers) and a shirt.[17] These were mostly small, relatively cheap items and they were given to the king by men and women who sold these types of accessories to him during the rest of the year. For instance, Alexander Howme, one of the king's shoemakers, gave him a pair of pantofles embroidered with Venice gold.[18] This short comparison of how Elizabeth and James used clothing to fashion their image reveals two very different ways of using conspicuous consumption. While Elizabeth actively used clothing to assert her position as queen, she did so using a relatively modest budget and the gift-giving process to ensure that others bore part of the cost. In contrast, James spent extravagantly on his appearance. However, cost alone could not compensate for his lack of interest in what he wore or how he wore it.[19]

Royal clothing was made from the best available materials but it still incorporated elements of fakery. This was most readily apparent in Elizabeth's case. The queen's body was shaped and moulded using bum-rolls and farthingales; it was embellished with fantastic gowns and her own hair was augmented with hair pieces and wigs.[20] Her wardrobe account for Michaelmas 1600 included 'Six fayre lardge heddes of heair' and for Lady Day 1602 another 'six heades of haire'.[21] In contrast, James's appearance was less deceptive, although his doublets were padded with bombast to create the fashionably rounded peasecod belly. Real royal conspicuous consumption was all about out-spending the nobility and using all available methods to make the monarch appear magnificent.

Magnificence

Shakespeare would have been familiar with the concept that a monarch should be magnificent and that clothing was essential for creating the required look of legitimate royal authority.[22] As a result, enterprising royal officials made money showing the royal wardrobe to visitors. In 1598 the German traveller Paul Hentzner went to the Tower of London, where much of Elizabeth's clothing was kept. After leaving his sword at the gate, he recorded seeing 'some royal dresses so extremely magnificent, as to raise any one's admiration at the sums they must have cost'.[23]

The sumptuary legislation of Henry VIII and Elizabeth I supported this idea by stressing the monarch's place at the top of society and defined that space by the wearing of, for example, purple silk, cloth of tissue and sable. However, magnificence was an ideal and it evolved under Elizabeth to include women, so allowing her to control potential rivals.[24] As such, royal dress was supposed to define and identify the monarch, and Shakespeare drew on this idea when he described:

> The intertissued robe of gold and pearl,
> The farced title running 'fore the king,
>
> (*H5*, 4.1.258–9)

These lines from *Henry V* encapsulate the richness of royal clothing, which announced the king to his subjects without the need for words. The lines also drew on fifteenth- and early sixteenth-century views of magnificence that fabrics incorporating metal thread, rare furs and large quantities of jewellery were necessities of royal life. This concept was rather outmoded by the time Shakespeare was writing, but it was pertinent for many of the Plantagenet, Lancastrian and Yorkist kings that he wrote about. Purple silk, for example, was seen as a royal prerogative in the sumptuary legislation of Henry VIII and Elizabeth.[25] This reflected the cost of purple dyes as well as the imperial and religious connotations of the colour.[26] However, Elizabeth and James rarely wore purple except on occasions of state, and Shakespeare only made a few negative references such as the allusion to 'Dives that lived in purple' and then burnt in hell in the same robes (*1H4*, 3.3.32).[27] In spite of this, Henslowe's inventory suggests that this colour was sometimes worn by actors because he had a pair of French hose of 'purple velvet cut in dimonds Lact [lace] & spangels' and another pair of 'purpell velvet lact with gould spanish'.[28]

From the chronicles that he drew upon, Shakespeare would have been aware of monarchs who failed to be magnificent – the best-known example being Henry VI's appearance in an old blue robe.[29] While this robe might have stressed Henry VI's piety, worn as it was on Maundy Thursday 1471, and blue being the official colour of royal mourning in the fifteenth and early sixteenth centuries, it failed to assert his political strength as king.[30] As the author of the *Great Chronicle* noted, it was 'More lyker a play than the shewing of a prynce to wynne mennys hertys'.[31] Shakespeare could have observed James's sartorial failures personally. Giovanni Scaramelli, the Venetian ambassador, observed that 'from his dress he would have been taken for the meanest among his courtiers, a modesty he affects, had it not been for a chain of diamonds round his neck and a great diamond in his hair'.[32] James, who chose not to compete with Elizabeth's flamboyant dress, used jewelled accessories to signal his status and offset his rather simple clothes with magnificent diamonds.

Jewellery was a mark of status and wealth at the Elizabethan and Jacobean courts.[33] After attending a Jacobean masque, Orazio Busino, chaplain to the Venetian ambassador to London, noted that the women in attendance had 'strings of jewels on their necks and bosoms and in their girdles and apparel in such quantity that they looked like so many queens'.[34] While these might have been genuine and their own, they may also have been borrowed, hired or fake. However, they evidently impressed Busino and that was the intention, as these women sought to emulate the queen's opulence. While there were no references to jewellery in Henslowe's list, there were numerous doublets, sleeves, cloaks and hose decorated with metal lace.[35] This would have conveyed a sense of wealth (although some was only copper lace), and of drama, as it glinted under the candlelight for indoor evening performances at Blackfriars, the Inns of Court or one of the royal palaces.

However, too much interest in clothes could prove a distraction from the things that mattered for a monarch. Shakespeare's Henry V observes that a monarch should not be distracted from honour by clothes: 'It earns me not if men my garments wear: / Such outward things dwell not in my desires' (*H5*, 4.3.26–27). Reminiscing about his youth, Prince Hal demonstrates how his clothes conveyed things about himself that he had come to regret, such as vanity and a distraction with frivolous things:

> What a disgrace is it to me to remember thy name! or to know thy face tomorrow! or to take note how many pair of silk stockings thou hast – viz. these, and those that were thy peach-coloured ones! or to bear the inventory of thy shirts – as, one for superfluity and another for use!
>
> (*2H4*, 2.2.12–18)

On one level, what he describes is incongruous because a fifteenth-century king would not have had 1590s fashions. However, the references to knitted silk hose, in new colours, and the shirts, so numerous that they required an inventory to record them all, would have been very recognizable to Shakespeare's audience and could have brought the clothing excesses of Elizabeth's male favourites such as Essex to mind. Elizabeth's own levels of expenditure on clothing left her open to charges of extravagance and from a clerical point of view this presented dangers for her soul. Towards the end of her reign:

> my lord of London preached to the Queen's Majesty and seemed to touch on the vanity of decking the body too finely. Her Majesty told the ladies that 'if the bishop held more discourse on such matters, she would fit him for heaven – but he should walk thither without a staff and leave his mantle behind him'.[36]

All of this served to stress that the monarch needed to a strike a careful balance between luxury and magnificence, so avoiding courtly excess, both on and off the Shakespearean stage.

Symbols of power

Clothes were one of the most important symbols of power, but it is important to ask: what made certain clothes specifically royal? The person wearing them, the quality, the novelty or that some items were exclusive to royalty? All of this was important for costuming stage monarchs, so the answer was a blend of all four, but the most significant was that the monarch was God's anointed, and once a garment had been worn on the sovereign's body it became special.[37] As a recipient of coronation, the sovereign was 'Twin-born with greatness' (*H5*, 4.1.230), with the physical and spiritual aspects of their body being made manifest.[38] That said, most of the basic garment types that Elizabeth and James wore on their corporeal bodies could have been found in the wardrobes of any moderately well-dressed person of the period: linens, underpinnings (for women), outer garments, accessories, and a selection of pins, laces, aglets, and points used as means of positioning and fastening the different elements.[39] Shakespeare made Cleopatra appear like any woman of the period when she instructs, 'Cut my lace, Charmian, come!' (*AC*, 1.3.73).

While any garment could be infused with royal magnificence after being worn by the monarch, certain items were traditional symbols of power. The robes of state were the archetypal royal attire, and the sovereign had no choice but to wear them. Made from cloth of gold, cloth of tissue, purple and crimson velvet and ermine, these robes were worn for ceremonies, which reinforced the monarch's authority. Alive, the sovereign wore these robes for their coronation, the opening of parliament, and the feasts of the order of the garter.

After death, the monarch's effigy wore the robes during the funeral. The portraiture of Elizabeth and James reveals that they were regularly painted in their robes, often with the regalia, and these portraits were copied and purchased for display in town halls, Oxford colleges and aristocratic homes.[40] These robes were such a symbol of royal office that they were listed first in Elizabeth's inventory of 1601. The same inventory recorded that she had kept and preserved the robes of her dead brother and sister.[41]

The most significant set of royal robes were those made from cloth of gold which were worn at the moment of coronation. Elizabeth's consisted of 'one Mantle of Clothe of golde tissued with golde and silver furred with powdered

FIGURE 2 *James in his robes and regalia from* James I. The workes of the most high and mightie prince, James by the grace of God, King of Great Britaine, France and Ireland, defender of the faith, etc. *London, 1616. By permission of the Folger Shakespeare Library.*

Armyons' which was worn with 'one kirtle of the same tissue the traine and skirts furred ... with a paire of bodies and sleeves to the same'.[42] While Shakespeare referred to Henry V's 'intertissued robe of gold and pearl' (*H5*, 4.1.258), there was nothing like it in any of the playhouse inventories, which is perhaps not surprising, as cloth of tissue was the most expensive fabric available. However, Edward Alleyn's inventory of *c*.1602 did include 'A crimosin Robe strypt with gould fact with ermin'.[43] This was probably a peer's parliament robe bought at a probate sale but it still would have been a garment that was visually striking. It would have had a train and as such it would take up space on stage, forcing other actors to give the wearer room to move. The size or rather the length of the robe imbued it with power that transferred to the monarch when worn. This power derived from the cost of the fabric and the idea that the length of the train was proportional to the wearer's rank.[44] Shakespeare also used the word 'robe' to suggest imperial power, and examples of this feature in *Titus Andronicus* (for example, when Marcus 'offers robe' to Titus, the stage direction after 1.1.189) and when Cleopatra tells her attendants to 'Give me my robe. Put on my crown' (*AC*, 5.2.278). The term 'mantle' was often interchangeable with 'robe' and Shakespeare exploited this in *King Lear* to explore different facets of royal power.[45] Shakespeare went one step further in the epilogue to *Henry V* when he hinted at the problems caused by minority rule by the reference to 'Henry the Sixth, in infant bands crowned King' (*H5*, Epilogue, 9) and his swaddling was juxtaposed with his crown.

Shakespeare frequently referred to other markers of power including the crown, sceptre and orb. The imperial state crown, worn by Elizabeth and James, was arguably the most potent symbol of Tudor and early Stuart royal authority.[46] When inventoried in 1574, it weighed 98 oz and in 1649 it was valued at £1,110.[47] For these monarchs, it was linked to ceremonies that asserted and reinforced royal authority: coronation and, pre-reformation, crown-wearings on the key days of the liturgical year. In Shakespeare's plays, these positive images are stressed but also contrasted with the symbolism of the removal or loss of the crown. King John seeks to have himself re-crowned but is reminded by Pembroke that 'you were crown'd before, / And that high royalty was ne'er pluck'd off' (*KJ*, 4.2.4–5). In contrast, transfer of the crown is central in the scene linked to Richard II's deposition where the discussion about the crown is reinforced by the stage direction 'Re-enter York, with Richard, and officers bearing the regalia' (*R II*, after 4.1.161).

Shakespeare challenged the primacy of the royal crown by presenting his audiences with a hierarchy of crowns: the coronation crown, the smaller, personal crown, and the coronets of the nobility, which were smaller still – 'I saw Mark

Antony offer him a crown – yet 'twas not a crown neither, 'twas one of these coronets' (*JC*, 1.2, 235–7). More significantly, he stressed that the crown could become a burden to its wearer, as in *King Henry IV, Part 2* when Prince Hal asks:

> Why doth the crown lie there upon his pillow,
> Being so troublesome a bedfellow?
>
> (*2H4*, 4.5.20–1)

Significant as the robes and regalia were, the monarch usually wore fashionable, everyday clothes.

The quality and quantity of these garments obviously set the monarch apart in reality, ensuring that their authority was

FIGURE 3 *Couple in fashionable clothing from* Royal, military and court costumes of the time of James I. *By permission of the Folger Shakespeare Library.*

respected without the need for the permanent use of the markers of their rank, such as crowns and robes. They had new clothes for all key occasions and they expected to change their clothes several times a day. Recall, for example, earlier mention of the many fashionable garments that they purchased. Within the theatre, since these costumes would have been expensive, the authenticity of the costumes may well have often been a matter of the relative quality of 'royal garments' that the company might have had. Royal costumes worn by the characters would have depended in part on the demands of the plot and the budget for the performance.[48] The references to 'Harey the v velvet gowne' and 'Harye the v satten dublet, layed with gowld lace' in Henslowe's list suggest investment in the costumes for this royal hero.[49] Shakespeare also explored how these clothes were worn in his reference to Hamlet, prince of Denmark, wearing:

> his doublet all unbraced
> No hat upon his head, his stockings foul'd,
> Ungarter'd, and down-gyved to his ankle,
>
> (*Ham*, 2.1.78–80)

Shakespeare offered a more nuanced view of how a particular style of dress could mould the wearer when he gave Henry V the words: 'I will deeply put the fashion on, / And wear it in my heart' (*2H4*, 5.2.52–3).

Actual and stage royalty also adopted fashionable informal wear such as nightgowns or loose gowns. Usually worn in semi-private in the morning and evening rather than for sleeping, they provided a monarch with an opportunity to step away partially from their more ceremonial persona. This could be problematic as in 1597, when Elizabeth I chose to receive the French ambassadors in her nightgown but was concerned and asked, 'What will these gentlemen say to see me so attired?'[50] In spite of Elizabeth's doubts, the nightgown and loose gown, which was worn for informal wear rather than for sleeping or prior to going to sleep, had gravitas because they were made from expensive, patterned fabrics as in the case of 'One Nightegowne of verie riche rose coulor wroughte veluett wroughte with golde lace with furre' made for James I, costing £148 2s 3d.[51] When a Shakespearean character wore a nightgown it implied the passage of time because nightgowns were usually worn in the evening, night or early morning. The nightgown also indicated a semi-private space because this is where they were usually worn, and in turn, a sense of intimacy, secrecy or wakefulness. For instance, *Henry IV, Part 2*, included the stage direction 'Enter the King in his nightgown, with a page' (3.1.0) and other characters enter in this way, including Julius Caesar (2.2.0).[52]

While Elizabeth and James dressed in current fashions, Shakespeare's theatrical monarchs covered a much wider chronological range, spanning from 'historic' Roman/early British to medieval and then to near-contemporary royalty such as Henry VIII.[53] This raised the question of whether the same markers or signs of royalty could be used on stage, regardless of when the play was set. While this question is impossible to answer, hints from within the plays, Henslowe's papers and the revels office suggest that certain objects (such as crowns) went across time and place, being equally applicable for Julius Caesar and Richard III, for classical Rome and London.[54] Ordinary clothing in contrast was more mutable and could be used in different ways according to the dictates of the text and the performance. In *Hamlet* Shakespeare implied that the prince was dressed in black as a sign of mourning and of his wish for revenge.[55] While Elizabeth wore black as a fashionable colour she also wore it as a public expression of mourning in 1584 after the death of her suitor, the Duke of Alençon.[56] In contrast, clothing was used to explore the theme of need throughout *King Lear*. In the middle of the play, Lear challenges contemporary ideas of royal magnificence when he asks, 'Is man no more than this? Consider him well. Thou ow'st the worm no silk, the beast no hide, the sheep no wool; the cat, no perfume' (*KL*, 3.4.101–4).[57]

Kingship and female rule

The scale of Elizabethan and Jacobean court pageantry was vast regardless of the monarch's gender and it was played out through the streets of London. The royal household, along with the court, civic and clerical elites, processed dressed in red cloth for royal coronations and black for royal funerals.[58] The coronation procession was something Shakespeare would have experienced in 1604 when he was given four yards of red cloth for a cloak to wear as he walked in James I's cortege on 15 May.[59] He must have been aware of funeral processions and it may have been this pageantry that he sought to evoke in *King Henry VI, Part 1*, with references to 'Hung be the heavens with black' (1.1.1) and 'We mourn in black' (1.1.17). Staging these events in the theatre was challenging but possible, as the funeral of Henry V, the coronation procession of Anne Boleyn and the christening of Princess Elizabeth in *Henry VIII* demonstrate (stage directions after 4.1.37 and at the start of 5.4).[60]

Although royal spectacle was concerned with stressing the authority of the monarch, early modern clothing was highly gendered. While Shakespeare experienced male and female rule, it was the theme of kingship that dominated his plays. His History plays presented a sequence of English kings with very different levels of ability to rule, thus providing him with rich material with which to work. Shakespeare also moulded his view of kingship and royalty according to whether he was writing for the house of Tudor or Stuart. Plays for Elizabeth focused on English history, including *King Richard II* and *King Richard III*, and the Tudor lineage, while those for James looked at Scottish interests and the relationship between the king's two crowns, most notably *Macbeth*.[61]

A defining feature of early modern kingship was leadership of the royal army, ensuring peace at home and success against foreign aggressors. This was acknowledged by placing the figure of the king in armour on horseback on the obverse of the royal seal. However, while this martial image had suited Henry

VIII and was epitomized by his armour which was still in the Tower of London, it was problematic for Elizabeth as a woman and for James as an advocate of a peaceful foreign policy. While it was accepted that Elizabeth would pass this role to her male courtiers and favourites, it was more problematic for James when he did the same, not least because he had to compete with the increasingly bellicose, yet chivalric views of his son Prince Henry. If Elizabeth and James could be seen as failing in their military role, Shakespeare invited his audience to consider historic royal military prowess. Frequent mentions of arms and armour stress the development of Prince Hal's character.[62] They also mark his military successes in the references to 'His bruised helmet and his bended sword' (*H5*, 5.Chorus 18). In a similar way Cleopatra rewards the valiant Scarus with 'An armour all of gold. It was a king's' (*AC*, 4.8.27). In spite of the references Shakespeare made to armour, the Admiral's Men owned relatively little, including 'j greve armer' and 'iij payer of bases' which could be worn with armour, while Henslowe made a payment of 20s to 'the armerer for targattes'.[63] Good-quality armour was expensive and it is possible that Henslowe hired armour as the revels did. For the Shrove Tuesday performance in 1572, Morris Pickering and William Jennings received 51s 6d from the revels for the hire of 'certeine Armour for the playe oof parries & Vienna to furnish the triumph therin'.[64]

While James avoided wearing armour, contemporary ideas about masculinity and rank ensured that even he wore a rapier on formal occasions.[65] The sword's social significance explains why Henslowe took 'a Raper & hangers' on 14 December 1598 as security for a loan of 8s.[66] The sword's association with violence was also noted in society and may explain why many of Shakespeare's references to swords, especially in a royal context, depict them as a symbol of political turmoil. Taking one example, from *Richard III*: 'Is the sword unsway'd? / Is the King dead? The empire unpossess'd?' (*R3*, 4.4.469–70).

Although Elizabeth as a queen regnant had proved exceptional, historically, female rule was viewed suspiciously. Elizabeth I described herself as a 'prince' or, as Judith Richards would term it, 'a female king', and her femininity was apparent to all who met her or saw the Ditchley or the Rainbow portraits.[67] She exploited the female wardrobe, including the French gown, loose gown, straight-bodied gown, doublet and round kirtle, so that she could tailor her appearance to the occasion throughout her forty-four-year reign.[68] In contrast, James I's choice of clothes once he was King of England was relatively conservative and his suits, demonstrating a marked fondness for pale-coloured satin, and consisting of doublet, breeches and a short cloak, changed little over the course of his reign.[69] Elizabeth was more flamboyant than James, but she knew how to manage her appearance far better than he did.

Most of Shakespeare's queens are queens consort (the wife of the sovereign rather than monarch in their own right) and he used these royal women to explore various themes associated with femininity and authority.[70] In *Henry VIII* he chose to stress the domestic symbolism of Katherine of Aragon's role as wife by presenting her sewing and through her comment 'Your graces find me here part of a housewife' (*H8*, 3.1.24). In reality, Katherine continued to make Henry VIII's shirts even after he had married Anne Boleyn.[71] As such, Katherine of Aragon's domesticity contrasts strongly with the assertive behaviour of Queen Margaret in *King Henry VI, Parts 2* and *3*.[72]

Elsewhere Shakespeare used his queens to comment on female failings. First, Henry VI's queen complains that Eleanor Cobham, Duchess of Gloucester, is dressed more regally than she is, so stealing her position. The Duchess' clothes reveal her ambition to all that see her: 'Strangers in court do take her for the Queen. / She bears a duke's revenues on her back' (*2H6*, 1.3.80–1). Consequently, Cobham's spectacular fall was presented to the audience visually. Denied the symbols of power that she had assumed illegitimately, she appeared barefoot, dressed in a penitential white sheet, with verses pinned to her back and a taper in her hand (stage direction after 2.4.16).[73] In *King Lear*, it is the revealing nature of some female clothing that receives criticism through the king's comments to his daughters Goneril and Regan:

> Thou art a Lady;
> If only to go warm were gorgeous,
> Why, nature needs not what thou gorgeous wear'st,
> Which scarcely keeps thee warm.
>
> (*KL*, 2.2.459–62)

This critical allusion to the fashionable low neckline favoured by Elizabeth and then Anne of Denmark allowed Shakespeare to air contemporary debates about the immorality of such styles. While the boy actors portraying Goneril and Regan might present a counterfeit image, the royal foibles that they performed were all too real.

Disguisings and disguise

The term 'disguising', used to describe a costumed performance at court, supports Gosson's view of performers, whether courtiers or professional actors, as counterfeiters.[74] The popularity of these entertainments at court meant that the crown owned one of the largest collections of theatrical costumes at the time. While royal ownership of these costumes gave them a degree of legitimacy, it also indicated that the monarchy condoned the counterfeit element embodied by these garments. Administered by the office of the revels, these costumes were paid for by the crown, and the quantity and quality reflected how individual monarchs viewed these entertainments at court. Expenditure under Elizabeth was relatively restrained, but it increased significantly under James when his wife and children performed in court theatricals.[75] The revels office not only provided costumes for the performances it devised at court, but also brought in productions, which were:

> thoroughly apparelled and furnished with sundry kinds and suits of apparel and furniture, fitted and garnished necessarily and answerable to the matter, person and part to be played.[76]

For instance, nine plays were performed between Christmas and Shrovetide in the years 1579–80. The revels supplied new costumes for some, while others made use of existing items and the rest were 'wholly furnished in this office with many garments newe made manye altered and translated'.[77] Old revels costumes could also be passed on to professional actors, as in the case of some 'frockes and priestes gownes with wide Sleves' of crimson damask which were 'translated twice agayne in to torche bearers and vsed by players and to them geven'.[78]

In addition, royal revels costumes were loaned to other interested parties. Whether the master of the revels actively sought to control how royal characters were dressed for these private performances is hard to gauge. However, it is clear that the revels staff did brisk business renting out costumes. For example, John Arnold, yeoman of the revels, was accused of depriving Thomas Giles, a haberdasher, 'of his living here by, who having apparel to let and cannot as cheaply let the same as her highness mask [costumes] are let'.[79] Giles' complaint that these clothes were being worn 'for the most parte' by 'the meanest sort of men' which was 'to the grett dyscredytt to the same apparell' is reminiscent of Gosson's concerns.

The concept of the clothes gaining a degree of prestige either by being royal property or more importantly being worn by the monarch was echoed in a letter dated January 1595 from the Head and Fellows of Trinity College, Cambridge. They informed Lord Burghley that:

> we intend ... in our college to set forth certain comedies and one tragedy. There being in that tragedy sundry personages of great estate, to be represented in princely attire, which is no where to be had but within the Office of the Robes at the Tower.[80]

Here they make the link between the status of the character and the quality of their clothes, with the added suggestion that princely characters required clothes that had actually been worn on the royal body and they were 'no where to be had' but in London.

Actors performing before the monarch had to wear good-quality costumes.[81] This is demonstrated by the Lord Chamberlain's request for a play for Twelfth Night in 1601. It was to be 'furnished with rich apparel' in addition to having 'great variety and change of music and dances, and [be] of a subject that may be pleasing to her Majesty'.[82] Different but equally important considerations would have influenced the costumes provided for six maskers sent to Scotland in September 1589 to celebrate the marriage of James VI to Anne of Denmark. They were supplied with sumptuous coats of purple gold tinsel guarded with purple-and-black-striped cloth of silver.[83] The complex demands of this occasion, the fact that it was for a royal wedding, that the groom was the unacknowledged heir to Elizabeth's throne and that it was taking place just two years after the execution of his mother, Mary Queen of Scots, may help to explain the necessity for such high-quality costumes.

Performances earlier in Elizabeth's reign and staged away from the capital did not always receive the same level of expenditure or demand for quality as royal weddings did, as is evident from the costumes supplied for the summer progress to Kent in 1573.[84] The accounts of the yeoman of the revels included payments for:

> yolow Cotton to lyne the Monarckes Gowne at viijd the yard xij yards – viijs
> Canvasse for his gerkins – xvjd
> Carsy Lyning & hollon for his hosen – iijs
> Silke to sett on the gardes – vs
> Thredd to sowe those iij garmentes – iijs.[85]

While these items are much cheaper than the fabrics and accessories for many royal costumes, the above example reveals that this 'monarch' was still fully equipped with a suit of new clothes for the performance.

One point is often cited about theatre costumes in the early seventeenth century: that Philip Henslowe spent £561 on 'apparel and properties' in the six-year period between 1597 and 1603.[86] This observation demonstrates that costumes represented a significant investment for the theatre companies, and they are supported by Thomas Platter, a Swiss writer who visited London in 1599. After attending a performance at the Globe he reported that 'the actors are most expensively and elaborately costumed'.[87] Henslowe's accounts also reflect that clothes were relatively expensive and that they retained their value, thus making them well suited to be given as gifts, left as bequests or used as security for loans.[88] At one level, creating an image of contemporary royalty on stage was relatively simple – the actor needed to be well dressed (or better dressed than those around them), preferably with crown and mantle. The companies evidently succeeded too well on occasion and their investment in costumes could be used against them. In July 1613, Sir Henry Wotton described the 'pomp and majesty' of the costumes in Shakespeare's *King Henry VIII* including 'the knights of the Order with their Georges and Garter, the guards with their embroidered coats and the like', thus making 'greatness very familiar, if not ridiculous'.[89] Wotton's comment suggests that contemporaries considered stage depictions of royalty being all too real. Elizabeth and James were remarkably tolerant of comments about themselves on the stage, and in 1605 Samuel Calvert observed that 'The play[er]s do not forbear to represent upon their stage the whole course of this present time, not sparing either King, state, or religion'.[90]

The rich and distinctive nature of royal dress could be challenged on stage and it was a theme that Shakespeare explored on several levels. First, other people could dress as the king or as a claimant to the throne. As Richard III notes during the battle of Bosworth: 'I think there be six Richmonds in the field: / Five have I slain today instead of him' (*Richard III*, 5.4.11–12).

More significant were the occasions when Shakespeare chose to present the monarch incognito; the best-known instance is when Henry V wears Erpingham's cloak as a disguise prior to the battle of Agincourt.[91] As the soldier Williams notes in *King Henry V*, 'Your majesty came not like yourself', reinforcing the contemporary view that you should be able to tell a person's rank by appraising their clothing. As a result, he argues, Henry had to accept the consequences:

> you appeared to me but a common man – witness the night, your garments, your lowliness; and what your highness suffered under that shape, I beseech you take it for your own fault and not mine, for had you been as I took you for, I made no offence;
>
> (*H5*, 4.8.50–5)

Equally, by questioning an individual's right to wear royal clothing, it was possible to challenge their right to rule as when Douglas asks Henry IV, 'What art thou / That counterfeit'st the person of a king?' (*1H4*, 5.4.26–7), or by questioning the English claim to the French throne with the reference to 'borrow'd majesty' in *King John* (1.1.4). Both speeches also bring Gosson's words 'the compass of a lie' to mind. Finally, and most unsettling, clothing could be used to deceive the viewer about an individual's true nature and as a metaphor for deceit. This theme is developed to good effect when Richard III informs the audience, 'And thus I clothe my naked villainy' (*R3*, 1.3.336).

From the point of view of staging a play, putting royalty in disguise removed or reduced the need for sumptuous clothes for that character. Equally, when the plays were being performed in front of the monarch, it was important that the actors dressed as royalty would not rival the sovereign. Royalty disguised was also a dramatic theme with contemporary relevance for Elizabeth and James. For example, in 1568 Mary Queen of Scots resorted to disguise twice in an attempt to escape from Lockleven Castle. She tried dressing as a laundress on 25 March, but her white hands gave her away.[92] But on 2 May she succeeded, and disguised in a red kirtle and a simple hood she made her escape.[93] Once free she sought to return to her previous, regal appearance, just as actors were expected to take off their costumes after the end of a performance.

Conclusion

By selecting Richard II as the subject of a play, Shakespeare could explore the question of deposing the king. Always a dangerous topic, it was especially so in the politically charged 1590s. John of Gaunt's reference to Richard II as the 'Landlord of England' rather than her king (*RII* 2.1.113) presents him as a false monarch.[94] Even if the deposition scene were not performed, the idea itself had resonance for the childless Elizabeth I. While her comment 'I am Richard II, know ye not that?' may relate to her recent portrait in her cloth of gold coronation robes, wearing the regalia and with her hair loose about her shoulders (which may have been modelled on the full-length coronation portrait of Richard II at Westminster Abbey), rather than to Shakespeare's play; she cannot have welcomed a renewed focus on the Succession question.[95] This example encapsulates how Shakespeare explored the concept of royalty in his plays, and how monarchy was inextricably linked with clothing, image, self-presentation and ceremony.

Sir Philip Sidney felt that the theatre sought to undermine the mystique of monarchy because playwrights increasingly mingled 'kings and clowns' and in so doing 'thrust in clowns by head and shoulders, to play a part in majestical matters with neither decency nor discretion'.[96] Shakespeare could have begged to differ. While his plays were intended to entertain, they also made insightful comments on the nature of royal power and authority. He was well placed to witness Elizabethan and Jacobean monarchy being performed on a grand scale with a huge budget, so ensuring it appeared 'majestical'. Through a skilful use of words, costumes and props, ranging from robes, mantles, the crown, sceptre, the throne, cloth of estate, and engagement in pageantry, Shakespeare conveyed an idea of monarchy. Equally, he summed up how blurred the boundaries were between royalty in reality and how it was presented in the theatre in the mocking exchange between Falstaff and Prince Hal in the tavern scene:

> FALSTAFF This chair shall be my state, this dagger my sceptre, and this cushion my crown.
> PRINCE Thy state is taken for a joint-stool, thy golden sceptre for a leaden dagger and thy precious crown for a pitiful bald crown.
>
> (*1H4*, 2.4.374–8)

Undeniably counterfeit on one level, this was a cutting, well-observed political comment on another. The result was Shakespeare's very distinctive view of how clothing created an image of English and then British royalty. If the Sanders portrait is a painting of Shakespeare, *c.*1603, it provides evidence of a man for whom the visual self and royal patronage were very important.[97] His doublet, trimmed with silver lace, and the fine linen collar reflected a man who had secured lucrative work for the crown, while his uncovered head acknowledged James as his patron. This patron's royal image was real, not counterfeit, and James VI and I deserved, in Gosson's words, 'the title of a Prince'.[98]

Suits of Green: Festive Livery on Shakespeare's Stage

Erika T. Lin

In *The Merchant of Venice*, when the clown Lancelot decides to leave Shylock's household, his new master, Bassanio, bestows livery as a sign that the clown has been accepted into his service: 'Take leave of thy old master and enquire / My lodging out. [*to a Follower*] Give him a livery / More guarded than his fellows': see it done' (2.2.144–6).[1] Livery – distinctive clothing marked out by colour, cut and insignia – both identified persons as members of particular households and served as partial payment of servants' salaries.[2] This twofold notion of livery as both symbolic marker of identity and financial compensation for services rendered is of special interest for it links costumes in Shakespeare's theatre to early modern festivity. Sixteenth- and seventeenth-century holidays were often observed with sartorial games that involved both mimetic roleplaying and monetary exchange. In local parishes, participants would wear livery to signal their allegiance to festive monarchs and to assist with community fund-raising. In commercial theatre, roleplaying depended on costumes that likewise circulated both as semiotic markers and as economic objects.

This chapter analyses how festive livery practices shaped audience experiences and dramatic narratives in the professional playhouses. Theatre, I argue, did not simply depict household livery within the imaginary worlds of plays; rather, it integrated the social functions of festive livery into its own performance practices. I begin with a brief discussion of the anonymous play *George a Greene, the Pinner of Wakefield*, which offers an especially useful introduction to calendar customs and their connection to the public stage. Bearing in mind these overlaps, I then examine how livery works in Shakespeare's *The Merchant of Venice*. Leveraging spectators' familiarity with festive roleplaying, the play positions commercial theatre as a holiday game in which playgoers are also participants. Rather than simply referring to livery through fictional narratives or literary allusions, stage costumes are themselves figured as a form of festive livery. By integrating holiday practices into its own semiotics and actor–audience dynamics, early modern theatre enabled not only the dramatic *representation* of livery practices but also their socially efficacious *enactment*.

George a Greene, the Pinner of Wakefield, first staged at the Rose Theatre in London in 1593, centres on the exploits of a 'pinner', or 'pinder', an official in charge of impounding stray animals. Its protagonist was a well-known folk hero who also appeared in a number of ballads.[3] Among the play's many twists and turns is an episode in which George's servant, Jenkin, receives clothing as thanks for 'conjuring' his master's beloved. The servant's reward, a 'sute of green, and twentie crownes besides' (Sig. D4r), exemplifies livery's dual function as signifier of household affiliation and as financial compensation.[4] Later, in an unrelated episode, livery again appears in the play when Robin Hood and his merry men disguise themselves and trespass upon George's field in order to provoke him into a fight. The altercation ends with the outlaw inviting the pinder to join his band of merry men:

George, wilt thou forsake Wakefield,
And go with me,
Two liueries will I giue thee euerie yeere,
And fortie crownes shall be thy fee.

(Sig. F1v)[5]

In offering not only clothing but also monetary payment, these scenes underscore the economics of allegiance. However, livery was not a neutral form of currency. It was both payment for services rendered and, as Ann Rosalind Jones and Peter Stallybrass demonstrate, 'a form of incorporation, a material mnemonic that inscribed obligation and indebtedness upon the body'.[6] Jenkin's reward as George's servant is to be physically marked as George's servant; Robin Hood's men must accept gifts of clothing that reinscribe them as Robin Hood's men.

The bestowal of livery in *George a Greene* resonates with actual holiday practices in early modern England. In the Thames Valley and in the west of England, as Alexandra Johnston has described, the 'combined producer and stage manager of the festival events' was known specifically as 'Robin Hood',[7] a figure who was both the main administrative coordinator and the chief actor in the roleplaying entertainments. At parish celebrations, Robin Hood and his men would often be clothed in 'Kendal green'.[8] The original actors in the play *George a Greene* were probably also dressed in this colour: Henslowe's theatrical inventories record 'vj grene cottes for Roben Hoode', 'j green gown for Maryan' and numerous other items clearly meant for the famous outlaw.[9] When George a Greene and Robin Hood offer green livery to their men within the fictional narrative, their actions highlight this material overlap between commercial theatre and parish festivity.

Beyond the similarity in colour, there was also a similarity in function. Both professional theatres and seasonal celebrations employed clothing as symbolic markers of identity, yet in both cases these signifiers pointed to shifting and multiple signifieds. Allegiance to the local parish Robin Hood was temporary, confined to holiday time. Sartorial markers in the theatre were similarly ephemeral and changing. Green clothing might distinguish a member of Robin Hood's band in one play while serving a very different function in another, and the same actor wore different costumes not only on successive days, but also, given the prevalence of doubling, within a single play.[10] Moreover, both in playhouse performance and in parish festivity, livery served as an object of economic exchange. During holiday celebrations, paper livery badges were sold to spectators in exchange for a small donation, and according to notorious anti-theatricalist Philip Stubbes, revellers wore 'badges & cognizances in their hats or caps openly' (Sig. M3r).[11] As part of their fundraising efforts, parishes might sell anywhere from a few hundred to a few thousand badges bearing the insignia of Robin Hood – quite large figures when compared with population records.[12] In the theatre, livery similarly served as a financial vehicle. Early modern actors were, quite literally, traffickers in the used-clothing trade: theatrical producers, such as Philip Henslowe, were also pawnbrokers and second-hand clothing dealers. Some of what they bought was, in fact, *real* livery – clothing bestowed on servants as compensation for their labour – and these they sold to the acting companies for use onstage.[13] Costumes were frequently the most costly investment that players had to make. Whereas the writing of a play usually cost around £6, a woman's gown might cost up to three or four times that amount.[14] Modern theatrical productions often involve costumes that are specially designed and sewn for a particular show; in the early modern playhouses, procuring a costume for use only in a single play was an unsound financial decision.

The theoretical implications of this material circumstance shed light on theatre's relation to festivity. Even as costumes were essential for constituting and differentiating among roles, they could be transferred from one play to another only when divested of fixed symbolic meaning. Both qualities were central to the economic viability of the theatres. Livery in the festive context functioned in similar ways. During real-life holiday observances, livery badges operated as markers of identity. At the same time, the actual purpose of selling these badges was to raise funds for parish needs. Participants were well aware that such symbols of allegiance were temporary and non-binding; it was only because livery badges were *not* 'real' that they could be sold. Both professional theatre and seasonal festivity needed livery to work in two contradictory ways at once: livery's symbolic resonances depended on traditional understandings of clothing as an identity marker, but at the same time, this semiotic function had to be erasable in order for livery to serve as an object of economic exchange.

This tension between the semiotic and economic functions of holiday livery undergirds the actor–audience dynamics of a range of plays whose festive roots are not necessarily as obvious as those of *George a Greene*, and it helps explain the popularity of cross-dressing, disguise, class inversion and other tropes of sartorial exchange in early modern drama. In Shakespeare's *The Merchant of Venice*, Bassanio orders Lancelot 'a livery / More guarded than his fellows" (2.2.144–6). The term 'guarded', which the *Oxford English Dictionary* defines as 'Ornamented, as with lace, braid, embroidery, etc.',[15] not only has strong festive connotations but also applied particularly to upstart servants and fools. One of Henry VIII's acts of parliament in 1509–10 ordered that 'No servyng manne waytyng uppon his Maister ... were [i.e. wear] eny garded Hose', and in the anonymous 1609 play *Euerie Woman in her Humor*, one character states, 'I grieue to see this double garded age, all side coate, all foole'.[16] Although we cannot be sure, Lancelot's livery may also have involved stripes of colour, for a letter printed in Richard Hakluyt's *The Principall Navigations, Voiages and Discoveries of the English Nation* (1589) describes 'smal fishes ... with gardes blew and greene round about their bodies' as being 'like comely seruing men'.[17] A combination of the two colours would be especially poignant, since blue livery was associated in early modern England with servants[18] and green with holiday festivity. Regardless of colour, however, the use of guarded livery for the clown is significant: within the dramatic narrative, it marks Lancelot as a servant and a fool; that same livery in the playhouse takes the servant and fool roles and combines them into the stage clown, whose costume operates as a kind of *theatrical* livery, alerting spectators to his dramatic function.

Livery is further integrated into the dynamics of onstage performance when Lancelot and Shylock first appear together after the servant's switch in employers. The stage direction reads, '*Enter Jew and his man that was*[,] *the Clown*' (2.5.0.s.d.); and as he walks on, Shylock declares, 'Well, thou shalt see, thy eyes shall be thy judge / The difference of old Shylock and Bassanio' (2.5.1–2). Within the dramatic fiction, these words emphasize differences between the two households – mirroring the cultural and racial differences thematized in the play as a whole. On the actual stage, however, Shylock's comment draws attention to the servant's change in costume. Since Lancelot's new allegiance is visually marked by new livery, it is the audience whose 'eyes shall be [their] judge / The difference of old Shylock and Bassanio'. Sartorial change in the fictional narrative is here imagined as actor–audience *ex*change in the playhouse.

This emphasis on players' costumes (and playgoers' interpretations of them) replicates precisely the issue at stake shortly before this episode, when Lancelot's father first approaches his son.[19] Mistaking him for a 'young gentleman' (2.2.34, 65), the blind Gobbo repeatedly addresses the clown as 'Master' (2.2.29, 34) even as he insists that his son should be referred to as mere 'Lancelet' (2.2.51, 54), since he is 'No master, sir, but a poor man's son' (2.2.46). The humour in the scene depends on the marked contrast between spectators' ability to deduce identity from visual signifiers and the old man's incapacity to do the same. The father is 'sand-blind' (2.2.69) and 'know[s] ... not' (2.2.65, 69) the son; the audience, by contrast, can tell the difference between a base clown and a 'gentleman'. Theatrical spectatorship is here defined as both the accurate interpretation of clothing and the affective enjoyment of their *mis*identification. During parish festivities, those unable to read sartorial signifiers properly could not participate in holiday livery games. In the playhouse, theatregoers are implicitly positioned as knowing participants, those who understand the rules and are willing to play.

Such participation is crucial to the class inversion central to this interchange in Shakespeare's play. When Lancelot determines to leave Shylock's service, he complains that the Jew, despite his wealth, has left the clown 'famished in his service. You may tell every finger I have with my ribs' (2.2.99–100). Bassanio, by contrast, supposedly 'gives rare new liveries' (2.2.102–3), and Lancelot thus seeks to become one of the Christian's followers. The clown is also concerned about the moral consequences of serving his erstwhile master, since the Jew 'is a kind of devil' (2.2.21). When Lancelot beseeches Bassanio to take him on as a servant, then, he is motivated by livery in both its senses: as material remuneration, new livery will help the 'poor man's son' (2.2.46) improve his 'fortune' (2.2.104, 150, 156); as a signifier of affiliation, Bassanio's livery will render Lancelot's service morally legitimate.[20] The scene with Old Gobbo capitalizes on these two meanings of livery by stressing both the financial dimension of Lancelot's service as well as the way dress serves as an identity marker – one that playgoers, but not Lancelot's blind father, are able to interpret correctly.

Moreover, the two functions of livery are here overlaid across each other – and humorously reversed. That is, the very identity markers that Old Gobbo misinterprets are, in fact, signifiers of wealth. The blind man mistakes his son for a gentleman precisely because he insists on the fixity of Lancelot's economic position, even as his error raises the very option of class mobility and the circulation of its signifiers. This inversion is significant both for the subsequent exchange with Bassanio and for what it suggests about the commodification of festive performance. Theatre was precisely that arena in which the mingle-mangle of high and low was derided. This topsy-turvy logic of the stage is embodied by the clown's inappropriate exchange of employers and his concomitant shift in livery. By leaving Shylock and entering Bassanio's household, Lancelot hopes to improve both his moral and financial situation, yet the rich Jew is the one to whom the poor Christian is indebted. The reversal of fortunes that attends these two characters later in the play can be seen to apply also to the clown in the subplot at this early juncture in the narrative. As Bassanio stresses when agreeing to employ Lancelot, the latter's choice inverts the expected order:

> I know thee well. Thou hast obtained thy suit.
> Shylock thy master spoke with me this day
> And hath preferred thee, if it be preferment
> To leave a rich Jew's service, to become
> The follower of so poor a gentleman.
>
> (2.2.135–9)

The clown obtains his 'suit' – a pun collapsing his ambitions and the clothing he hopes to receive – but that 'suit' is not suitable, in that what should be upward economic mobility heads in the opposite direction instead. Within the fictional world of the play, such reversals are mistakes that render Lancelot and his father both fools. On the playhouse stage, however, such inversions of degree are constitutive of the entertainment: the upending of social hierarchies within the fictional representation is precisely what audiences have paid to see. Here, dramatic narrative depends on spectators' willing reading of livery as semiotic marker. Class inversion within the imaginary world of the play exists in dynamic relation to actual audience participation. It is not just that viewers must decode costumes that represent livery; rather, playgoer cognition and affect become the motivating forces that ultimately drive the plot. In this sense, parallels between household livery within the dramatic fiction and costumes on the playhouse stage can be viewed as the legacy of a medieval theatrical tradition incorporating audiences into the narrative itself. Livery, in other words, is not merely a feature *of* the story but an integral structural component *constitutive* of the performance experience.

This presentational dynamic links the festive undercurrents of the clown scenes, the central narrative of the money-lender and the commercialization of theatre. Indeed, there is even some evidence that potentially connects Shylock's story with Robin Hood livery practices. Scholars have noted narrative and linguistic similarities between an episode in *A Gest of Robyn Hode*, an anonymous long poem first published in the early sixteenth century, and a medieval miracle tale known as *The Merchant's Surety*. In *A Gest*, a poor knight receives livery from Robin Hood as well as a loan of £400, although as collateral he can only pledge 'Our dere Lady' (line 267).[21] In *The Merchant's Surety*, an impoverished Christian merchant borrows from a Jewish money-lender and offers the Virgin as his bond; after falsely claiming not to have received repayment, the Jew's dishonesty is revealed, and he converts to Christianity. In the Middle English tale, the Jewish money-lender, Abraham, functions as what Adrienne Williams Boyarin describes as 'a symbol of the "letter of the law" '. She notes that his 'too-literal understanding of what is *legally* acceptable and provable ... is a large part of Abraham's *spiritual* failure'[22] – a theme that, I would note, is applicable also to Shylock. Moreover, both in Shakespeare's play and in the Robin Hood tale, livery implies a form of debt, yet social and economic hierarchies are inverted as in the festive tradition. In *The Merchant of Venice*, ruin becomes fortune, and base clowns are taken for well-born gentlemen. In *A Gest of Robyn Hode*, the yeoman outlaw bequeaths livery to the nobleman and stresses that 'It was never the maner, by dere worthi God, / A yoman to pay for a knyght' (lines 150–1).

This sort of inversion, characteristic of early modern festive livery, also informs how sartorial practices shaped the way actors' bodies were understood – as circulating objects similar to costumes. In the scene in *The Merchant of Venice* immediately preceding the episode with the clown and his father, Morocco specifically refers to his 'complexion' (2.1.1) as the 'shadowed livery of the burnished sun' (2.1.2). His line plays on the notion that bodies are like clothes but with a further reference to the use of blackface make-up in the early modern playhouse.[23] The irony is that Morocco's dark skin is indeed put on and can thus be taken off. His face can, in this sense, circulate since it functions quite literally like costume. Livery is thus precisely the right metaphor to use in this instance: Morocco may declare that he 'would not change this hue' (2.1.11) except for Portia, but his too-careful reliance on surface appearances ultimately leads him to choose the wrong casket, as a result of which his 'heat' (2.7.75) is dampened and his 'suit is cold' (2.7.73).

In the scene when Old Gobbo encounters Lancelot, faces are likewise changed and exchanged and binaries reversed. After the father finally recognizes his son, he declares, 'Lord worshipped might he be, what a beard hast thou got! Thou hast got more hair on thy chin than Dobbin, my thill-horse, has on his tail' (2.2.87–9). Just as the blind man earlier mistakes his base son for a well-born gentleman, Old Gobbo here inverts high and low around the issue of Lancelot's facial hair. In early modern England, beards were kept in the tiring house and worn like costumes to indicate age, gender and social status.[24] Old Gobbo's comment highlights the mobility of beards as sartorial signifiers. Transposing Dobbin's tail to Lancelot's chin, as a lowly clown might put on the clothes of his betters, the blind man's remark implicitly compares Lancelot's face to a horse's behind. When the clown vents his folly, he behaves, to put it bluntly, like an ass.

Indeed, this metaphor is underscored when Lancelot replies, 'It should seem, then, that Dobbin's tail grows backward. I am sure he had more hair of his tail than I have of my face when I last saw him' (2.2.90–2). The line's overt meaning is that the clown's beard is either cut short or completely smooth-shaven; Gobbo, that is, has mistaken his son's hair for his beard. The comment also gestures toward some amusingly vulgar stage business, however. To identify the speaker as his son, the blind father is usually assumed to have run his fingers over Lancelot's face or head.[25] Yet the clown's remarks also imply that Old Gobbo may as well have touched not Lancelot's head but his 'tail'. In his folly, the clown reverses front and back, high and low; his 'beard', which should grow on his face, is like that which 'grows backward' on his behind, à la Chaucer's 'The Miller's Tale'. The crassness of this joke not only illustrates the early modern festive trope of the world turned upside down but also draws a parallel between the actor's body and what he wears. Like beards and other theatrical costumes, actors' bodies are here imagined as subject to changing and exchanging – and to consequent rises and falls in status and fortune. When Old Gobbo declares, 'Lord, how art thou changed!' (2.2.93), then, his comment foreshadows Lancelot's imminent change in employers as well as the change in livery that will accompany it. Onstage, this same line further suggests that the actor himself is like livery: he puts on new identities like a man puts on new clothes – and he is thus like an exchangeable object.

Such understandings of festive *in*version shed light on other sorts of *con*versions that also involve the sartorial. The transformation of Jew to Christian is the most obvious of these – and although beyond the scope of this chapter, I would argue that this conversion, so problematic to audiences and readers today, was specifically seen as festive in early modern England.[26] In addition, it is worth stressing that livery as holiday custom was closely associated with festive crossdressing. Maid Marian, in the Robin Hood games, was typically played by a boy in women's clothing, and various records mention transvestism in conjunction with the election of mock rulers at holidays.[27] Such festive customs bear on the issues of gender and sexuality raised by livery practices in *The Merchant of Venice*. Immediately after Lancelot's speech about wishing to join Bassanio's household because the latter 'gives rare new liveries' (2.2.102–3), Bassanio enters and instructs his men to 'put the liveries to making' (2.2.108–9). This comment most overtly refers to servants' uniforms;[28] however, it also gestures subtly toward the costumes for the masque and feast that Bassanio will shortly host. Couched between two other orders – to 'See these letters delivered' and to 'desire Gratiano to come anon to my lodging' (2.2.108, 109–10) – the reference to making liveries is situated within the sentence as if it were one of several preparations necessary for the upcoming entertainment.

This entertainment is not a court masque but rather a disguising in which revellers wear costumes. Its plot function in Shakespeare's play also calls to mind what Meg Twycross and Sarah Carpenter have referred to as 'amorous masking', a custom in which romantic courtship could take place with some degree of licence given the anonymity (whether real or assumed) of masked participants.[29] It is, after all, this very event that enables the cross-dressed Jessica to escape to join her beloved Lorenzo. Moreover, her male garb not only facilitates her escape but enables her to participate as a torch-bearer in the revels as well. Jessica provides her own 'page's suit' (2.4.33) through which she is 'thus transformed to a boy' (2.6.40), a line implying that the garments she wears underscore gender-crossing over changing household affiliation. Indeed, when she finally meets up with Lorenzo, Jessica is 'glad 'tis night you do not look on me' (2.6.35) and does not want to 'hold a candle to my shames' (2.6.42) for 'They, in themselves, good sooth, are too too light' (2.6.43). The conversation draws attention to the issue of sight by emphasizing that which is 'light', with its dual sexual and optical connotations in early modern England. As in the earlier scenes with Old Gobbo and Lancelot, the point here is about who can and cannot see: if 'love is blind, and lovers cannot see / The pretty follies that themselves commit' (2.6.37–8), then Lorenzo's assertion that 'fair she is, if that mine eyes be true' (2.6.55) is potentially festive reversal, especially given that Jews supposedly had darker skin but were in practice indistinguishable from Christians.[30]

Thinking about costumes as festive livery, then, helps us make sense of a whole range of narrative tropes that appear repeatedly in early modern plays. In *George a Greene*, the pinder is united with his beloved specifically when his boy disguises himself as a woman to smuggle her out of her father's house. The play also directly compares George's beloved, Bettris, to Robin Hood's Maid Marian, the traditional transvestite figure in holiday revels as well as a character in the play. In *The Merchant of Venice*, cross-dressing likewise resonates with festive practices. If actors' bodies, like Lancelot's beard, are mobile and exchangeable in the theatre, then cross-dressing – the exchange of boy actors for female characters – might be thought of as but one of the many exchanges in the play that are overlaid with significance for both the play's concern with commerce and its representation of identity and its marks. Jessica's appropriation of her father's bag of ducats, the choice of the three caskets, Portia's ring trick, Antonio's trials and tribulations as a merchant venturer – all of these aspects of Shakespeare's play might usefully be reinterpreted in light of the transposition of festive performance onto the professional stage.

In associating commercial theatre with holiday inversion and playhouse costumes with festive livery, actors used their own semiotic system to foster greater audience investment. Livery capitalized on the participatory connotations of financial contributions at parish festivities. In purchasing livery badges, spectators at summertime games became active co-celebrants and co-creators of the performance event. It is not merely that holiday rituals required financial backing, but rather that charitable donations were themselves a form of festive roleplaying. Livery badges signified both economic and theatrical support: they marked wearers as donors *and* as Robin Hood's followers. This overlap between the semiotic and economic functions of livery incorporated spectators at parish celebrations into the social body. That this form of participation was essential to group identity may be seen in Philip Stubbes's complaint that those who refused to purchase livery badges were 'mocked, & flouted at, not a little' (Sig. M3r).

In the professional playhouses, such forms of social pressure no longer applied in the same way. Audience members paid admission at the door. As in parish games, an economic contribution was required of spectators, but that monetary investment no longer guaranteed active participation in the roleplaying itself. The theatrical support of playgoers had to be solicited in other ways. Connecting costumes in the public theatres to seasonal livery practices transformed the entrance fee into a contribution to a fictive community, an offering imagined as akin to participation in a holiday game. Paying for admission, in other words, was not a socially neutral transaction but implicitly positioned playgoers as responsible neighbours generously donating to the communal cause. Financial support, social investment and theatrical participation were intertwined. By linking their own performance practices to holiday rituals in this way, actors appropriated the authority of festive traditions – what early modern writers would have referred to as 'ancient customs' – for the new and financially risky institution of the commercial theatre.[31]

Professional playing was, in this sense, quite conservative, growing out of and reinscribing traditional social formations. Such continuities between drama and seasonal customs indicate more than simply the existence of overlapping and contemporaneous cultural practices; rather, they suggest that generic distinctions between theatre and festivity are, for this period, very difficult to sustain. Although the historical processes through which they eventually diverged are too complex to assess here, the plays I have examined in this chapter do highlight one important factor contributing to this separation: differences in the material constraints of the parish and the playhouse altered the implicit exchanges at the heart of performance and thus the economic valences of dramatic representation. In the playhouse, spectators' contributions, whether in the form of personal energy or material resources, did not directly benefit the local community, as was the case in the parish setting; instead, *imaginative* exchange took the place of *actual* exchange. Audience investment, financial or otherwise, in the performance event resulted not in some concrete manifestation of genuine social bonds – say, a new roof for the parish church – but in ephemeral affective experiences. Those experiences, while certainly a part of festive roleplaying games, acquired a new fungibility in the commercial playhouses.

By integrating festive livery into its own actor–audience dynamics, early modern theatre slowly transformed roleplaying from a ubiquitous practice into an exchangeable commodity, from a popular custom shot through the fabric of community life into an economic object set apart for commercial consumption. Costume, like livery, could be traded only when divested of the very semiotic fixity that made it what it was. By folding this contradiction into the presentational dynamics of the stage and by enacting it over and over again, the very act of performance gradually changed performance itself – enabling playing to come into its own as the ontologically distinct entity that today we call *theatre*.

'Honest Clothes' in *The Merry Wives of Windsor*

Catherine Richardson

And *Honi soit qui mal y pense* write
In em'rald tufts, flowers purple, green and white,
Like sapphire, pearl and rich embroidery,
Buckled below fair knighthood's bending knee:
Fairies use flowers for their charactery.
                    (*MW* 5.5.69–73)[1]

So says Mistress Quickly, dressed as the Queen of the Fairies, taking *The Merry Wives of Windsor* through its final shift of energies to this small, embroidered verse oasis of calm in Act 5, scene 5. By the time she does so, the audience has been on a fairly extensive journey through early modern England's complex relationships between clothing and moral status, and Quickly's bejewelled and perfumed garter finds its visual and olfactory opposite in Falstaff's description of his experience in the buck-basket: 'By the Lord, a buck-basket! Rammed me in with foul shirts and smocks, socks, foul stockings, greasy napkins.' It is the contention of this chapter that the connections between social and moral identity that clothing can articulate shape *Merry Wives* in fundamental ways: just as the garter symbolizes a coherent elite code of moral authority, so the fresh and dirty linens that preoccupy the characters in much of the rest of the play allow Shakespeare to articulate the gendered connections between non-elite dress and morality. In a play that has an enormous social range – from knights to citizens to maids – but that concentrates its attentions on the Pages and Fords in the middle of society, this is particularly important. The non-elite moral codes which were so central to such middling-status households in particular are perhaps less familiar to us than their elite counterparts: they appear less clearly defined and articulated largely because they circulate in oral discourses around shame and reputation such as those of the ecclesiastical courts, where they are often negotiated through the materiality of dress. Their reconstruction reveals a play whose jest is more serious than we have previously realized; a drama that draws striking parallels between theatrical representation and offstage practices of communal shaming.

In order to explore these issues, this chapter deals with two pairs of clothed images whose visual impact establishes the moral dynamic of the play. The first pair is the horns and the kerchief, the head coverings around which male and female reputation are negotiated; the second is the set of starched and pinned linens that cover the body to form the image of the good housewife, versus the dirty, disorderly linens, disconnected from the body, that epitomize her polar opposite. One of each of these pairs is a shaming image that destroys reputation, whereas the other both secures and advertises it.

I begin by suggesting that the way in which characters are clothed and reclothed in *Merry Wives* constitutes a specific comedic strategy that shapes the play's exploration of the gendered relationship between shaming and mirth – between, as Mistress Page puts it, being 'honest' and being 'merry' (4.2.100). But I argue that, in order to understand the complexities of *Merry Wives*' interplay between language and costume, we need to situate such disguises in relation to extra-theatrical discourses of reputation and shame expressed through dress. Such discourses, in both didactic literature and documentary sources (especially the testimonies given in the early modern courts), help us to understand how the costume of the play would have been seen as expressing gendered moral reputations. These discourses have two functions: they give access to the relationships between clothed images and inner moral states, and they reveal the significance of dress in articulating sexual violence against women. Finally, I contend that the play stages the tensions between the onstage and offstage functions of dress: clothing's methods of making gender in the theatre and its role in defining morality outside the playhouse walls.

Merry Wives signals its focused interest in these questions of reputation through an almost obsessive repetition of the language of moral status, shared by the majority of its characters. The play uses emphatic reiteration more generally as a kind of reverberation – setting important concepts echoing around its scenes. While this is the case with various words, by far the most frequent occurrences are of the word 'honest'.[2] With its cognate words honesty and dishonesty, it appears twenty-nine times in the play, its instance picking up in frequency and gaining emphasis from 1.4 onwards. Initially present in general terms and applied to both genders (Slender talks of 'honest, civil, godly company'; Quickly calls Fenton 'an honest gentleman'; and Anne, Mistress and Master Ford, Rugby, Master Page, Falstaff and Quickly herself are so named), it becomes focused in its reference to aberrant sexual identities. The wives jokingly desire only 'villainy' that 'may not sully the chariness of our honesty' (2.1.87–9) and state that 'wives may be merry and yet honest too' (4.2.100), but the men positively descant on the word.[3] It is Ford himself, of course, who makes best use of the term – 'If I find her honest I lose not my labour' (2.1.215), he says of testing his wife; as Brook he confides in Falstaff that she might only 'appear honest to me' (2.2.211) and suggests the knight 'lay an amiable siege to the honesty of this Ford's wife' (223–224). Faced with the buck-basket a second time, he shouts, 'behold what honest clothes you send forth to bleaching!' (4.2.114–15), and mocks his wife as 'Mistress Ford, the honest woman, the modest wife, the virtuous creature' (121–2). Given to a kind of public railing and a lack of restraint, Ford employs a discourse that stands on the knife edge of slanderous utterance, both with his wife, and with the disguised Falstaff whom he calls 'A witch, a quean, an old cozening quean!' (4.2.162), shouting, 'I'll prat her! Out of my door, you witch, you rag, you baggage, you polecat, you runnion, out, out!' (174–6). This kind of speech threatens his own reputation as a responsible citizen of the town, as his wife's sarcasm makes clear: ''Tis a goodly credit for you!' (179–80).[4]

We can add to these instances the similarly heavy use of a discourse of shaming and reputation. It begins with the wives in the first two scenes of Falstaff's disguising: 'You're shamed, you're overthrown, you're undone for ever!' (3.3.88–9) says Mistress Page as Ford approaches the house, 'defend your reputation, or bid farewell to your good life for ever' (109–10), and then later, at the identical moment in 4.2, repeats 'you are utterly shamed ... better shame than murder' (39–41). The discourse then migrates to address the knight himself in the forest: Mistress Ford says to Mistress Page as they plot Falstaff's final downfall: 'I'll warrant they'll have him publicly shamed, and methinks there would be no period to the jest should he not be publicly shamed' (4.2.209–11). Also related are Falstaff's ironic discussions of honour and male reputation. When he argues with Pistol in 2.2, for instance, he rants repetitively in the following terms in the course of two speeches: 'I took't upon mine honour'; 'you stand upon your honour!'; 'keep the terms of my honour precise'; 'hiding mine honour in my necessity'; 'under the shelter of your honour!'. Taken together, these examples demonstrate a play saturated with the language of the communal definition of reputation. It is within this linguistic field that the clothing of the play's characters gains meaning, and its density shows the essential seriousness of the ideas of honesty versus shaming that *Merry Wives* articulates.

This is a play whose comic structure is built around the doubly clothed body of the actor, its meaning made from the interplay of character and disguise, and the second half of *Merry Wives* is structured around a series of disguises that give it an episodic feel. Most obviously, there is Falstaff in the buck-basket, as the fat woman of Brentford and finally as Herne the hunter; but there is also Ford disguised as Brook, and the Windsor residents dressed as fairies, with Anne Page's complexly costumed elopement: from Act 3 onwards these episodes form a series of scenes focused on a central disguised figure that indicates that the reclothed body offers a dominant way of understanding the development of the comedy.

While these striking images of the alter egos that clothing offers are given equal weight in terms of their form, each gaining roughly equivalent 'theatrical exposure' in front of the audience, their narrative and metaphorical functions are rather different. Ford's disguise, for instance, 'belongs to the main "Italianate" plot of the jealous husband and the deceits in love'.[5] His reclothing is a device that generates comedy as it allows him to witness first hand Falstaff's extravagant plans for his wife's unfaithfulness and the knight's rather too frank appraisal of his own character. Anne's disguise too is a traditional comic tool that facilitates the triumph of romantic love over arranged marriage and the passions of youth over parental control. Shakespeare typically complicates matters by adding three suitors and three rival outfits, but the traditional elements of comic disguise – that is, the concealment of identity from some of the characters, but not from the audience, for the purposes of altering plot development – remain firmly in place. So far, *Merry Wives* uses disguise in a fairly conventional way.

While Anne's and Ford's disguises do raise questions about identity and true knowledge of others, the allusive potential of Falstaff's disguises far surpasses these more traditional clothing roles. The three scenes that constitute his shaming as a lecher offer rich and complex amendments to and explorations of character, ones which investigate connections between clothing and moral identity within the community. His appearance in the stag's horns has long been recognized as a triumphant comic realization of a series of metaphors and repeated references to different textual sources that have been bubbling close to the surface of the play from the point at which Falstaff propositions the wives.[6] I want to extend these arguments by discussing how his horned image functions in relation to non-elite discourses of reputation, before going on to show how it is connected to his disguise as the witch of Brentford. I argue that his two different head coverings fit together as a pair of gendered stereotypes of sexual reputation. I work backwards through Falstaff's three central scenes of re-dressing, therefore, in order to tease out a contemporary sense of the complex relationship between moral identity and clothing.

Through the horns which Mistress Quickly obtains for the fat knight, *Merry Wives* clarifies the debt its plot owes to Fabliau tales of young men cuckolding older husbands, and the figure of Actaeon-turned-deer pursued by his own hounds. These familiar stories, circulating textually and visually outside the theatre, are given material form – made tangible – in Falstaff's final head covering. And those horns also give shape to the feverish nightmares of Ford, finally putting to rest his fears of wearing them himself when they appear on someone else's head. As Graham Holderness puts it, they turn Falstaff 'into the deer that's pursued by the hunt, crowning him with the horns of ridicule he was hoping to pin, as the badge of the cuckold, onto their husbands'.[7] Although Falstaff thinks himself dressed as the potent stag for a last triumphant liaison, the wives costume him in Herne's huge horns in order to shame him in front of an audience of their husbands and neighbours as a 'public sport' – the disguise they use is both the symbol of shame and its method.

Tracing the development of this imagery allows us to see the discursive weight it carries, to assess how significant notions of cuckoldry are in the play, and to see how they fit with *Merry Wives*' explorations of honesty. Mentions of the cuckold ring through the language of the play with bell-like insistence: Pistol sets the idea of the cuckold in motion when he first tells Ford about Falstaff's letter to his wife: 'Prevent, or go thou like Sir Actaeon he, / With Ringwood at his heels. / O, odious is the name!' 'What name, sir?' Ford replies, slow on the uptake, to be informed, 'The horn, I say' (2.1.106–10). Ford himself in 3.2, now much quicker, is eager to 'divulge Page himself for a secure and wilful Actaeon' (3.2.39), and Falstaff calls Ford 'the peaking cornuto' who dwells 'in a continual larum of jealousy'. After his first meeting with Falstaff, Ford, disguised as Brook, demonstrates the verbal expression of this alarm as he begins one of his agitated Tourette's-like speeches focused on the word 'cuckold'. 'But cuckold? Wittol? Cuckold! The devil himself hath not such a name!' (2.2.283–4), he says, and ends with 'Fie, fie, fie! Cuckold, cuckold, cuckold!' (296–7). He does the same with the word buck when he sees the washing in 3.3: 'Buck? I would I could wash myself of the buck! Buck, buck, buck! Ay, buck! I warrant you, buck – and of the season too, it shall appear' (144–6). Horn, buck, cornuto, Actaeon and cuckold: as this list makes clear, a good part of the play's linguistic texture is made up of reminders of the shameful image of the horned man, and the horns in which Falstaff is dressed draw all these mentions into themselves in a crescendo of the loss of male sexual reputation.

The horns, in other words, become a focus for different discourses on the theme of male honesty within the play, and this is a feature of *Merry Wives*' use of key items of costume which, I argue later, extends to female reputation through the other significant item of dress in these key central scenes, the kerchief. Such items of costume offer a visual economy of purpose – an epitomizing quality essential to comic energy; they are subject to metaphorical elaborations. And in Falstaff's horns, literate tales meet oral discourses of shame, allowing the play to negotiate the relationship between its high and low, its foreign and its English subtexts and allusions. The image of the cuckold and his horn was part of the most common discourse of the communal, social implications of unruly relationships between men and women – of identifying, distinguishing and thereby managing domestic rupture. It had a universal social range that wove in and out of print and oral tales, and a significant public presence in the early modern court. Examining the contemporary manifestations of the cuckold imagery suggests how the play's conjunction of costume and discourse might have functioned on the early modern stage.

Although discourses of cuckoldry circulated widely in early modern culture, it was in the increasingly commonly used ecclesiastical courts that they became a part of the explicit establishment of moral norms. In the evidence that witnesses gave there, we can catch echoes of oral tales and significant gestures circulating in contemporary communities. Just two examples must suffice here, but similar discourses of male shaming can be found in the records of any ecclesiastical court from this period. On 23 July 1613, the twenty-two-year-old Elizabeth Stone came to court in Oxford to depose that 'about Michaelmas Last' in her mother's chamber, she heard John Brickland 'tell her said mother that Robert Hill ... was a Cuckold yf there were anie such in Oxford for Jenkins hath given him an Acteons head & cornuted hime to a heire, & doeth vse his wyfe ... as ordinarily as her husband doeth'.[8] This case is typical in its sense of the local impact and definition of identities – 'yf there were anie such in Oxford'. It is, however, unusual in its use of what might be seen as the literary language of sexual sin – its mention of Actaeon and of the Italian for cuckold, 'cornuto'. This bringing together of the prosaic world of masculine insult and the learned world of classical allusion comments interestingly on both the migration of written narratives into shaming speech in the textually savvy urban spaces of Oxford, and the familiarity and logic of the play's similar move.

In another case from the rural community of Besford in Worcestershire, John Goscome, a seventy-five-year-old farmer, deposes about the shocking behaviour of his son. Thomas, he says, 'doth not s[t]icke to slaunder him ... beinge his owne naturall Father, callinge him Cockolde and holdinge vpp his

Fingers vppon his browe in Forcked manner signifieinge him to be a Cockolde. And divers others he hath in this manner abused.' John's description of the way his son uses his fingers to make the sign of the horn gives us a sense of the familiarity of the image as popular gesture, and its links to violent and offensive behaviour, as he adds that Thomas 'hath alsoe beaten this deponent and his mother in law'.[9] Although not an everyday article of dress, the horns were a familiar potential addition to men's public image, clothing them in the shame of dishonesty.

These cases also demonstrate how inextricably linked were men's and women's reputations: crucial to our understanding of *Merry Wives* is the pairing of the image of the horn with discourses of female honesty. The 'mother in law', actually John's second wife Joanna, confirms that her step-son called his father cuckold, but also that he called her whore. The two insults are paired partly because a 'cuckold' necessitates the presence of a 'whore', and partly because they are the gender-specific terms of slander – terms intended to injure reputation. As a result of these slanderous utterances, 'there is a publicke voyce and Fame as of divers other dissolute behaviours', Joanna states, and Elizabeth Stone's testimony, given above, concluded with the assertion 'that the speakinge of the said wordes must needes be a scandall to the good name & credite of the said Mary whoe for all the tyme of the deponentes knowledge of her hath bine accompted an honest woman'. This identification of a woman's honest reputation and the damage done to it by slander is a preoccupation of a court system that was in the middle of an enormous increase in just such litigation at the time that *Merry Wives* was being written.[10] The image of the cuckold's horns is inextricably paired with these discourses of female shame and honesty, and in the play the latter offer a series of insistent verbal reminders of a coherent moral code through which communities policed aberrant sexual acts. Shaming horns, this evidence shows, are an important visual marker of reputation for men, policing the boundaries of moral repute in ways that are both similar to and different from the use of external signifiers of women's reputations.

We need to ask how early modern communities evaluated honesty. It was a nebulous concept which defined ideals of behaviour for both genders – the *Oxford English Dictionary* defines it as 'all kinds of moral excellence worthy of honour' (3a) – but for women it was mainly focused on their chastity. As chastity is not 'empirically demonstrable', Allen Brown says, 'truth is generally a consensual affair, a matter of narrative credibility and rhetorical prowess'.[11] But an honesty whose focusing dynamic was the chaste female body had to have its external signifiers, and early modern men and women were prepared to read carefully for material proof. Narratives about morality are often constructed around outward material signifiers of the honesty of the body underneath. If we are to understand the representation of this central aspect of gendered identity on the stage, then we need to reconstruct the significance of women's outer appearance from other sources, as we have done for the cuckold's horns.

Dress could signify both honesty and dishonesty. To begin with prescription, many of the gestures that connote chastity in didactic literature were related to dress. Writers like Henry Smith listed apparel as one of the five things 'thou must mark' if 'thou wilt know a godly man or a godly woman'. He linked women's honest dress to 'an honest face' because 'a modest countenance and womanlie shamefastnes, doe commend a chast wife'. This fact was apparently to be observed in the word 'Nuptiae' which 'importeth a couering, because the Virgine which should be married, when they came to their husbands, for modestie & shamefastnesse did couer their faces' like Rebecca before Isaac, who 'cast a vayle before her face, shewing that modestie should be learned before marriage'. In other words, honesty is seen through the dress that represents obedience, tying the two concepts inextricably together. As 'the ornament of a woman is silence', so 'a modest woman is knowne by her sober attyre': silence adorns her modest dress like an accessory.[12] Women's physical and metaphorical clothing, their virtues and their head coverings, become densely intertwined in this influential kind of writing about the role of wives.

Outside the pages of advice literature, concepts of 'honesty' also cling to clothing in ways that suggest its power to represent female identity. John Thomas of St Peter's parish in Canterbury wills that his 'Servaunt and mayde Alice at her departing from her mystres my wyf ... be clothed well and honestely and a marc of money'.[13] Thomas Strowde, making his will in Elham in Kent, left money towards his daughter Jane's marriage to Thomas Byrde, 'on condicion that the sayd Byrde wold leve her worthe xxti nobles incase she dyd overlyve the said Byrd and also sayd that he wold honestly apparell her'. It is variously stated that 'the value of her apparell cometh to 4li', or that it costs '5 marks at the leste to be honestly apparelled'.[14] Honest clothing permits women to adopt an appropriate public identity – to demonstrate their moral nature through their dress. In these examples the notion of sartorial honesty connects social and moral appropriateness around women's dress to its financial implications – it costs more to dress a woman of higher status honestly than it would her poorer neighbour. This takes us to the heart of the play's concerns with Mistress Page's and Mistress Ford's status as honest wives who hold the strings of full purses. An honest reputation connects moral behaviour to social status, and dress is one of its most important expressions.[15]

Such a metaphorical reading of garments suggests their potency in representing moral states – this is a less obvious but potentially equally powerful version of the male horns of shame. In the courts we can see these readings linked to gestures that suggest how they might be put to such work on stage where women's honesty is often called into legal question implicitly through the loss of significant items of clothing. In an unpleasant assault case at the assizes, Jane Smith says she was 'sitting in the doore of Lance Smith' when she saw three women fighting, and 'went in to parte them and the said Smith puld the Coyfe [coif, a close fitting cap] of[f] ... Mary Northes head'. Jane's final statement is that she 'went in with a stone and hitt her the said Mary North with an intent to parte them.' Isabel Masser says she saw 'Smith and her daughter vpon the said Mary North and heard the said Mary North Cry Murther they both of them the said Smithes standing by with her Coyfe of her heade'.[16] This small item of dress works silently to characterize both perpetrators' and deponents' sense of its significance in the construction of appropriate gendered identity. North is effectively scalped when her coyfe is removed, and the violence is directed against her identity as an honest woman: rather than putting on the horns, they take off her head covering. These deponents take as read the significance of such an item of dress, just as we can clearly see the metaphorical potential of Falstaff's horns.

Appropriate display of linen items, especially but not exclusively on the head, could be used to define a woman's honesty,[17] but they could also symbolize the obedience on which proof of that honesty was based. When William Cleveley lay sick in his bed by his hall fire, he made a nuncupative testament (a verbal will) in which he gave his father his wearing apparel, but 'with that ... Jane [his wife] pulled her kercheiffe [headcloth] of[f] her head *as beinge discontent* and threw it on the grounde' and friends and neighbours 'persuaded her to be quiet'. Those present, in other words, both read her gesture as signifying discontent, and used it in their retelling of the event in order to demonstrate her emotion to the court.[18] Obedient wives are kerchiefed as a mark of their respect for their husband's authority, and this case demonstrates their awareness of the function of head linens as a symbol of submission or rebellion. Studying a play that represents women who constantly test the boundaries and definitions of honest female behaviour necessitates careful attention to this kind of evidence.

These head coverings, then, constitute the opposing pair to the image of the horned man, and *The Merry Wives of Windsor* uses them to explore key aspects of female status. The depositions give a complex but clear sense of the importance of linen in the construction of women's honest

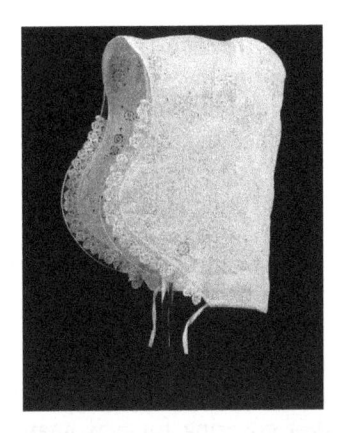

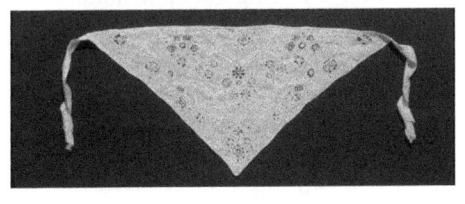

FIGURE 4 a and b *Linen coif and forehead cloth, embroidered with linen thread, coif edged with bobbin lace, T.57-1947,* © *Victoria and Albert Museum, London.*

reputations – for their public identity as wives – as their heads were always covered when in company. A recent analysis of surviving early modern linens has shown the complexity of the decoration of headwear which was set against its honest simplicity of form for the middling sort and above, and the coif and forehead cloth shown here suggest the visual impact of linen embroidered in a way that demonstrates skill but resists vain shows of extravagance.[19] Plainness is a relative term, referring to the form and its appropriateness for a working context, rather than its decoration. These objects give a visual context to what is happening in performance during Falstaff's preposterously inflated wooing of Mistress Ford in 3.3.48–54:

FALSTAFF	Let the court of France show me such another! I see how thine eye would emulate the diamond: thou hast the right arched beauty of the brow that becomes the ship-tire, the tire-valiant, or any tire of Venetian admittance.
MISTRESS FORD	A plain kerchief, Sir John: my brows become nothing else, nor that well neither.

Falstaff offers her a vision of herself in the courtly headdress that was one of the articles of clothing attacked by moralists, while she contrasts this with a 'plain' kerchief – the appropriately modest covering for a woman of her status.[20] The discussion picks up on her husband's threatening boast from the previous scene: 'Well, I will take him, then torture my wife, pluck the borrowed *veil of modesty* from the so-seeming Mistress Page, divulge Page himself for a secure and wilful Actaeon, and to these violent proceedings all my neighbours shall cry aim' (3.2.36–40, my italics). As was the case in the domestic manuals, the veil is both a material thing and a metaphorical expression of sartorial honesty appropriate for the middling sort. But Ford's comment shows the double nature of the object: its covering is both modest and potentially deceitful.[21]

These textual and material appearances of headcloths that might signal modesty or deceit become significant in a more complex way in 4.2 when Falstaff exits the house in his second reclothing. Here, his head is covered as he is dressed as the fat woman of Brentford in a scene that, the episodic nature of the play's visual set pieces suggests, we should see as connected to his later horning. Here, head coverings become the stuff of disguise – 'he might put on a hat, a muffler and kerchief, and so escape' (64–8), says Mistress Page. When Mistress Ford remembers that 'My maid's aunt, the fat woman of Brentford, has a gown above' and Mistress Page adds 'there's her thrummed hat and her muffler too' (71–5), half the disguise is in place. But Falstaff is still missing the 'plain kerchief', which is essential to disguise his gender. Mistress Ford offers, therefore, that, 'Mistress Page and I will look some linen for your head'. As Falstaff exits to the chamber to 'put on the gown the while' (76–9), it is their own head linen which the wives find to dress him in, making a woman of this man by mixing the signs and symbols of their honesty with the liminal attire that defines the outer garments of 'the witch of Brentford'. Does Mistress Ford find linen on the stage for him, or does she remove the head covering she is currently wearing in which to dress him, thus leaving her own head shamefully bare? What turns men into women in the theatre makes women respectable outside it, and that crossover of cloths, migrating from the head of Mistress Ford to the head of the greasy fat knight in order to facilitate his escape, becomes a visual symbol of the tensions between theatrical and non-theatrical gender definition, and between mirth and honesty. Under this one object, ostensibly just the convenient answer to a pressing comic problem, meet the respectable and unrespectable, notions of covering and deceiving, and expressing and denying gender. It is, in other words, an object just as flexibly susceptible to multiple readings and metaphorical interpretations as the stag's horns, but one that operates mainly at the level of oral tales about female reputation.

However, these meanings also point up *Merry Wives*'s even more intimate vestimentary exchanges, setting clean against dirty linen, and considering the metaphorical potential of their relationship in a sophisticated way. Linen was an important negotiator of that crucial early modern distinction between inner and outer garments, because on the head and around the collar and cuffs, what was close to the body nevertheless showed through to the public gaze. Absorbing 'the dirt and secretions of the body beneath', linen shirts and smocks 'were indelibly marked by their association with the body' to the extent that 'the second skin of cloth became metaphorically indistinguishable from the body's "natural" covering'. Personal cleanliness was entirely bound up with the laundering of linen, and the regular changing of underwear, dependent as it was on ownership of additional garments, defined status through a crisp, whitened exterior.[22] Thomas Bentley, in *The Monument of Matrons*, makes these garments part of a routine of prayer based around dressing and undressing in the early morning: 'Putting off your neerest garment, praie thus', he says; 'Most gratious and mercifull Saviour Jesus Christ, thou knowest how we be borne, cloathed, and clogged with the greevous & heaviee burden of the first woman Eve who fell awaie unto fleshlinesse ...', and then, 'Beholding your nakednesse, praie thus ... cloath me with thine innocencie, and holie vertues; and so cover my filthinesse ...'. The movement of the prayers turns upon the changing of linen, ending: 'Putting on your neerest garment, praie thus: ... O cover thou my nakednesse and shame with the fine linnen robe of his righteousnesse and vertue ... Yea, make thou my linnen cloaths as white as snowe, and shining like the light.'[23] The whiteness of linen comes to signify the election (in the theological sense) of the body and soul it covers. This idea of a nearest garment makes clear the extent to which smocks and shirts (loosely gendered alternatives in an age before what we know as underwear) stood for the individual they clothed, both body and soul, their cleanliness paired with the spiritual purity of their wearer.

Bringing these ideas about the morality of personal linen together with the expression of gendered honesty and shame discussed above, we can now fully explore the metaphorical possibilities of Falstaff's presence in the buck-basket. The symbolic interpretations of this scene have always been seen as strong.[24] Mistress Page's supposed pragmatism lights upon the method by which the foul is cleansed and purified when she says, 'Look, here is a basket: if he be of any reasonable stature, he may creep in here, and throw foul linen upon him, as if it were going to bucking; or – it is whiting time – send him by your two men to Datchet Mead' (3.3.119–22). Falstaff's physical and moral purification are twinned. But the solution she suggests is also a socially specific way of dealing with his problematic sexuality. The processes of washing and starching linen were crucial to the maintenance of a household of some social standing, and they provided a clear, visual way of demarcating the distinctions between the middling sort and those below them, not through the sumptuous outer fabrics of the elite but through the careful attention paid to inner garments. The middling sort looked different to those below them precisely because they were invested in these practices. The focus of the wives' solution on the domestic processes around laundering clothes draws into play the moral dynamics of non-elite status: greater whiteness conflated higher standards of laundry with higher moral principles.

When Falstaff returns to his room at the Garter in 3.5, his comic monologue imagines the laundering through which he has been put for the audience: ''Sblood, the rogues slighted me into the river with as little remorse as they would have drowned a blind bitch's puppies' (8–9). The events take on, however, a rather different focus later in the scene in his reiteration of his escape to Brook: 'By the Lord, a buck-basket! Rammed me in with foul shirts and smocks, socks, foul stockings, greasy napkins, that, Master Brook, there was the rankest compound of villainous smell that ever offended nostril' (82–6). It is not the washing, but his presence in the dirty laundry on which he concentrates in this instance. The description Falstaff gives her husband is fundamentally bodily, the knight's roasted flesh both caused and covered by his contact with the household's linens. And these include 'foul shirts and smocks, socks, foul stockings', in other words the second skin of Ford's family, and especially his wife – the items that have lain closest to her flesh. The wives clothe him dirtily, disguising him by covering him in linen until he is invisible: 'Help to cover your master, boy' (3.3.133), Mistress Page says to Robin. Thinking about Falstaff's time in the basket as a clothed disguise, like his other humiliations, helps us to understand the extent of the moral complications of this play and the way it pushes the boundaries of acceptable behaviour. It both shames him, through his contact with women's clothes, and shames the wives through his proximity to their intimate linens.

Ford's intemperate, hysterical response to the buck-basket's reappearance in 4.2 is apparently motivated by this unseemly, dishonest reclothing of the fat knight in his wife's smock and stockings. His language is freighted with the discourse of reputation – 'behold what honest clothes you send forth to bleaching!' (114–15) – and his neighbours' responses to the basket's unpacking give a clear sense of the inappropriateness of Ford's action: ''Tis unreasonable! Will you take up your wife's clothes?' (133–4), Evans says. The double entendre has often been acknowledged here – taking up a woman's clothes revealed her naked private parts. The comedy of the image is frequently used to shame those who engage in illicit sexual activity. In the case quoted above of the son who accused his father of cuckoldry and his stepmother of whoredom, he is said to have described a couple 'in a bushe or Brake in Asham Feilde with her clothes vpp and his breaches downe'. This familiar topsy-turvy image of clothes up and breeches down brings a shaming kind of humour to tale-telling about sexual incontinence, and it constitutes slander to repeat it in such a way as to suggest adultery.[25] Mistress Ford's comment on her husband's actions is pertinent in many different ways, therefore: 'Are you not ashamed?' (130), she says. Falstaff's presence and Ford's response to it are both careless in their dealings with intimate garments – both men are too close to soiled linens – and understanding the material representations of potential dishonesty gives us a much fuller sense of the titillating power of *The Merry Wives of Windsor*'s comedy.

There are also, however, aspects of this scene where the material evidence pulls against the comedy, or at least opens up its much darker side, and these are illuminated by examining how clothing operates as a way of discussing the violence done to the body, a method which substitutes sartorial for corporeal description. When Ford orders the basket to be emptied in 4.2, the audience is not offered a passive display of dirty laundry; rather the scene challenges comedic boundaries in its negotiation of violence. His rage, the emotional heart of the play, is perpetrated upon the linens within the buck; he vents his impotent frustration at his inability to find Falstaff on its contents. 'Pluck me out all the linen' (141), he says, and that harsh word 'pluck' is striking. It meant not only to pull the feathers off a chicken in order to make it bare, it also carried now-obsolete sartorial allusions. The late-sixteenth-century game called 'pluck at the crow' involved pulling at the clothing and hair of one of the players – it was a determinedly violent action on the borders of jest and cruelty.[26] In 4.2, Ford both beats Falstaff and plucks harshly at his wife's linens. If clothing stands for the body, then violence perpetrated upon it cannot be separated from the person whose shape it bears, and this takes his actions to the very edge of reason.

The link between 'near garments' and violence draws parallels with aspects of the numerous sexual abuse cases which were tried in early modern England. For instance, Margaret Braster offered the Somerset Quarter Sessions a narrative that uses description of her clothing as proof of a physical attack. She says that 'yesterday about 3 of the clocke in the afternoone there came one Thomas Ingland of Shepton Beauchampe to this Informants house there beinge noe body att home att the sayd tyme but this Informant and three Little children: and sayth that hee assaulted her and tore the wast bond of her Petticoate from of[f] her Body'.[27] Women often use descriptions of violence done to their dress as a way of negotiating the shame of assault.[28] Elizabeth Dyer, a domestic servant of the parish of St Dunstan's in Canterbury, was sent for 'a halpeny pot of beere' one morning to John Roydon's house, who 'willed this deponent to goo dowen into the seller' with him to fetch it. Elizabeth says that 'shee ys a shamed to speak' what he said next, so she substitutes his actions for his words: he 'came to this deponent And put his hand into her placket he plucked up her smoke [smock] And [l?]ent his hand to this deponents bare privitys'.[29] As in the cases involving women's head coverings, a modern court might consider the clothing detail here tangential. But describing violence done to dress in fact makes it possible to discuss lasting marks of abuse without depicting the body, and it quantifies moral and psychological injury in the material financial terms of damaged possessions. Reading Ford's violent plucking of the clothes in the basket in similarly metaphorical ways reveals the low, ungentlemanly and dishonourable (both violent and crude) nature of his behaviour. But it also shows how dangerous his emotion is to the women's reputations: the coming apart of women's dress symbolizes a moral unravelling because it stands for the very physical threat to body and reputation.

Finally, then, we can compare the contrasting images of linen on stage in this play, in order to assess Shakespeare's use of costume in his definition of the wives' honesty. Starched and pressed linen was layered on women's bodies in order to produce the whitened, perfected exterior of the 'honestly dressed' housewife.[30] Holbein's portrait miniature of Jane

FIGURE 5 *Hans Holbein, Mrs Jane Small, formerly Mrs Pemberton, P.40&A-1935, © Victoria and Albert Museum, London.*

Small, wife of a wealthy London merchant, boldly displays the relationship between the crispness of her linen and the demureness of her expression in an aesthetic form (the portrait) usually reserved for the elite. The parts of *Merry Wives* that expose linen undo that image spectacularly, revealing (rather than concealing) clothing's debt to its processes of construction and exploding the crucial focus on the totality of effect involved in being honestly dressed. But it is the juxtaposition of this disarray with the constant stage presence of Mistress Ford and Mistress Page that holds their morality at the focal point of the play's dangerous comedy. The merry wives of Windsor do not dress up; they do not don disguises. Throughout these scenes of dirty linen and images of shame, they control the stage as whitened, starched and correctly pinned images of the honestly dressed middling-status housewife, doing so as their linen migrates to the head and body of a disreputable old knight. The complexity of the play's exploration of their honesty lies in the staged pairing of clean and dirty linens.

There is a good deal at stake in the honesty of these wives. Recent work on the play has made a significant case for its engagement in early modern political discourse, revealing the dual dangers of Mistress Page's 'honest' and 'merry' formulation: both mirth and honesty were perceived as having dangerous social potential. Harriet Phillips has argued for the political potency of the latter half, suggesting that the nuances of contemporary meanings of 'merry' 'came to stand in for a host of desires and intentions in varying degrees of proximity to sedition'.[31] We can see these political nuances in relation to the mirthful games of shaming explored above. Phil Withington advocates a widening of the sexual elements of 'honesty' to include its social determinants. He carefully reveals the word's political overtones in relation to notions of good citizenship, arguing that the wives' honesty 'cannot be reduced to their sexual probity ... but also involves the kind of discretion, discourse and social agency associated with civic humanism'.[32] The analysis offered here reveals an additional layer to *Merry Wives*' broad concerns with communal stability, by suggesting that this is a play interested in considering the relations between the two terms (mirth and honesty), precisely in order to examine how shaming works to contain aberrant behaviour. The comedy of the play's disguises is essentially political in nature.

Shaming, through wearing the horns, recalibrates honesty in ways that show the social work that comedy does. But this chapter has revealed strong connections between horns and linens that indicate the extent of the play's flirtation with the idea of shaming the wives too – violently plucking out their dirty linen in public in ways that bring them close to the equivalent of wearing the horn. This domestic politics of shaming balances the jest of *Merry Wives*, and the chapter therefore extends debates about the play's political discourses in a material direction: looking at clothing's functions onstage in this play gives insight into the specifically theatrical ways in which drama engages in communal discourse. It indicates a mode of staging in which key actions take place within the context of sartorial reminders of the opposing poles of honesty and dishonesty which formed a coherent moral code for early modern townspeople, negotiated by a process of shaming.

If we look across the play – from the buck-basket to the kerchiefed witch, to Falstaff horned – we can see its stage images echoing off one another just as its linguistic fields do. Focusing on dress in *Merry Wives* makes it possible to explore how the material elements of a play – its properties and costumes – extend its metaphors, sharpen its social commentary and characterize its gender dynamics. It shows what was at stake in the gestures around clothing; the extent to which the play's subtle evaluations of appropriate behaviour depend upon this fertile interplay between text, object and stage image, and just how closely Shakespeare might have expected his audience to watch the things he staged, as well as listening to the words he wrote.

How to Do Things with Shoes

Natasha Korda

Among the scattered dress-pins, buttons, beads, hooks, bits of copper lace and silk fringe, and other remnants of costume unearthed in the Museum of London Archaeology's (MoLA's) excavations of England's first commercial playhouses, now stored at the Mortimer Wheeler House in London, lies an unusually intact artefact: a slip-on left shoe found at the Rose Theatre, just over twenty centimetres in length or roughly the size of an Elizabethan adolescent boy's or woman's foot (see Figures 6 and 7).[1]

What are we to make of this shoe, which has stepped out of Shakespeare's theatre world and into ours, as if challenging us to recall and attend to the 'stuff' that theatrical illusions are made of – or in the case of shoes, quite literally 'made *on*' (*Tempest*, 4.1.156–7)?[2] Situated at the point of contact between the actor's body and the stage, shoes continually call to mind, with each strut, step, stride or stomp across the boards, the material substrate upon which theatre is grounded. They remind us that theatre is neither reducible to nor does it float

FIGURE 6 *Left slip-on shoe, with zigzag slashes across vamp and pinked patterning on heel, found in Museum of London Archaeology excavation of Rose Theatre. Length 20.5 cm. Photograph: Andy Chopping. By permission of Museum of London Archaeology.*

magically above the material world, but rather is defined by its points of contact and modes of interaction with that world.

The epithet 'treading the boards' (or the stage), which has long been synonymous with the actor's art, suggests the reliance of that art upon footwork and footwear.[3] Yet previous studies of gesture in Shakespeare's theatre have focused almost exclusively on 'the Art of Manual Rhetorick' or chironomy,[4] following the broader tendency to privilege hands over feet in Western culture since classical antiquity.[5] As described by Tim Ingold, this hierarchy defines the primary purpose of bipedal locomotion as the liberation of the hands to become agents of the intellect: the feet merely 'undergird and propel the body

FIGURE 7 *Bottom view of Rose shoe, with double-soled, welted construction (treadsole missing). Photograph: Andy Chopping. By permission of Museum of London Archaeology.*

within the natural world' so that 'the hands are free to deliver the intelligent designs or conceptions of the mind *upon* it'.[6] Reinforced by everything from Darwinian science to modes of transportation, structures of the built environment, and technologies of footwear, Ingold demonstrates, the triumph of the head and hands over the heels has become 'deeply embedded in the structures of public life in western societies' as well as 'mainstream thinking in the disciplines'.[7] Its influence may be seen not only in theatre history, as noted above, but in the study of material culture, which seeks to put us in touch with the past, while defining this 'touch' in manual terms through its focus on the artisanal skill manifested in the crafted object.

What might the Shakespearean stage look like if viewed from the perspective of the feet? We would do well to recall that this was the vantage from which the majority of early modern theatregoers – the groundlings and those in the lower galleries – would have watched the 'two hours' traffic' of plays unfold on the raised platform of the thrust stage in the public amphitheatres. What form did actors' foot-traffic take? And how was it variously enabled, enhanced or impeded by changing technologies of footwear? What did actors do with shoes onstage? And how might this inform what we – scholars and theatre practitioners – in turn do with them? This chapter sets out to investigate such questions by stepping outside established disciplinary parameters in attending to foot-skills as well as hand-skills, worn shoes as well as crafted shoes. To pursue this avenue of inquiry, it traces the footsteps of actors through early modern playtexts and other documents of theatre history in an effort to reanimate the shoe as an artefact of performance.

To understand the functional requirements of theatrical footwear on the Shakespearean stage, we must grasp the varied forms of footwork upon which actors relied. A survey of Dessen and Thomson's *Dictionary of Stage Directions in English Drama, 1580–1642* reveals just how much attention was paid to actors' feet in performance, although the precise nature of the foot-skills deployed is not always clear, as when an actor is instructed to '*Practise footing*' in Richard Brome's *The Court Begger* (c.1639–41).[8] The term 'footing', which encompassed everything from 'walking', 'pacing' and 'stepping' to 'dancing' and the 'action or manner of placing the feet' to support the body (*OED*, 'footing, *n.*' 1.a, c, 4.a, b), provides an apt rubric for the varied forms of footwork enacted onstage. In *The Court Begger*, Dainty's cue-line reveals that the 'footing' in question here is an impromptu dance lesson, when he says to Cit-wit and Swain-wit: 'I'll make [i.e. devise] the dance and give you [i.e. instruct you in] all the footing.'[9] Onstage dancing was extremely popular during the period: there are nearly 350 examples of stage directions to '*dance*' in extant early modern playtexts. Actors were required to master imported dances popular at court, such as *'The Spanish Pavin'* (209), the French *'Coranto'* (56), the German *'Almaine'* (235) and the Italian *'Lavolta'* (142), as well as more rustic, native forms (i.e. *'The two dance a gig devised for the nonst [i.e. nonce]'*, *'The Morris sing and dance'*, *'Dances Sellenger's round'* [65]), and specialized choreography (i.e. *'dance anticly'*, *'dance a short and nimble antic to no Music'*, *'dance in several postures'*, *'dance expressing a fight'* [65]).[10] Players and playwrights deployed the distinctive rhythms and tempos of different dances to varied dramatic effects: the Pavin conveyed a slow and stately tone, the Lavolta enlivened with exhilarating jumps, the Coranto hastened dramatic pace with tripping steps and hops, and so forth. Stage directions sometimes offer specific instructions as to the tone, rhythm, and volume of the dance required, such as *'a soft dance to the solemn measure'* (206).[11] The effects of such rhythms and tempos on audiences would have been quite visceral, as the vibrations of sound generated by actors' feet, amplified by the 'wooden O', resonated up through the feet and bodies of theatregoers.[12]

Yet the sophisticated foot-skills upon which actors relied were by no means limited to dance: stage directions reveal a diverse lexicon of expressive foot movements used to ground motion and emotion, and to build dramatic character from the ground up. Just as particular hand gestures were associated with particular emotions – as when 'we clappe our Hands in joy, wring them in sorrow, [or] advance them in prayer and admiration'[13] – so too were gestures of the feet. Stamping the feet, for example, was commonly associated with anger (e.g. *'She reads the letter, frowns and stamps'*, *'chafing and stamping'*, *'they stamp and storm'*, *'she stamps, and seems to be angry'*, *'stamps and goes out vexed'* [213]), quaking or trembling of the legs with fear (e.g. *'He stands staring and quaking'*, *'Divers Senators passe by, quaking and trembling'*)[14] and leaping with joy (e.g. *'leaping in great joy'* [130]).[15] The degree to which dramatic character was grounded in footwork is suggested by

Lady Percy in *Henry IV, Part 2*, when she says of the late Hotspur, 'He was indeed the glass / Wherein the noble youth did dress themselves. / He had no legs that practis'd not his gait' (2.3.21–3). Social identity was conveyed through stance, gait and carriage, as Autolycus facetiously acknowledges when he asks, 'hath not my gait in it the measure of the court? ... I am courtier *cap-a-pe*' (*WT*, 4.4.734, 738).

Footwork was likewise a crucial indicator of gender. In the Induction of *The Taming of the Shrew*, the Lord instructs his page to 'usurp the grace, / Voice gait, and action of a gentlewoman' (Ind.1. 130–1) when the boy impersonates Sly's wife. Contemporary etiquette dictated that the female gait should be moderate in stride as well as light of foot, a delicacy notably absent from Kate's assertive, 'princely gait' (2.1.254) in the main play. In Jonson's *Epicene*, Truewit abhors women who 'stalk i' their gait like an ostrich, and take huge strides' (4.1.36–7).[16] If boy-actors were required to moderate their strides when adopting female roles, so too were female characters in breeches-wearing parts required to lengthen theirs. In *The Merchant of Venice*, Portia's transformation into Balthasar thus requires that she 'turn two mincing steps / Into a manly stride' (3.4.67–8). Masculine footwork onstage entailed more athletic forms of footwork as well, including leaps, runs and turns (e.g. '*leaps over the stool and runs away*' [130], '*turns suddenly*' [240]), scuffles and skirmishes (e.g. '*In scuffling ... change Rapiers*' [189], '*enter againe in Skirmish*' [202]), marches (e.g. '*the soldiers march and make a stand*' [138], '*They march about the Stage*' [140]) and kicks (e.g. '*kicks her out*', '*Kicks him and thrust him out*' [123–4]), among others. Such choreography and blocking are suggestive of the ways in which actors used their feet to take possession of stage space, and deployed foot-skills as vehicles of power or status. If assertive footwork conveyed puissance onstage, staggering or stumbling conveyed weakness or subordination (e.g. '*staggers on, and then falls down*' or '*staggers with faintness*' [213]). Yet ungainly footwork of this kind required no less skill on the part of the actor; rather, it required what we might call a *sprezzatura* of the feet, or dissimulation of the practised skill necessary in order to make footwork appear spontaneous.

When the court-aspirants of The Court Begger '*Practise footing*' onstage, they humorously highlight the arduous, yet ordinarily hidden, labour of rehearsal required to make footwork seem nonchalant. As codified by Castiglione, the *sprezzatura* of the 'courtier cap-a-pe' stipulated the avoidance of 'over nimble footinges' and 'to[o] busie trickes': above all, graceful footwork had to avoid the appearance of being *work*.[17] The disgraceful absence of such unstudied finesse on the part of Dainty's pupils as they '*practise about him*'[18] onstage is underscored when Cit-wit, attempting to follow Dainty's choreography, '*dances, looking on his feet*'.[19] Whether Cit-wit is looking down at his own feet or is staring too fixedly at those of his instructor, his breach of decorum reveals, by negative example, the studied effort that skilled footwork elides. The scene concludes with Dainty ushering his pupils offstage, '*Footing*' as they go, to 'practise, and be ready' for the play's final masque.[20] The unpractised footwork of the play's characters is contrasted with that of its actors, whose polished foot-skills are on display throughout The Court Begger. In an elaborate dance routine in Act 4, scene 2, for example, the actor playing Ferdinand '*Ris[es] from his chair and cavort[s] about*' the stage boasting, 'So now a Dance! I am all ayre – Ahaigh – Ahaigh / I thanke thee *Mercury* that hast lent thy wings / Unto my feete.'[21] He proceeds to dance '*a conceited Countrey Dance, first doing his honours, then as leading forth his Lasse. He danceth both man and womans actions, as if the Dance consisted of two or three couples.*'[22] Unlike Castiglione's courtly dancer, actors were licensed – indeed expected – to execute 'over nimble footinges' and 'to[o] busie trickes' onstage, as Ferdinand does here in dancing the parts of '*two or three couples*' simultaneously.

The canon of decorum governing actors' footwork was of necessity far more flexible than that which confined the courtier, and was both role- and genre-specific. Hamlet cautions the 'tragedians of the city' (2.2.330) against 'o'erstep[ping] ... the modesty of nature' (3.2.20) by 'strut[ting]' like buffoons onstage (l.34). The studious Dane here displays his knowledge of Quintilian's *De Institutio Oratoria*, which proscribes stomping, stamping, strutting, 'running up and down', jumping, hopping, standing 'on tiptoe' and 'Holding the feet too far apart', as 'Gesture[s] of comedy rather than of oratory'.[23] Such excessive and unwarranted gesticulations of the feet ought to be shunned not only by orators, according to Quintilian, but also by 'more serious actors [*histrionibus ... gravioribus*]'.[24] Yet even serious actors were at times obliged to 'o'erstep' the measured strides of orators in executing tragic roles, as Hamlet's leap into Ophelia's grave so memorably demonstrates.[25]

Given the attention commanded by such flamboyant feats of actors' feet on the raised platform of the thrust stage, it is not surprising that they were known to wear eye-catching and fashionable shoes and stockings. With footwear as with footwork, they walked a fine and constantly shifting line between grace and affectation. Anti-theatrical writers routinely castigated players as sartorial upstarts, citing their showy shoes and stockings as evidence of theatre's frivolity. Stephen Gosson's *Plays Confuted in Five Actions* (1582) dubs theatres 'markets of bawdry', and compares them to 'the royall exchaung[e]' where one may 'take a short stock[ing], or a longe, a falling band, or a French ruffe'. His catalogue of the expensive trifles sold at the Royal Exchange and flaunted by actors is adduced as evidence that the 'soule of ... playes is ... mere trifles'.[26] For Gosson, theatre's lack of substance is epitomized by actors' flimsy footwear: he thus derides the 'waste of expences in these spectacles that scarce last like shooes of browne paper'.[27] Yet even Gosson acknowledges, if only to admonish, the allure of such 'spectacles', claiming that the Devil 'sendeth in Gearish apparell maskes, vauting, tumbling, daunsing of gigges, galiardes, morisces' to beguile the eyes of spectators.[28]

Whereas moralists admonished actors' fancy footwork and footwear, fashionable gallants were all too willing to pay extra to sit onstage, the better to ogle them – or so Thomas Dekker claims in *The Guls Horne-booke* (1609). They are said to perch 'on the very Rushes where the Commedy is to daunce' in order to 'examine the play-suits lace' up close during the performance, while showing off the 'most essenciall parts of a Gallant', namely their own 'good cloathes' and 'proportionable legge[s]'.[29] Henry Fitzgeffrey's 'Play-house Observation' of Blackfriars (1617) similarly describes fashionable gallants, dressed in the latest trends in imported footwear ('His Boote speakes Spanish to his Scottish Spurres'). One such dancing dandy heads straight 'from the Dauncing-schoole' to the theatre, entering the playhouse 'with a Coranto grace' and 'skipping too and fro' with excitement as he watches the play.[30] Although these satirical accounts must be taken with a grain of salt, they suggest that the popularity of dancing schools created an audience deeply appreciative, if not demanding, of displays of expert footwork and fashionable footwear onstage. Barnabe Rich similarly describes a gallant 'newly come from the Dauncing Schoole', who can 'treade a tricke of one and twentie follies' and 'will speake of Playes, Players, and who be the best Actors'.[31] The fashionable gallant's study of the 'Skipping Arte[s]' renders him eager to see the latest foot-skills and attires displayed onstage, and knowledgeable about 'the best Actors' who exhibit them.

The celebrity that professional players were able to achieve through fancy footwork and footwear is exemplified in the careers of Richard Tarlton (d.1588) and William Kempe (d.in or after 1610?), actor-clowns famed for their robust athleticism and post-play jigs. Tarlton, a member of the Queen's Men, was a Master of Fence, and is described in Henry Chettle's *Kindharts Dreame* (1593) as renowned for 'standing on the toe, and other tricks'.[32] According to Samuel Rowlands, he was also known for wearing attention-grabbing 'great clownish slops', a style of round, full, padded breeches later adopted as a fashion trend among gallants: 'In every streete where any Gallant goes, / The swagg'ring slop, is Tarltons clownish hose.'[33] If Tarlton's wit, as Peter Thomson argues, worked 'to draw attention to the functions and appurtenances of the human body's lower half', so too did his 'clownish slops'.[34]

Will Kempe may likewise have cultivated extravagant legwear, as Henslowe records a loan to him of five shillings in August 1602 'to bye buckram to macke a payer of gyente hosse'.[35] Kempe, a member successively of Leicester's, Strange's, Chamberlain's and Worcester's Men, was renowned not only for physical clowning, tumbling and jigging, but also for famously taking his foot-skills on the road in his celebrated 130-mile Morris dance from London to Norwich in February 1600, recounted in his *Nine Daies Wonder* (1600).[36] The pamphlet advertises Kempe's extraordinary footwork and footwear from first page to last. The title page woodcut features him frozen mid-air, his thighs accentuated by slops, and his calves adorned with several rows of bells (traditionally worn by Morris dancers). He boasts that he is 'head-master of Morrice-dauncers', whose 'pace in dauncing is not ordinary', and claims that 'so light was my heeles, that I counted the ten mile no better than a leape'.[37] At the pamphlet's end, he informs his audience that at 'the Guild-hall at Norwich ... my buskins, that I then wore and daunst in from London thither, stand equally devided, nailde on the wall'.[38]

The fortitude of Kempe's footwear metonymically figures that of his footwork: the 'wonder' of his 'nine daies' performance lives on, memorialized by his buskins. The boots' survival and display stands as an implicit rebuke to Gosson's claim that actors' 'spectacles ... scarce last like shooes of browne paper'. Indeed, insofar as 'buskins' or *cothurnoi* were the footwear traditionally worn by actors on the ancient Greek and Roman stages, Kempe's monument evokes the ancient and enduring heritage of actors' footwork and footwear. A similar claim is made in Thomas Heywood's *An Apology for Actors* (1612), where the 'Antiquity' of the actors' profession is allegorically figured by their 'buskend Muse' Melpomene.[39] According to Heywood, the poor condition of Melpomene's buskins in his day, far from reflecting actors' low status, is caused by anti-theatrical writers' 'utterly despoyl[ing]' them of their 'wonted

Jewels and ornaments'; in protest, her garters are now imprinted with the motto: '*Behold my Tragicke Buskin rent and torne, / Which Kings and Emperors in their tymes have worne.*'[40] Heywood's defence seeks to restore the 'ancient Dignity' of actors by repairing and adorning their muse's buskins so that she may once again 'pac[e] with a majesticke gate'.[41]

That legwork and -wear were considered foundational to the actor's profession, and propelled some of its first celebrities to fame, helps to explain the large sums that actors invested in silk hose and stockings, as evidenced in Philip Henslowe's 'diary' or account-book. In consecutive entries for loans made on 10 and 12 December 1597, we find Henslowe 'lent unto Robart shawe for to by cop[per] lace of sylver to lace a payer of hosse ... the some of xvjs' and 'L*ayd* owt for ij gyges [i.e. jigs] for shawe & his company ... the some of vjs 8^d'.[42] The ornate hose for which Shaw paid sixteen shillings were most likely breeches made by a tailor, rather than stockings (or netherstocks) made by a hosier, but Henslowe's accounts include numerous loans to players for silk stockings as well.[43] On one occasion, Henslowe sold actor Thomas Downton a pair of colourful silk stockings out of his own stock of apparel:

> Sowld unto Thomas downton A payer of longe sylke stockenes of crymsone coller to be payd for them xxiiij s Redey money wch he yet owes unto me I saye wch he had of me th*e* 3 of marche 1598.[44]

The entry is crossed through to indicate that Downton eventually paid Henslowe the considerable sum of twenty-four shillings for his crimson stockings. The many stockings in Henslowe's accounts reflect the broad range of colours fashionable at the time (including 'fleashe color', 'yelow coler', 'blacke', 'whitte', 'genger coler', 'sylvercolor', 'orangecoler' and 'sewater grene'), and were variously valued at from five to twenty shillings.[45]

To gauge the bedazzling effect that actors' legs, adorned in flamboyant silk stockings, would have had on spectators, it is important to recall that they were a relatively new fashion at the time. Although imported silk stockings were occasionally worn at court prior to Elizabeth's reign, the first pair manufactured in England, according to Edmund Howes' augmented edition of Stow's *Annales* (1615), were presented to Elizabeth by her silkwoman, Alice Montague, as a New Year's gift in 1560/61. So delighted was the queen that she announced:

> [']indeede I like silke stockinges so wel because they are pleasant, fine & delicate, that henceforth I will weare no more cloth stockinges,['] and from that time unto her death, the queene never wore any more cloath hose, but only silke stockings.[46]

The perfect match of form and function, knitted silk stockings were form-fitting, moisture-wicking, warm and durable. The fashion appears to have caught on, and become increasingly ornate, by the 1580s, as Stubbes complains in his *Anatomie of Abuses* (1583):

> Then have they nether-stocks to these gay hosen, not of cloth (though never so fine) for that is thought to[o] base, but of Jarnsey [i.e. Jersey] worsted, silk, thred and such like ... and so curiously knit with open seam down the leg, with quirks and clocks[47] about the ancles, and sometime (haply) interlaced with gold or silver threds, as is wunderful to behold. And to such insolency & outrage it is now growen, that every one (almost) though otherwise verie poor having scarce fortie shillings of wages by the yeer wil be sure to have two or three paire of these silk nether-stocks, or els of the finest yarne that may be got, though the price of them be a Ryall or twentie shillinges, or more ... The time hath beene, when one might have clothed all his body well, for lesse then a pair of these nether-stocks wil cost.[48]

Stubbes's 'outrage' at the 'insolency' and expense of the fashion trend is coupled with the acknowledgement that such sumptuous silk stockings are nonetheless 'wunderful to behold'.

By the early 1590s, fashionable silk stockings appear to have become a trademark of the professional players. In Robert Greene's *A Quip for an Upstart Courtier* (1592), which takes the form of a dispute between velvet breeches and cloth breeches, a player arrives wearing a cloth gown adorned with lace, 'which he quaintly bare[s] up, to shew his white Taffata hose and black silke stockings'. He is followed by two boy-actors who carry his 'sword of choller' and his 'daunsing papier of delight', representing the Janus-faced actor through the contrasting arts of footwork (fencing and dancing, respectively) upon which he depends. The player is accompanied by his close 'Comerade', the 'Usher of a daunsing Schoole', who likewise 'live[s] by [his] legges', and is 'given over to the pumps and vanities of the world'.[49] Flamboyant legwork and legwear are cast as vital tools of their allied trades.

The considerable financial investment of players in silk stockings may likewise reflect the emphasis placed on shapely legs as an attribute of youthful, robust male beauty: in *Romeo and Juliet* the Nurse praises Romeo by exclaiming, 'his leg excels all men's' (2.5.40–1), and Dekker, as mentioned above, includes 'a proportionable legge' among the 'essenciall parts of a Gallant'.[50] Old, feeble and unattractive men were by contrast characterized by their 'decreasing leg[s]' (*2H4*, 1.2.181) or 'shrunk shank[s]', which were too narrow for 'youthful hose' (*AYL*, 2.7.160–1). In *The Two Gentlemen of Verona*, Thurio hears that Silvia finds his leg 'too little' and vows, 'I'll wear a boot, to make it somewhat rounder' (5.2.5–6). By satirizing male vanity regarding legs onstage, players were effectively able to have their silk stockings and wear them too. Perhaps the most famous example of this strategy appears in *Twelfth Night*, which deflects anti-theatrical criticism onto the anti-theatrical Malvolio himself, who is made to don ostentatious, cross-gartered, yellow stockings.[51]

Given the many payments and loans for silk stockings and hose in Henslowe's accounts, the lack of any analogous expenditures on footwear, fancy or otherwise, invites further scrutiny. In the absence of such payments, we must search elsewhere for clues as to what actors wore on their feet. Playtexts offer hints, although their evidentiary value is not always clear. Hamlet famously teases a boy-actor in a travelling troupe for being 'nearer to heaven than when I saw you last, by the altitude of a chopine' (2.2.427–8), referencing the towering *cioppini* worn by Venetian courtesans.[52] Has the boy-actor's growth spurt enabled him to doff his chopines, as Hamlet's remark implies? And are we then to construe his remark as a reference to contemporary theatrical practice? Hamlet later facetiously asks Horatio, 'Would not this, sir, and a forest of feathers ... with [two] Provincial roses on my raz'd shoes, get me a fellowship in a cry of players?' (3.2.277–80), referring to decorative shoe-roses made of ribbon and to the practice of razing or 'pinking' shoe-leather in ornamental patterns, respectively, both innovations from France. Did actors indeed wear fashionably 'raz'd', raised and beribboned footwear, as Hamlet suggests? If so, how are we to accord these delicate attires with the demanding athleticism of their footwork onstage?

The heightened, hyperbolic language of Hamlet's references to actors' fancy footwear and headgear ('the *altitude* of a chopine', 'a *forest* of feathers', etc.) seems intentionally overstated, as if he were 'o'erdoing Termagant' (3.2.14), if not out-Gossoning Gosson. References to such attires in playtexts suggest that they were reserved for specific occasions (such as inset masques), or for satirical effect (as in the lampooning of social upstarts). In *A Midsummer Night's Dream*, Bottom instructs the rude mechanicals to wear 'new ribbons' on their 'pumps' (4.2.34–5) when they perform their playlet of Pyramus and Thisbe. Such 'new ribbons' hobble Simon Eyre's wife Marjorie when they come untied in Thomas Dekker's *The Shoemaker's Holiday*: 'Thou goest too fast for me Roger,' she says, then asks, 'Hans pray thee tie my shooe' (3.2.1, 25).[53] In Jonson's *The Devil is an Ass* (1616), the 'puny devil' Pug ingratiates himself with Fitzdottrel – a sartorial upstart who wears 'Garters and roses' worth 'fourscore pound a pair' as well as 'Embroidred stockings' (1.1.127–8) – by donning enormous shoe-roses himself. A stage direction indicates that '*[Fitzdottrel] looks and surveys [Pug's] feet over and over*' and comments, 'those roses / Were big enough to hide a cloven foot' (1.3.8–10). In such scenes, outlandish foot attires are turned into hilarious show-stoppers by revealing socially aspirant characters' lack of both grace and *sprezzatura*. In so doing, they afford opportunities not only for satire, but also for displays of comedic footwork by skilled actors.

Playtexts reveal that the social aspirations of female characters onstage could sometimes indeed be measured by the altitude of their chopines. In *The Devil is an Ass*, Wittipol impersonates a Spanish Lady wearing '*Cioppinos*' (4.4.69), prompting Lady Tailbush to ask: 'I should think it hard / To go in 'hem madame ... / Do you never fall in 'hem? ... / ... I sweare, I should, / Six times an hour' (ll.72–4).[54] The practical difficulty of 'going' or walking in chopines posed an obstacle to their use onstage except for satirical effect, as did their association with the sexual 'falls' of foreign courtesans.[55] Most of the references to chopines are thus not surprisingly found in satirical plays performed by the children's companies.[56] Several of them poke fun at the way cork-soled shoes creak, as when Birdlime in Dekker and Webster's *Westward Ho* (*c*.1604) says to Mistress Justiniano, 'why prettie soule tread softlie, and come into this roome: here be rushes, you neede not feare the creaking of your corke shooes' (2.2.64–7).[57] The cork-soled shoes worn by boy-actors were probably not as tall as those worn by Venetian courtesans: Stubbes describes those worn in England, which were more commonly known as pantobles or pantofles, as 'bear[ing] them up a finger or two from the ground'.[58] Less cumbersome than platformed chopines were heeled shoes, which began to appear onstage soon after coming into fashion at court (Queen Elizabeth got her first pair in 1595).[59] In *The Shoemaker's Holiday*, Marjorie's social aspirations are reflected not only in her fancy French shoe-ties, but also in her desire for shoes with soles of 'corke' *and* 'woodden heele[s] too' (3.2.29–30).

Inset masques in plays performed on the professional stage, which became increasingly common in the early decades of the seventeenth century, may have offered additional opportunities for the display of ostentatious foot attire. In Brome's *The Court Begger*, Swain-wit suggests that the fancy 'footing' choreographed by Dainty and performed in the play's final masque may have been complemented by ostentatious footwear. He asks Philomel, Lady Strangelove's maidservant, 'shall we have no silken things, no whim whams / To Dance in tho'[?],' to which she replies, 'my Lady has tane care for all.'[60] The 'silken things' and 'whim whams' (i.e. 'trifle[s]' or 'ornament[s] of dress'; see *OED*, 'whim-wham, *n.*', 1) worn in inset masques probably included fancy foot attires like those found in the Revels Office accounts documenting masquing attire at court, which include numerous payments for sumptuous 'Maskinge shewes [i.e. shoes]' made in various styles out of velvet, silk and satin in a stunning array of colours (e.g. 'gold and redd velvett' and 'Purple Clothe of Silver') and adorned with gold and silver lace, spangles, ribbons and buttons.[61] The most common style worn by female masquers were 'shorte buskyns' (also known as 'startoppes'), which reached just above the ankle to be glimpsed beneath their gowns as they danced. Men typically wore 'longe buskyns', which reached to the mid- or upper calf and were topped with colourful, ornamented hose.[62] Because masque costumes were only supposed to be worn once in the same form, they were frequently 'translated' or taken apart and remade until they became so worn as to be no longer usable, at which point they were marked 'not chargeable' and often given to professional players as 'ffees' or payments-in-kind for court performances.[63] In this way, the luxurious footwear worn in court masques may have found its way onto the professional stage to adorn the feet of dancers in inset masques.

Although the professional stage emulated fashion trends at court, its budgetary constraints were far more modest than, and its performance requirements quite different from, those of court revels. The demands of the professional repertory required that all but the most exceptional costumes be worn multiple times and endure outdoor exposure in the open-air amphitheatres. The athletic foot-skills upon which actors relied would likewise have required sturdier footwear than the silken 'whim whams' worn in court masques. The footwear found in the Rose and Globe excavations would appear to accord with these demands: in addition to the slip-on shoe mentioned above (Figures 6 and 7), several other near-complete shoes, parts of two buskins and many shoe fragments are all made of sturdy, bovine leather (showing signs of considerable wear), and all have doubly reinforced 'welted' soles.[64] However, shoes made of leather, although more durable, are also more difficult to fit, as bovine leather is less flexible than fabric. The shoe upper in Figure 6 has a deliberately cut hole at the toe, apparently 'to accommodate a toe deformity or bunion', reflecting both the difficulty and necessity of a shoe fitting properly.[65] Because leather conforms (and deforms) with the foot of the wearer over time, leather shoes are less amenable than other costume elements to being worn by multiple wearers. These constraints may help to explain the absence of footwear in Henslowe's diary, as professional actors may have preferred to supply their own to ensure proper fit.

Theatrical footwear on the professional stage would have had to combine durability with flexibility to accommodate the nimble and athletic forms of footwork described above. A number of the shoes found at the Rose reflect enhanced flexibility through the technology of 'pinking' – or scoring and perforating leather with decorative slits and eyelet holes.[66] The slip-on shoe in Figure 6 has such perforations across the vamp as well as on the heel. This technique, first used on shoes and leather garments as a practical means of easing their stiffness, eventually took on a purely decorative function in revealing the contrastive colour or texture of stockings, shirts or garment-linings worn underneath, a fashion trend that reached its height across Europe in the late sixteenth and early seventeenth centuries.[67] In *The Second Part of the Anatomie of Abuses* (1583), Philip Stubbes decries decorative pinking, claiming that shoes are 'pincked, cutte, karved, rased, nickt, and I cannot tell what' only 'to the ende they may seeme gaudie to the eie'.[68] Hamlet associates the fashion with actors in particular when he claims that 'raz'd shoes' would get him 'a fellowship in a cry of players' (3.2.279–80), while intimating that fancy yet flexible shoes are among a player's most valued and valuable assets.

Pinking could do only so much, however, to ease the discomfort of shoes made of overly thick, stiff or heavy leather. Romeo emphasizes the importance of light, nimble shoes to sprightly footwork when he tells his companions, 'You have dancing shoes / With nimble soles, I have a soul of lead / So stakes me to the ground I cannot move' (1.4.14–16). Romeo's punning identification of the sole as the 'soul' of the shoe suggests that a 'nimble sole' animates the foot, sets it in motion, enabling it to dance, and in so doing, enlivens the soul of its wearer. The light, flexible soles of dancing shoes in Shakespeare's day were made of cork. Thomas Heywood refers to cork-soled shoes as nimble and fit for dancing in both *The Foure Prentices of London* ('as fine a paire of heeles, as light and nimble, as any the neatest corke shoe in all the Towne turnes up') and *The Rape of Lucrece* ('They weare so much corke under their heeles, they cannot choose but love to caper').[69] As single-soled shoes were reinforced with treadsoles at the end of the sixteenth century to accommodate the friction caused by road paving, cork midsoles were added to cushion the foot, allowing for a thicker yet lighter sole, as seen in several of the shoes found at the Rose Theatre (see Figure 7).[70]

Although it is impossible to know with certainty whether any of the shoes found in MoLA's excavations of early theatres ever trod the boards on the feet of an actor, they nonetheless prompt us to think about Shakespeare's theatre-world in new ways – indeed from the ground up – by attending to the ways in which shoes mediate the human actor's contact with its changing environment, and the ways in which the actor's body continually shapes and is reshaped by that contact. The dramatic transformations of shoe styles and technologies that took place during Shakespeare's lifetime have a great deal to tell us about a material world in transition, and how the feet that trod the boards of the early modern stage brought the varied emotions it stirred to life in and through motion.

'Apparel oft Proclaims the Man': Dressing Othello on the English Renaissance Stage

Bella Mirabella

When Iago complains to Roderigo that 'three great ones of the city ... Off-capped to' Othello to make Iago his lieutenant, Shakespeare immediately signals the importance of clothing and dress in his play. In fact, in the first sixty-four lines of the play Iago makes at least six references to attire including 'bombast' stuffing for doublets, and, most tellingly, Iago's portrayal of himself as one only 'trimmed in forms and visages of duty', and, who, if he let his 'outward action' reveal his 'heart / In complement extern', would have to 'wear [his] heart upon [his] sleeve', because, as he reveals, 'I am not what I am' (*Oth*, 1.1.9; 12, 49, 60–4).[1] This comment is particularly important, not only because it reveals the essence of Iago, but also because it is a reference to clothing's power to disguise or present one's true self. In this chapter I propose that

Shakespeare's many references to dressing and attire in the play emphasize that how Othello was dressed – whether in English or Moorish garb, for example – would have profoundly affected how his character and thus the play itself would have been perceived and understood.

As way of background, and with regard to Moors, it is important to remember that in August 1600 the Moorish ambassador, Abd el-Ouahed ben Messaoud ben Mohammed Anoun (1558–?), made a visit to the court of Queen Elizabeth I, on a mission from the king of Morocco, 'Muly Hamet' (Mulai Ahman al-Mansur), who hoped the English would participate in a joint invasion of Spain. The ambassador and his retinue of sixteen, including prisoners to be returned, stayed in England for six months.[2] There were other Moors in England as well, and according to Nabil Matar, the English had an intense relationship with the Moors generated through trade, piracy and the tense business of taking each other captive. But it was a complex relationship, one that Matar describes as a mix of 'anxious equality and grudging emulation', which in part may have stemmed from the reputation the Moors had as fierce warriors, as well as England's desire for political clout in the Mediterranean.[3]

The cultural popularity of the Moors in England is reflected in the fact that they appear in a number of plays, including George Peele's *The Battle of Alcazar* (1594), Thomas Dekker's *Lust's Dominion, or the Lascivious Queen* (1600) as well as Shakespeare's *Titus Andronicus* (1588–93) and *The Merchant of Venice* (1596–8).[4] In his 1587 *Description of England*, William Harrison notes the sartorial influences of Moors when he describes 'Morisco gowns and Barbarian sleeves' as two of the more desired fashion items of the day. It is likely that Harrison refers to Moorish Blackwork embroidery, which was sewn with black silk on white linen.[5]

Given the powerful presence and influence, both cultural and political, of Moors in England, it is easy to speculate about the ambassador's visit as a potential influence on Shakespeare as he wrote *Othello*, first performed in 1604. In this chapter I

FIGURE 8 *Abd el-Ouahed ben Messaoud ben Mohammed Anoun, Moorish ambassador to Queen Elizabeth I, 1600*, © *The University of Birmingham Research and Cultural Collections. Artist: unknown.*

want to use the visit of the Moorish ambassador and his entourage to initiate an exploration of male fashion and the construction of English masculinity in the latter half of the sixteenth and early seventeenth century. I also want to consider Moors, and Moorish dress, particularly the clothing of el-Ouahed depicted in a painting made during his visit.

My examination of English dress and masculinity will in part focus on a comparison of the draped attire of the Moorish ambassador with the English 'uniform' of doublet and hose represented by the portraits of Robert Dudley and Walter Ralegh.[6] These two constructions of masculinity – English and Moorish – created through the use of what I call 'hard' and 'soft' apparel, represent concepts of masculine power inspired,

I suggest, by the political ideals of concealment for the Moors and constraint for the English.[7] I want to use these ideas about masculine attire to consider the implications of how Othello might have been dressed on the stage, not only with regard to the theatrical effect of his appearance, but also to speculate about the sartorial choices the Moorish general might have made. In order to do this I will consider three possibilities: the first is Othello dressed like Aaron in the Henry Peacham drawing (1595) based on *Titus Andronicus*; the second consideration is of Othello dressed similarly to the Moorish ambassador, el-Ouahed; and the third speculates about what it would mean to have Othello dressed in doublet and hose.

As way of background and before addressing Othello's clothing, I want to explore briefly: Moors and attire; the key issues for the English regarding foreign dress; and the elements of doublet and hose. With regard to Moors, we face the challenge of unravelling the knot of confusion about their identity. I cannot possibly do justice to the 'notorious indeterminacy' of the term 'Moor' that Michael Neil notes, nor to the complexity of the inquiries that such scholars as Eldred Jones, Nabil Matar, Emily Bartels, Martin Orkin and Neil have made into the where, when and why of Moors, but there are some parameters I can set out.[8] The term 'Moor' is a word Europeans used to describe many different kinds of people, but for this chapter, I want to limit it to describe those Berbers and Arabs who come from the Barbary Coast, which is another European term used to describe Northern Africa – that is, Tunisia, Algiers and Morocco – which was called the Maghrib by the Arabs. Moriscos were those Moors who invaded Spain in the eighth century, who inhabited al-Andalus in southern Spain, and who had, importantly, been converted to Christianity.[9] And while some Moors could be dark-skinned, not all were. In 1549 Andrew Borde, for example, describes the inhabitants of Barbary as 'whyte mores and black moors'.[10]

An important source of information about the Moors in Shakespeare's time was John Pory's 1600 translation of Johannes Leo Africanus' *A Geographical History of Africa*, originally published in Rome in 1526 at the wish of Pope Leo X, who baptized Africanus and changed his name. Africanus was born (1492-4) as al-Hasan ibn Muhammad al-Wazzan in Granada, Spain and was expelled with his family, who went to live in Morocco.[11] As if he were writing about Othello, Africanus describes the inhabitants of Barbarie as 'strong', 'valiant' and 'honest', 'destitute of all fraud and guile', who embrace 'all simplicitie and truth'. However, he also includes the fact that 'no nation in the world is so subject unto jealousie', who will more readily lose their lives than put up with any disgrace 'in the behalf of their women'.[12]

With regard to the sartorial influence of Moors, their goods were regarded as the 'gold standard of luxury' for Christian monarchs, and their textiles were apparently the 'unambiguous' 'sign of respectability and propriety' in Castilian clothing.[13] Exquisite silks and intricate embroidery were prized fashion items throughout Europe. Antoine de Lalaing, a Flemish courtier who travelled with Philip the Fair to Spain in 1501, comments on silks 'worked in the Moorish fashion ... beautiful for their multitude of colors and the variety of their work'.[14] An Italian traveller, Hieronimi Vicecomitis, who attended the wedding of Princess Margaret of Austria and Prince Juan of Spain in 1497, notes how beautifully dressed King Fernando and the prince were 'in the Moorish fashion (*la morescha*) with brocade mantles and doublets, with various embroideries and ornaments and with their head veiled in the Moorish fashion (*al modo moresco*)'. He continues that 'such varied and beautiful fashions' were 'a marvelous thing'.[15] These items were so highly desired that after King Philip's order to expel the Moors from Valencia in 1609, there was, among the Spanish, a frenzied selling and buying of 'rich clothes in the Moorish style', described as 'jewels', that had been left behind by the Moors in the rush to leave. And although the Spanish Christians hated the Moors enough to exile them, they nonetheless coveted 'towels worked in gold, wonderfully made shirts, very fine pieces of linen'.[16]

Flowing gowns were an essential of Morisco attire, particularly the cloak, called the *marlota*.[17] In his *Habiti*

Antichi et Moderni, Cesare Vecellio, commenting on the clothing of those Moors living in Barbary, writes that noblemen dress 'very elegantly and richly, wearing gowns of lisaro and other kinds of white cloth', as well as a turban, and a 'fazzuolo under their beard'. It seems from this description that Vecellio had read Africanus, since he mentions that they are 'courageous', 'free of guile' and 'jealous'. Describing the wealthy Moor, Vecellio notes that he is accessorized with gold earrings, 'a band of gold with jewels of great value' worn across the chest, 'scimitars and bows and arrows', as well as a white turban.[18] Both men wear long flowing robes with ample sleeves, and these items, along with the turban and weaponry, coincide with the Moorish ambassador's attire.[19]

These illustrations and descriptions help explain why the Spanish coveted the clothing and textiles of the Moors, in the same way that the English desired foreign clothing. Queen Elizabeth herself, according to James Melville, one day wore 'the English weed, another the French', and was particularly pleased that Melville thought 'Italian dress' 'became her best'.[20] Wearing foreign dress was certainly an issue in early modern Europe and has been the subject of current scholarship.[21] For the purposes of this chapter, however, I want to explore two specific points as background to Othello's possible attire: that foreign dress, just like Moors and Moorish culture, could be both alluring and dangerous, and how wearing the attire of the Other could be a threat to self, soul and heart.

Clearly, one of the biggest fears for critics was the loss of self, or being 'translated' as Thomas Dekker says. In a passage from the *Gull's Hornbook* (1609), Dekker advises his gallant that proper attire can be attained, in part, by translating himself out of his 'English cloak' and wearing, instead, 'a light Turkey grogram'.[22] Such an act of translation indicates that the gallant must physically rewrite himself, displacing his English self with the Turkish garment.

William Harrison, dismayed over the 'fantastical folly' of changing fashions, highlights the 'mutability' of the self and the problems of *trans*formation and *de*formation. People are 'transformed from the cap even to the very shoe', he writes, turning themselves into 'monsters'.[23] Philip Stubbes agrees, writing that the 'newfangled fashions rather deforme, then adorne'. Dress can 'disguise us', he writes, and then 'become us', turning the wearers into 'savage beastes, and brutish monsters', no longer 'sober and chaste Christians'. In a similar vein, Borachio in *Much Ado About Nothing* calls fashion a 'deformed thief'.[24] Stubbes recognizes that clothing has the power to alter the body as well as the spirit.

In a similar vein, Federico Fregoso, in Baldessare Castiglione's 1528 book *The Courtier*, says that a man's 'appearance' represents 'what sort of man he wants to seem ... even by those who do not hear him speak or see him perform anything at all'. Clothing is a kind of silent language that can represent 'personality', a statement that prefigures Polonius' advice to Laertes in *Hamlet*, that 'apparel oft proclaims the man' (1.3.71).[25] Clothing for Castiglione is not just a pretty outer shell; it is a visualization of the essence of the person wearing the clothing – it is their very 'personality'. Later in the text, Pietro Bembo says that outward beauty is the true sign of inward goodness and a sign of the true character of the soul. Erasmus makes a similar point when he writes in 1530 that clothing is the 'body's body' from which one can 'infer the state of a man's character'.[26]

For some English observers, true character is found in the rejection of things foreign, and the embrace of a true English past and its apparel. Harrison, for example, yearns for a purer, 'merrier' time when the Englishman was known both abroad and at home 'by his own cloth and contented' 'with his fine kersey hosen', his 'coat, gown, and cloak of brown-blue or puke', 'without such cuts and garish colors as are worn in these days'.[27] Stubbes longs for the good old days when men wore 'blacke or white Frize coates, in hosen of huswiues cloth' rather than velvets and satins.[28] In Robert Greene's *Newes both from Heaven and Hell*, Cloth Breeches contends that throughout England, one will find 'goodman Cloth breeches at home keeping good Hospitalitie'.[29] In an anonymous sixteenth-century ballad called 'The Old Cloak', a husband and wife debate over whether the husband needs a new cloak. The wife ultimately wins by arguing for the usefulness of the old garment, comparing it to King Stephen's inexpensive breeches that 'cost him but a crown'. Wanting her husband to learn from such a humble example, she reprimands him: 'It's pride that puts this country down: / Man, take thy old cloak about thee!'[30] Such a lesson praises the virtues of frugality and humility – the old stalwart values embodied in simple, plain cloth, lost in a time of fashion craziness. This is, in fact, the very ballad and the very part about Stephen that Iago sings while he seduces Cassio to drunkenness (2.3.85). Here Iago upholds the old values while tearing down the new fashions, represented by both the fancy Florentine who has taken his promotion, and the Moorish general who has put Cassio in Iago's place.

An examination of the details of English and European apparel for men shows that courtiers, for example, were expected to be well dressed since expensive attire announced 'gentility'; those who defended the crown and life at court argued 'for the morality of male display'.[31] Clothing represented an image of masculine virtue, an image based on shaping the body through hard clothing. Dudley's picture in Figure 9 demonstrates certain consistent characteristics of English male apparel – the use of lace at the wrists and the neck, accessories of war, such as a sword and rapier, usually a head covering, and sometimes gloves, a handkerchief or a small bag – but the two items that are completely necessary and from which one does not diverge are a doublet that comes to a sharp point and tight-fitting hose. And while the fashion changes slightly as the sixteenth century progresses, often with a softer collar, the doublet and hose remain, as the 1602 painting of Sir Walter Ralegh and his son reveal in Figure 10.[32]

In Shakespeare's *As You Like It*, for example, the doublet and hose are the essentials needed to make Rosalind's pretended maleness real. At one point she notes that 'doublet and hose

FIGURE 9 *Robert Dudley, First Earl of Leicester,* © *National Portrait Gallery, London. Artist: unknown.*

ought to show itself courageous' (2.4.6–7), while at another point she protests that she is still female, and although she is 'caparisoned like a man' she does not 'have a doublet and hose' in her 'disposition' (3.2.192–3).[33] Rosalind's choice of the word 'disposition' seems telling here – more than the parts of a sartorial uniform, the doublet and hose are the essentials that constitute English and, for that matter, European maleness, and she, wanting to hold on her to femaleness, needs to resist the power of these sartorial elements.[34]

The total look, centred as it is around the doublet and hose, presents a body that can appear stuffed, stiffened, exaggerated and constrained. It is a body that has been moulded in what Jane Ashelford has called 'a most extreme and artificial shape',[35] a shape in which the body parts often appear

FIGURE 10 *Sir Walter Ralegh,* © *National Portrait Gallery, London. Artist unknown.*

discontinuously separated from each other, such as Dudley's head, which appears to be separated from his body by ruff and the collar of the doublet. This separation seems to draw the eye to individual segments of the male body in an image that is, according to Anne Hollander, 'visually startling and abrupt'. Such fragmentation suggests that we are meant to notice the breaking apart of the body and focus on the eroticized individual elements such as the codpiece,[36] which serves as a visual end point to the hardened doublet.

Some doublets were so stiffened with bombast, made of 'horsehair', 'rags, cotton, flax', even bran, that, according to Stubbes, the men could 'hardly either stoop down, or decline themselves to the ground'.[37] While padding might conceal bodily imperfections such as a fat or sagging belly, the very idea of bombast, figuratively and linguistically, points to false matter, something that takes up space but has no significance, as when Iago tells Roderigo that Othello is not to be believed, because his 'bombast' language is 'stuffed with epithets of war' (1.1.12–13). With regard to linguistic stuffing, Dekker and Middleton make a reference to 'huge bombasted plays, quilted with mighty words to lean purpose'.[38] Whether referring to material reality or metaphorical figures, the visual image of swelling doublet, intended to make men look large and imposing, is in part undermined by the implication of vacuity.

The stiff, hard construction of both line and fabric is modelled after military garb, resembling armour or a 'veritable *cuirasse*'.[39] The desired result was to present a visual image of constrained power – hard, immovable and unshakeable male strength – that endures, impervious to outside challenges. In fact, the unbendable quality of the doublet that worried Stubbes is central to the English look, which in part counters another of Stubbes' worries, that the English have lost their 'hardnesse' and have become weak, 'effeminate', no longer the 'puissant, valorous and hardy men' of the glorious English past.[40] For men like Ralegh and Dudley, the doublet and hose embodied a visually erotic and iconic image of male power.

While the portrait of Dudley in Figure 9 focuses on the upper body, anyone looking at the painting at the time would have known that the doublet led inevitably to the legs, so splendidly on display in the painting of Ralegh and of Queen Elizabeth with her male courtiers.[41] The qualities of the firm doublet are erotically enhanced by the over-exposed presentation of the legs, emphasized through fitted and revealing hose, constructed to accentuate the curve of the leg, particularly the calf. The word 'hose' is used to describe the clothing that covered the lower portion of the male body, which could consist of breeches or upper hose, or lower hose, also called nether hose or stockings.[42] As breeches became shorter in the later sixteenth century, the legs became even more prominent, as a true sign of male beauty, strength and worth. In a discussion of the ideal male shape, Bernardo Bibbiena in *The Courtier* worries about 'these legs of mine which do not seem to me to be as good as I would wish';[43] in *Romeo and Juliet*, the Nurse must admit that Romeo's value is measured by the perfections of his body – with a 'leg that excels all men's' (2.5.40–1) – and in *Much Ado About Nothing*, Beatrice, discoursing on the qualities of an ideal man with her uncle, says that 'With a good leg and a good foot, uncle, and money enough in his purse, such a man would win any woman in the world' (2.1.13–15).

In a period where women's legs were conspicuously hidden, and men's legs conspicuously displayed, it almost seems that 'sartorially speaking, only men had legs', as Susan Vincent has commented.[44] The ubiquitous presence of male legs clearly distinguishes the masculine from the feminine, but also draws attention to the necessity and strength of those legs to move men through the world physically, politically, socially and metaphorically. The presentation of male legs in portrait after portrait seems a visual symbol of domination, taking a stand, claiming and occupying space.

The constrained hardness of the doublet coupled with the ubiquitous musculature of the legs comes together in a story told by Robert Carey while he was fighting in France with Essex in 1592. Carey recalls a tense moment when the British soldier, Sir Ferdinando Gorges, dressed only in 'his doublet and hose, and his rapier by his side', rallied a few of his soldiers, 'leaped over the trenches' and fought off the enemy, saving Carey and his fellows, who would have 'been cut into pieces' had not it not been for the 'worth and valour' of Gorges.[45] He was able to fight so valiantly without physical armour, because the doublet and hose have their own integral protection: worth and valour. The tight-fitting firmness of the clothing is a symbol of reliable character and constrained power that can hold itself steady and unmoving, but is ready to act when challenged.

In comparison to the hard construction of the doublet and hose, the line and construction of el-Ouahed's costume is soft;

his body is cloaked, concealed in flowing robes of simple black and white, a head wrap and a turban. The shape of his body is hidden behind the folds of fabric, as are his legs, and, except for hands and face, very little is revealed. He is wearing the expected dress of his culture, but how would the English have viewed him? A draped look, emphasizing an excess of flowing fabric, recalls the garb of the ancient world. Such a look was popular into the Middle Ages, but by the time of Queen Elizabeth I and King James I, long robes were often reserved for funerals or other ceremonial occasions. In Renaissance painting, for example, draped clothing was often 'an imitation of reborn antiquity', associated with and used to represent holy figures such as Jesus or saints. Anne Hollander points out the connection between 'draped cloth and lofty concepts', such as nobility; and while draped clothing in itself did not make anyone more noble, the drapery can suggest the idea of a 'better and more beautiful life'.[46]

While the softness of the flowing robes remained familiar in some religious and ceremonial situations, the entire ensemble of the Moorish ambassador was certainly foreign to the English. But it was also the idea of softness itself that had negative connotations, both figural and literal, and these troubled the English. For example, in contrast to the image of the virtuous and steady male, women, according to John Knox, were morally soft. 'Womankind is imprudent and soft', he writes, imprudent because she lacks wisdom and reason, and soft because 'she is easelie bowed ... easily persuaded to any opinion especiallie if it be against God'.[47] In some ways, then, soft clothing was a challenge because it not only blurred the visual look between men and women, but because it was associated with the moral weakness of the female. In his 1611 Italian/English dictionary, John Florio defines the Italian word for softness, *morbidezza*, as 'wantonnesse', 'lasciviousnesse', 'ranknesse' and effeminacy, and in 1605, Francis Bacon expressed a similar sentiment, writing that idleness of action comes from 'some weakness of body or softness of spirit'.[48] Delivering a sermon to James in 1619, John Williams, Dean of

Salisbury, declared that soft and rich clothing is reserved only for those 'magistrates and other remarkeable persons' who serve Kings, whereas he rails against other more ordinary folks who will be morally corrupted by looking at or wearing such raiment. Later, in 1641, Richard Braithwaite confirmed Stubbes' ideas about a loss of hardness, writing, 'Soft cloathes introduce soft minds. Delicacy in the habit, begets an effeminacy in the heart'.[49] Softness is thus troublesome; it might indicate gentility and status, but it can also lead and point to moral weakness of character. One way to counter the threat of corruption was with a look of steady, hard constraint that literally signalled moral uprightness.

In August 1594, Philip Gawdy wrote to his brother from court that the Queen, through the Lord Chamberlain, had announced that 'no man shall come into presence, or attend upon Her [Majesty] ... wearing any long cloke beneath the knee, or thereabouts', indicating perhaps disdain for men in long robes, which obscure a hard body and a well-made leg.[50] Or perhaps such a prohibition stemmed from the disapproval of soft clothing as well as fears over the concealment that a long robe facilitates. The ambassador's body is concealed, and if one is expected to read an Englishman through the contours of his tightly held body, what can one understand about the ambassador? His body is hidden, accessorized with an elaborate strap holding a prominently displayed sword with what appears to be a dragon's head handle. The military accessories, presented against black-and-white garments, complemented by what might be a fierce or seductive expression, complete this dramatically complex presentation of an imposing figure – mysterious, secretive, defiant and menacing.

Such concealment of intention, and the difficulty of assessing what lurks behind the eyes and clothing of a man, was certainly the concern of the future James I who, in 1599, composed *Basilikon Doron*, a letter for his son Henry, advising him how to be an effective leader. Included in the letter is the necessity of appropriate dress; James touches on the issues of military garb, the problem of secrecy and the importance of honest clothing. He also advises against wearing 'ordinary armour' with clothing, using only those military accoutrements that are 'knightly and honourable', such as 'rapier-swords and daggers'. Besides the fact that more weaponry at court can bring 'confusion in the country', his real concern is over those who might wear 'traitorous, offensive weapons', secret weapons that can conceal a 'secret evil intention'.

James was also concerned that hidden weapons might inspire the wearer to glance in 'their enemies' eyes to strike terror into their hearts', which might explain el-Ouahed's glance. But the real intention of concealment, James contends, is betrayal under the mask of trust. Echoing Castiglione's idea that a man's outer appearance should mirror inner virtue, James condemns those whose 'outward badge' does not reveal who they really are.[51] James' fears are realized in the character of Iago, whose external self masks the inner one and who declares, 'I am not what I am.' While el-Ouahed might not have been concealing anything, James' concerns point to how the English might have felt about the ambassador and his appearance. There had been a rumour of el-Ouahed's connection to a murder, and this thought, combined with concealment of his attire, wrapped up with secrets, a 'reticence' to reveal information and the role that concealment plays in the military with secret weapons, as well as in spying and surveillance, could have encouraged mistrust.[52]

Such concerns would have affected how the audience perceived Othello, his dress and appearance in contrast to Cassio and Iago. Their attire on the stage would have revealed their status, and it is likely that Cassio most likely resembles Dudley or Ralegh, wearing a padded doublet, stuffed with bombast, very possibly made of foreign fabric, all calculated to resemble his military position. And then there would be the hose, tightly covering and prominently displaying his well-turned legs. The splendour and beauty of the entire look is designed to signal the virtues of his class. Recall that Iago is aware of Cassio's beauty, complaining that the Florentine 'hath a daily beauty in his life / That makes me ugly' (5.1.19–20). Iago, on the other hand, would most likely have been dressed in the simple attire of King Stephen he praises in Act 2. With his 'auld cloak about' him, Iago represents the plain yet traditional and enduring English values that Stubbes praised, values that are in stark contrast to Cassio's excessive look. Would either costume, representing choices for English men, be something Othello would have chosen to wear?

When Othello says 'Haply for I am black' (3.3.267), he identifies himself as dark, but Iago has done this early in the play when he calls the general 'an old black ram' (1.1.87), and later, luring Cassio to drunkenness, says they need to drink to the 'health of black Othello' (2.3.28–9). In making Othello, like Aaron in *Titus Andronicus*, black, Shakespeare has chosen to distinguish him from the Moorish ambassador, whose portrait shows him having light skin.[53] It seems that Shakespeare was aware of skin colour, since, in the Folio stage directions for *Merchant of Venice*, for example, Morocco is described as being a 'tawnie Moore'.[54] Whatever the reasons for Shakespeare's choice, the result is that Othello, according to the language used to describe him, resembles Aaron, causing him to stand out sharply against the white skin of the other characters.[55] Given the darkness of Othello, it is likely that the actor representing him on stage would have appeared with a blackened face, either through the use of oil, paint, soot or a fabric covering, such as velvet. Such a blackening might provoke anxiety in the audience, who, mindful of the white body of the actor underneath – 'the icon of true English soul' – are disturbed by its loss.[56] Recall the daughters of Niger in Ben Jonson's 1605 *Masque of Blackness*, who, although graced by the perfect beauty of their black hair, are 'black with black despair' when they realize that true beauty is the white skin of Britannia.[57] While Othello's black face is crucial to an understanding of how he was read and understood on the stage, I would suggest that how he was dressed was equally significant and that his attire goes beyond underscoring 'geographical difference as a function of sartorial taste'.[58] Othello's costume might signal that he is foreign-born, but it is the clothing and his skin colour working in concert with one another that reveal a fuller and more complete understanding of the character.

While it is difficult to say how he might have looked on the stage, I would like to consider three possibilities – the first to consider is Othello dressed similarly to Aaron in Henry Peacham's drawing, shown in Figure 11. The drawing, dated 1595, is believed to be a scene from *Titus Andronicus*.[59] The costumes of the characters seem to be a melange of different styles and periods, with the two figures on the left wearing contemporary English dress, and with Aaron and the Goths depicted in Roman armour. As Schlueter also notes, the drawing most likely 'depicts an actual theatrical wardrobe', and indicates what resources a theatre would have had.[60]

With regard to Aaron's image, a number of things are apparent: his military garb and sword, whether historically accurate or not; the soft skimpiness of his costume; and the darkness of his skin. With regard to his role as a general, it is

FIGURE 11 *The Peacham Drawing, by permission of Marquess of Bath, Longleat House, Warminster, Wiltshire. Artist: Henry Peacham.*

likely that Othello would have worn a sword and a rapier, which were also part of English male attire. Although the play mentions clothing and dressing a good deal, it does not offer specific details about what Othello might actually be wearing; but there is mention of head garb. Early in the action, when Othello is still self-possessed and confident, he defends his reputation through the image of removing his hat – speaking 'unbonneted' – to the world to illustrate that his merits and faults are clearly known, revealing his 'proud' 'fortune' (1.2.23). A little later, he ironically refers to his helmet turned into a skillet by housewives if he should ever lose control and let his passions 'taint' his 'business' and interfere with his ability to make clear judgements (1.3.273). Coming as it does so early in the play, such a statement, centred on a key element of his warrior garb – his helmet – the item that protects his head, brain, and thinking, signals the loss of Othello's rational senses, his profession, and his very self. It is also worth noting that later in the play when Othello has completely come under Iago's power, he bids farewell to 'the tranquil mind', to 'content', and to 'the plumed troops and the big wars' (3.3.351–2). Like Hamlet, who bids farewell to his books and former life after the visit from the Ghost, all is lost for Othello in a similar way, which he expresses through the loss of his profession and his former rational and warrior self visualized in the image of his helmet, once decorated with plumes of feathers.[61]

It is possible then that Othello could have been dressed throughout as a military man and perhaps even like Aaron, with chest revealed, bare legs and sword in hand. But how would the audience have read such a look? With bare legs, much of his skin is revealed and, in comparison to the other figures wearing doublet and hose, Aaron does not appear threatening but unprotected, vulnerable and perhaps a bit uncivilized. European male attire showcased the legs, but they are usually covered, whereas Aaron's bare legs underline his blackness.[62] Then there is the skimpy quality of the costume, resembling an undergarment, which the audience might have seen as shameful; recall, for example, how Iago mocks

Brabantio for appearing in his nightgown – 'for shame put on your / gown'! (1.1.84–5). Given Othello's stature in Venice, such a flimsy costume, with so much exposed, naked flesh, could have undermined his position within the play and in the eyes of the audience, who would have understood that Othello is not only a warrior, but also a grander, more elevated figure, whose attire would need to reflect that status. He confirms his status when he reminds Iago that he fetches his 'life and being / From men of royal siege' (1.2.21–2).

Perhaps a more honourable costume for Othello might have been one similar to that worn by the Moorish ambassador, draped in soft attire, with some kind of headdress that would have more accurately presented him as the noble figure he is. In England, as mentioned earlier, robes could be worn for ceremonial occasions, and in Venice, according to Vecellio, the robes of the nobility resembled the Roman toga and were a sign of honour. For example, Vecellio notes that other classes of men, such as merchants or doctors, often wore the drapery of the 'nobility because it confers great dignity'. However, Vecellio is careful to point out that under those robes, at the core of the costume, the men are wearing doublet, breeches and hose, which reaffirm the essence of the male look.[63]

For the English audience, a draped look might have granted Othello a grave nobility, as well as elegance and grace. It may have also made him appear powerful and perhaps superior. However, given the character's skin colour and completely foreign attire, the audience could have viewed Othello with ambivalence, being compelled by and suspicious of his look. The attire would certainly have contributed to the exotic and mysterious qualities of Othello's character – he is visible and present in the play, but he carries with him, just as the painting of el-Ouahed suggests, hidden secrets. The stories he tells of his 'travailous history', of 'battles, sieges, fortune', of cannibals and the Anthropophagi (1.3.131–45) all point to a life beyond Venice and London, beyond the ordinary, a life of the strange and unknown, a life that makes him a hero and unknowable.

Despite the association of draped attire with nobility, the negative connotations of softness with lasciviousness, weak will, mysterious concealment, hidden secrets and weapons, as well as the threat of treason, the 'secret evil contention' that James I notes, could have unsettled the audience. At the end of the play, Othello in fact reveals that he has had concealed weapons. One weapon is taken by Montano, who says to Gratiano, 'Take you this weapon / Which I have here recovered from the Moor'. But even after Othello is behind a guarded door, he reveals to Gratiano that he has a 'sword of Spain, the ice-brook's temper', the better of which 'never did itself sustain / Upon a soldier's thigh' (5.2.239–40, 253, 259–60). He intends to kill himself with the sword – 'Here is my journey's end' (256) – but instead wounds Iago. And although Lodovico commands, 'Wrench his sword from him', Othello has yet another hidden weapon, and with the words 'I took by th' throat the circumcised dog' (253), he succeeds. Othello does not use the weapons for treachery or treason, as James had feared, and at this final moment, when all is lost, trying to gain some control and re-establish his honour, he uses the hidden knife to kill himself. When Cassio says he had feared such an outcome, 'For he was great of heart', he confirms Othello's honourable self and his desire to re-establish that honour. Proud as he was, Othello – with the quintessential accessories of his military garb – would have wanted to take his own life rather than have it taken from him (5.2.353, 358).

With regard to the danger of soft robes, recall also John Knox's argument against the softness of the female, which indicates their weak moral fabric. Women – imprudent and unable to reason properly – are 'easelie bowed ... easelie persuaded to any opinion'. While everyone in *Othello* is easily persuaded by Iago, such an association seems particularly applicable to Othello, who, although he defends his ability to reason early in the play, is bowed by and susceptible to Iago's designs. And then there is the handkerchief, the softest of soft items, given to Desdemona by Othello, a gift from his mother, given to her by an Egyptian, crafted and woven with magic and sacred silk, and laced with 'mummy', the liquid from dead bodies (3.4.58–77). It is an astonishing accessory, a gift that with each giving increases in charm, carrying with it the power to secure love and to destroy it. Othello gambles his entire life on the strawberry-studded item. Like the soft handkerchief, Othello too, concealed in soft robes, remains mysterious unknowable, and Iago is easily able to manipulate both the Moor and the accessory. Iago has certainly softened and weakened Othello, and perhaps his clinging to the accessory indicates Othello's desire to hold on to his origins and his stronger self, but ironically, it is the very soft object that conveys his downfall.

If soft clothing could alternately indicate mystery, concealed power and threat along with moral weakness, what would it mean for both the character and the actor to be dressed in the upright, hard costume of doublet and hose? The argument here is that Othello, seeking to assimilate himself into Venetian society, would have chosen to dress like the other aristocratic males; after all, he has already been successful with such an approach – he has gained great success as a military man and has even acquired a Venetian wife. Further, it might have been difficult and expensive to approximate exotic draped clothing, and doublet and hose were certainly at hand, although it was apparently 'conventional to purchase special costumes for the actors who played prominent parts'.[64] In any event, the beauty and splendid quality of Cassio's look would suit the noble general, and the doublet's similarity to military armour would reflect Othello's profession.

In the beginning of the play, Othello does seem to have many of the qualities exemplified in doublet and hose – he is firm, strong, unbendable, alluring and erotically powerful. He is also calm and confident, able to contain his passions; he is not intimidated by Brabantio's threats or impending battle. Despite his desire for his young wife, he reassures the Duke and senators that his desires are tamed, 'the young affects' in him now 'defunct'. But, of course, it is in this passage that he also ironically declares that if he loses control of his rationality, his helmet should be turned into a skillet (1.3. 264–5). As the play continues, Othello does deteriorate and his harder qualities seem to decline into an emotional, moral and rational softness. This decline is once again signalled by a reference to headgear, and dramatically identified by Emilia, who, calling Othello a 'gull' and a 'dolt', says he is 'as ignorant as dirt' and unworthy of 'so good a wife'. In this terrible moment of recognition, Emilia calls Othello a 'murderous coxcombe', who must now wear the headgear of the professional fool (5.2.159–60; 231–2).[65] Capped with the soft comb of the fool, having lost the protection of his helmet and military profession, Othello is vulnerable; further, his earlier references to his headgear and rationality reveal that he is aware of the power of clothing to strengthen or weaken.

Recall the English attitude to wearing foreign dress – seductive but threatening with any benefit easily outweighed by the fear, as Dekker suggests, of being 'translated' out of one's nationhood and one's identity. Castiglione voices a similar concern – Italians, he writes, have 'exchanged' their own style of dress for the attire of foreigners, who have in turn invaded and 'subjugated' them.[66] Much before Dekker and Castiglione expressed their concerns, the ninth-century emperor Charlemagne had descried foreign fashions. Apparently dressing himself like the 'common people', Charlemagne condemned the practice of wearing the clothing of those he had conquered, which is the exact practice of the Spanish, who deeply desired Morisco clothing. To do so, Charlemagne argues, was dangerous, a devastating loss because, as he writes, 'If you take their clothes, they will take your hearts.' This statement of threat points to the power of clothing to transform; no mere outer covering, clothing is Erasmus' second body, and as such implies that you are indeed what you wear. When you wear another culture's clothing, you take on their identity and lose your own, and worse, you also lose your very heart.

These fears were not limited to Europeans worried about invasion from the Other. Muhammad ibn Khaldûn, the

Tunisian scholar and statesman born in 1332, and part of a powerful Moorish aristocracy in Andalusia, worried that the Muslim Moors had come under the sway of the Spanish and had lost their souls by imitating and adopting 'the customs and manners' of the 'victor in the use of their dress, mounts, weapons' and 'emblems'. Likening the Moors to the soul, ibn Khaldûn argues that the soul 'sees' and seeks the 'perfection' it thinks it perceives in the manner and clothing of the victor who is superior and, therefore, worthy of emulation. Such an action is misguided and a clear indication that the Moors have 'been dominated by others', he writes, and that they have lost their soul.[67] Certainly, ibn Khaldûn and Charlemagne's ideas about the power of dress to eliminate one's identity coincide with Stubbes' and Harrison's fears of deformation. Further, by putting their emphasis on the loss of heart and soul, ibn Khaldûn and Charlemagne coincide with Dekker and Castiglione in their concerns about translation, subjugation and replacement, underlining the devastation of such a transformation, a transformation that can have tragic consequences. Further, they offer both sides of this conflict from the perspective of the conquered and the victor, indicating that the danger is not lessened by a position of power.

Perhaps Othello would have deeply understood the conflicts associated with putting on doublet and hose, that by trying to approximate the ideal of English male hardness and constraint, he would lose his self. As both a character in a play and as an actor on stage, when he enters, dressed in the ideal uniform of European masculinity in black face, it is perhaps immediately clear that he has already been translated and subjugated, that he has lost his self, as well as his heart and soul. As he continues to deteriorate, he presents a figure that is shocking to those about him. Lodovico particularly voices this change when, seeing Othello strike Desdemona, he says, 'this would not be believed in Venice', and later laments – 'I am sorry that I am deceived in him' (4.1.241, 282). Perhaps this is telling – the persona that Othello had perhaps constructed for himself with doublet and hose, the one that conformed to the desires of the

Venetians, is also lost under the pressures of Iago, who continually reminds Othello of his difference. And, of course, Othello deceived himself into thinking he could live and work as a Venetian, in part, through wearing the expected male attire. In this way he could blend in, while also making the grand gesture of embracing the European construction of masculinity by abandoning his own. It is revealing that Lodovico uses a term of dressing to tell Othello that he has lost power, that his 'command is taken off' (5.2.331). Perhaps Lodovico's pronouncement suggests that Othello, by taking off his own traditional attire, has lost both his masculinity and his power.

While it is true that we cannot possibly know what Othello actually wore on stage, the three possibilities I have examined in this chapter reveal that his costume could serve as a prompt to the audience, revealing key elements of his character and his tragic choices. In defining the meaning of the Italian word for attire, *abiti*, in her book on Venice, Bronwen Wilson writes that apparel reveals 'attitude and behavior', that it 'invested bodies with meaning through the quality of the fabric and the tradition and conventions attached to dress'.[68] Such a definition certainly applies to Othello, who is an internally conflicted character caught between two divergent definitions of masculinity, presented through hard and soft clothing, and attitudes of constraint and concealment, each carrying with them traditions and conventions that frequently clash with one another – in many ways, Othello is destroyed in this clash.

PART TWO

Designing Shakespeare: Theatrical Practice and Costume

The Stylish Shepherd, or, What to Wear in *As You Like It*'s Forest of Arden

Russell Jackson

'He – for there could be no doubt about his sex, though the fashion of the time did something to disguise it . . .'

(Virginia Woolf, *Orlando*, 1928, opening sentence)

This chapter discusses (not altogether in chronological order) the costuming of a selection of Rosalinds since the late nineteenth century.[1] The emphasis is on the ways in which costuming for the role has related to a number of factors: the demands of the script; the interpretive choices made in the production; and the relationship between stage costume and customary apparel (or fashion) in the play's own time, the period chosen and the production's own time. At the outset it is important to suggest what 'the demands of the script' might be, or indeed what such a phrase really means. In this context, I am thinking of the priorities that a designer and director might establish, with some sense of what the play unavoidably requires, but it is important to distinguish between what these might have been at the time of its composition and first performance, and what they may have been since.

In *Impersonations* (1996), Stephen Orgel argues for – and applauds – a potential for disturbance on the part for the cross-dressed male actor:

> The transvestite actor was indispensible in Renaissance England, but (or perhaps, therefore) the figure was never fully naturalized. He was essential precisely as a construct, always available to interrogate, unsettle, reinterpret the norms, which were always conceived to be unstable – the interrogation, indeed, was an essential part of the never-ending attempt at stabilization.[2]

If this destabilization sounds like solemn business, it should be remembered that it is also the basis of sophisticated wit and a degree of irony. In John Lyly's *Galatea* (1583/4), written for the choirboys of St Paul's Cathedral, Melibeus the shepherd disguises his daughter Phillida as a boy in order to protect her from the attentions of Neptune, who requires the sacrifice of the best-looking virgin to assuage his wrath. Phillida is puzzled:

PHILLIDA   But how shall I be disguised?
MELIBEUS   In man's apparel.
PHILLIDA   It will neither become my body nor my mind.
MELIBEUS   Why, Phillida?
PHILLIDA   For then I must keep company with boys and commit follies unseemly for my sex, or keep company with girls and be thought more wanton than becomes me. Besides, I shall be ashamed of my long hose and short coats, and so unwarily blab out something for blushing at everything.

(1.3.13–23)[3]

There is much thickening of the plots, with Diana disguising Cupid as a woman. The sea-god, who knows a thing or two about disguise, is not so easily fooled:

> Do silly shepherds go about to deceive great Neptune, in putting man's attire upon women? And Cupid, to make sport, deceive them all by using woman's apparel upon a god? Then Neptune, that hast taken sundry shapes to obtain love, stick not to practice some deceit to show thy desire; and having often thrust thyself into the shape of beasts to deceive men, be not coy to use the shape of the shepherd to show thyself a god.
>
> (2.2.17–24)

Phillida encounters Galatea, another strategically disguised virgin, and takes a fancy to 'him' in a scene that concludes encouragingly with Phillida's line 'Come, let us into the grove, and make much of one another, that cannot tell what to think of one another' (3.2.61–2).

In Sir Philip Sidney's 'Old' *Arcadia*, completed in 1590, Pyrocles is disguised as the Amazon Philoclea. So effective is the transformation that 'Musidorus, that had helped to dress his friend, could not satisfy himself with looking upon him, so did he find his excellent beauty set out with this new change, like a diamond set in a more advantageous sort'.[4] Subsequently, the confusion does its work on Cleophila when 'the ornament of the earth, young Philoclea, appeared in her nymphlike apparel, so near the nakedness as one might well discern part of her perfections, and yet so apparelled as did show she kept the best store of her beauties to herself...' Unsurprisingly, this fetishistic figure affects not only Cleophila with a strange disturbance of cognition and affect, but also, as the narrator suggests in an aside, the readers:

> [T]he clouds of Cleophila's thoughts quite vanished, and so was her brain fixed withal that her sight seemed more

forcible and clear than ever before or since she found it, with such strange delight unto her (for still, fair ladies, you remember that I use the she-title to Pyrocles, for so he would have it) that she stood like a well-wrought image, with show of life, but without all exercise of life, so forcibly had love transformed all her spirits into the present contemplation of the lovely Philoclea.[5]

The emphasis on elaboration, although here in the equivalent of a masque costume, reflects another aspect of the cross-dressing figure: its potential for satire directed against fashionable young men and women. Shakespeare exploits this in *The Two Gentlemen of Verona*, when Julia discusses with her maid the disguise that will allow her to set off in search of her wayward lover, Valentine:

JULIA	Gentle Lucetta, fit me with such weeds
	As may become some well-reputed page.
LUCETTA	Why then your ladyship must cut your hair.
JULIA	No, girl, I'll knit it up in silken strings
	With twenty odd-conceited true-love knots –
	To be fantastic may become a youth
	Of greater time than I shall show to be.
LUCETTA	What fashion, madam, shall I make your breeches?
JULIA	That fits as well as 'Tell me, good my lord,
	What compass will you wear your farthingale?'
	Why e'en what fashion thou best likest, Lucetta.
LUCETTA	You must needs have them with a codpiece, madam.
JULIA	Out, out, Lucetta, that will be ill-favoured.
LUCETTA	A round hose, madam, now's not worth a pin,
	Unless you have a codpiece to stick pins in.

(2.7.39–56)

Barbara Hodgdon suggests that this dialogue:

reveals a kind of 'double voicing' in which both female character and boy player speak, sometimes from 'inside' the role, sometimes from 'outside' it, [so that] the exchange works to validate fictional femininity by insisting that masculinity itself is merely a 'passing matter', a function of fashion.[6]

Rosalind remarks that the 'swashing and ... martial outside' that she will assume as Ganymede will be no more than what 'many other mannish cowards have / That do outface it with their semblances' (1.3.117–19). Her subsequent satire on the conventional male lover (3.2.359–68) is matched by a 'character' of the female counterpart, the teasingly reluctant mistress (390–406), which includes the passing observation that 'boys and women are for the most part cattle of this colour' (396–7). This glancingly asserts the boy player's aptitude for the role Ganymede will assume. Meanwhile, Orlando is presumably as puzzled as Lyly's Phillida or Sidney's Cleophila, while the audience shares Ganymede's knowledge of the deception and the boy player's knowledge of himself as being, *as usual*, not what he seems. This raises an important point: the boy player's shape-changing is at once familiar (being what his audience expects in the theatre) and novel, by virtue of the playwright's innovative take on it, even as his work was lodged firmly on a stable tradition of destabilization.

It is worth noting that Orlando's response to Ganymede focused very much on the oddity of encountering such a well-spoken young man in this remote rural environment. Where does the 'pretty youth' dwell, he asks, and he observes that Ganymede's accent is 'something finer than [he] could purchase in so remote a dwelling' (3.2.329–30). In *Twelfth Night*, the emphasis is much more directly on the physical features of 'Cesario', and when Orsino sends him on his errand to Olivia in 1.4, his description of the young man's qualifications is sensuous:

> Diana's lip
> Is not more smooth and rubious; thy small pipe

Is as the maiden's organ, shrill and sound,
And all is semblative a woman's part.

(1.4.31–4)

It is hardly surprising that directors have found it appropriate to emphasise the possibility of homosexual attraction in the relationship between count and boy. Out in the woods, Rosalind has sometimes been exposed to the equivocal attentions of Jacques – for example, in Terry Hands's 1980 RSC production – but she is not as subject to the continual sense of the threat (and, of course, opportunity) of discovery that Viola experiences in her dealings with Orsino in every scene she shares with him and in her encounter with Feste at the beginning of 4.1.

On Shakespeare's stage, *As You Like It* offered at least three definitions of the figure of Rosalind: (1) a boy as a woman; (2) a boy as a woman as a boy; and (3) a boy as a woman as a boy pretending to be a woman. In the final scene, the first of these options reappears, although in the epilogue at least (1) and (2) are presented, with a reminiscence of (3). By the final scene and the epilogue, Rosalind (1) – the 'authentic' female Rosalind as impersonated on stage by a boy – has been augmented by the experience of the intervening acts, in which s/he has gone through the other permutations. Lesley Wade Soule's identification of the assumed character as 'Cocky Ros' is valuable here, as is her reminder that the play's self-consciousness is one of its 'frequent and unmistakeable signs of non-illusionistic popular theatre'.[7] Arguably, the audience's relationship with the performer and the role has been modified yet again in the play's final moments: in Shakespeare's theatre, as now, the actor's performance would be looked back on from the vantage of the epilogue as a tour de force, a considerable achievement of some complexity. As Juliet Dusinberre observes, 'disguise makes a woman not a man but a more developed woman.'[8] On a related and not insignificant point, Valerie Traub distinguishes between the attribution of homosexual desire to any of the characters and the provisional suggestion of it: although 'at various moments in the play [Rosalind, Orlando and Phebe] temporarily inhabit a homoerotic position of desire' the play's 'entire logic... works against such categorization, against fixing upon and reifying any one mode of desire'.[9] Allowing for the dynamic effect of such playfulness, the possibility has to be accepted that the play remains essentially conservative. In a seminal article published in 1988, Jean E. Howard contends that 'the representation of Rosalind's holiday humour has the primary effect... of confirming the gender system and perfecting rather than dismantling it by making a space for mutuality within relations of dominance'. That this is more complicated than may seem at first blush is suggested in Howard's contention that Rosalind 'plays out masculine constructions of femininity', and that in this she is not so much 'released... from patriarchy' as enabled in theatricalizing its assumptions to teach Orlando 'how to get beyond certain ideologies of gender to more enabling ones'.[10] Whether he comprehends this is a question neither Howard nor the play can resolve: one can only hope.

Consideration of the role's effect in theatre of the play's own time can draw on such reflections on its affective and intellectual complexity as a pleasing puzzle to take account of some other factors. The 'reading' in performance of Rosalind (1) is in accord with the customary means by which a woman is represented in the theatre, which the audience is at liberty to view as both 'reality' (what they habitually accept) and pleasurable artifice (especially with a familiar and favourite performer). The transformation to Ganymede (2) is witty, and the emphasis is as much on manner and status (what is someone with that refined accent doing here?) as it is on clothing. In the context of the play's other couples, courtliness and wit – the 'saucy lackey' recalling the forward boys of Lyly's comedies or Moth in Shakespeare's *Love's Labour's Lost* – set Ganymede apart from the common run of forest dwellers. Viewed against the 'reality' represented by Corin, William and Audrey, Ganymede and Aliena are privileged incomers: their efficiency as sheep farmers is taken for granted but invoked in passing only as necessary, and they rely on the shepherd (Corin), whose wages Rosalind 'mends'. At this level, the play shifts easily in and out of the more serious convention of pastoral as a way of writing about weighty matters under the guise of caring about sheep. Silvius and Phebe are another matter: one might suggest that Arden is full of surprises, one of them being the encounter with such poetically gifted conventional lovers who speak in verse but seem to be real country folk rather than a figment of the courtly pastoral imagination.

Three centuries later, with the theatre moving in the meantime into and then out of a succession of different conventions both of pictorial realism and of decorous feminine behaviour, the case is altered. Rosalind (1) now appears to be a simpler figure, except in all-male productions, and the actress (the old term is helpful here) is a 'real woman'. The specific skill and, arguably, homoerotic frisson, that went with the boy-actor's impersonation has gone, together with the counterbalancing factor of his being the 'normal' way to represent women on stage. Rosalind-as-Ganymede (2) becomes a demonstration of the actress's versatility, although changing concepts of 'feminine' decorum will affect that. The transformation from (1) to (2) may still emphasize status, but the disguise's ability to conceal gender becomes more problematic – or, put another way, a different kind of opportunity. The allure of the breeches role, whether exemplified in the Principal Boy of British Christmas pantomime, Mozart's Cherubino in *Le Nozze di Figaro* or Oktavian in Richard Strauss's *Der Rosenkavalier* (or even Orlando in Sally Potter's 1992 film of Woolf's novel), adds a new dimension but also assumes the burden of credibility. In *As You Like It*, both Rosalind and Orlando have to negotiate this carefully. It helps, perhaps, that it is Oliver and not his brother who is present when Ganymede faints at the news of her beloved's injury. However, shifting the play's action beyond a period sharing its assumptions about the 'feminine' disposition to faint may cause a momentary ripple to disturb the audience's acceptance of what is being said. Stronger than this, however, is the consideration of dress codes: for better or worse, Rosalind-as-Ganymede has to show her/his legs, an element of the disguise that caused anxiety in the nineteenth and early twentieth centuries, in terms of the actress's desire not to appear in tights, suggestive of 'lower' forms of entertainment such as British Christmas pantomime and nineteenth-century burlesque. This aspect of the role's costuming may have ceased to be grounds for moral anxiety, but a new range of possibilities present themselves: how sexy (that is, 'coming on') should Rosalind/Ganymede be? What balance is to be struck between the scopophiliac pleasures of the audience (not only the men in it) and the credibility of the play's situations? Is Orlando to find himself attracted to a boy, and how surprised should he be by realizing this?

The costuming of actresses (the gendered term is historically appropriate here) in the role can be approached with these factors in mind, with one additional consideration: how real is that forest? In Victorian and Edwardian productions, when scenic artists strove – sometimes with the help of nurserymen – to make the woods on stage as 'real' as possible, what was to be made of Ganymede's outdoor attire? Was disbelief suspended selectively? Did the audience really care, as they could at one and the same time admire the accomplishments of scenic realism and ignore (or perhaps relish) the femininity of the figure adopting a swaggering outside but revealing her gender-specific charms in the respectable and licensed context of a classic play?

A further development of the topic, beyond the scope of the present chapter, would be a more detailed and systematic collation of these images (and potentially many others) with examples of the fashions of the production's own time. Nevertheless, one general conclusion is that there is no such thing as 'modern dress'. All contemporary clothing, once adopted on stage, becomes costume, inseparable from the interpretative intention of the production, but constantly referring the viewer to connections beyond it.[11]

Practicality and legitimized allure: a female Orlando in 1885, Ada Rehan in 1889 and Lily Brayton in 1907

Three late Victorian and early twentieth-century examples suggest the equivocal pleasures of the cross-dressed actress in the period and, at the same time, the difficulties of reconciling practicality with modesty. In a famous amateur performance at Coombe Woods in 1885, Lady Archibald Campbell appeared as Orlando, with the professional actress Eleanor Calhoun as Rosalind: the play was co-directed by Edward William Godwin.[12] This was a fashionable event, allied to the artistic avant-garde – Whistler painted Lady Campbell in character, and Godwin was a leading light of furniture and interior design as well as a notable architect and man of the theatre. Its significance in the present context lies in a combination of factors: the credibility of Rosalind's disguise as a young man being supported by an Orlando played by a woman; the performance in 'real' woodland that carries out the ambitions of contemporary stage realism to a degree impossible even in the best-equipped of theatres; and the celebrity outside the professional theatre of at least one of the players, 'Lady Archie'. The last of these adds a distancing element comparable to that of a professional performer's celebrity within the theatre world, although the performance is a social and artistic occasion of a kind distinct from even the most glamorous London first night. In an engraving from the *Illustrated London News*, the thigh-high boots worn by Lady Archibald Campbell as Orlando seem suitable for the forest, despite a dainty heel of the kind familiar in contemporary footwear and especially notable in stage shoes and boots of the time. Rosalind, the professional actress Eleanor Calhoun, wears similar boots. The hair of both is dressed in accord with current fashion, especially in 'aesthetic' modes. As for Rosalind, Oscar Wilde reported that some found her 'too dreamy' but considered that:

even admitting that the vigour of the lad who tripped up the Duke's wrestler was hardly sufficiently emphasized, still in the low music of [her] voice and in the strange beauty of her movements and gestures, there was a wonderful fascination, and the visible presence of romance quite consoled me for the possible absence of robustness.[13]

In photographs, Ada Rehan, whose Rosalind was seen in New York in 1889 and London in 1890 and 1894, is usually posed in a studio against a background that represents the kind of stage realism aimed for in Augustin Daly's production. Her ankle-boots of soft leather have raised heels in the manner of theatrical footwear of the time; over a soft-collared white shirt she wears a waistcoat-like vest with slashed sleeves that show the white underneath, and over this a skirted tunic that reaches to about two inches above the knee. A hat with a feather is perched at a jaunty angle on top of luxuriant hair, and neither hair nor make-up attempt to disguise the familiar look of the actress. *The Times* (2 May 1894) remarked on her 'grace, vivacity, and charm', which imparted 'to the most delightful of pastoral plays an incomparable freshness and beauty', and Rehan's comic vitality was often celebrated by critics. Daly staged *Twelfth Night* and *The Two Gentlemen of Verona* with opportunities for decorous cross-dressing for Rehan, and even began preparations for her to play prince Hal in a conflation of the two parts of *Henry IV*.[14] George Bernard Shaw, who admired Rehan and loathed Daly's productions, commented that in *The Two Gentlemen of Verona*, 'Miss Rehan provided a strong argument in favour of rational dress by looking much better in her page's costume than in that of her own sex'.[15] Reviewing a later production, with Adelaide Neilson at the St James's Theatre, Shaw returned to the theme of 'rational dress', a subsidiary feminist cause whose other notable supporters included Oscar Wilde. One of the main causes of Rosalind's popularity was that 'she only wears a skirt for a few minutes' and 'the dismal effect of the change at the end to the wedding dress ought to convert the stupidest champion of petticoats to rational dress'.[16]

Oscar Asche's 1907 London production, in which the actor-manager played Jacques, was notable for the lavishness and realism of its woodland setting, in which artificial and painted greenery was supplemented by cartloads of the real thing, stored (and watered) on the theatre's roof during the day: the amateur reviewer Gordon Crosse describes the rise of the curtain for the second act as revealing 'an open space covered with fallen leaves surrounded by trees, with charming looking paths wandering away among them, and a fine effect of distance, the whole looking lovely under a moonlight effect'.[17] Lily Brayton, Asche's wife, was an energetic and gamesome Ganymede. *The Times'* review, noting the, at times, overdone energy of the production ('a jolly, more or less Shakespearean, lark') asked whether Rosalind was 'a romp' and commented:

> Miss Lily Brayton would have us think so, and as she makes an irresistibly charming romp it would be churlish to insist, for the time being, upon any other view of the character. We do not remember to have seen a Rosalind who went through the game of mock-wooing with greater zest. Certainly there should be a strong leaven of roguishness in Rosalind; but this one is more than a rogue, is, in fact, a bit of a minx.

> (8 October 1907)

Max Beerbohm, Shaw's successor as dramatic critic for the *Saturday Review*, concurred, marshalling a series of Edwardian slang expressions to convey the modernity of the effect:

> 'Jolly' is surely the right epithet for Mr Oscar Asche's production of *As You Like It*; and one might, I think, without risk of hyperbole, strengthen that epithet by the adverb 'awfully.' Yes, it is an awfully jolly affair, compact of good will and 'go' and 'snap' and 'Ginger.' Sharp's the word, and there isn't a dull moment.

In this context, it was hardly surprising that Rosalind should be 'a very clever, mettlesome performance, somewhat lacking in softness'.[18] An illustration shows a commendable practicality in Ganymede's loose, cross-gartered buckskin trousers and what seems like a sheepskin jacket, but her footwear seems more suited to the stage than the forest, especially when compared with Orlando's sturdier boots. The most striking aspect of the photograph, however, is the undisguised femininity of her hair and face.

Fashionable androgyny in 1936: Elisabeth Bergner in Paul Czinner's film

Elisabeth Bergner's was the 'definitive' Rosalind in German-speaking theatre between 1925 and her exile in 1933. The film, directed in England by her husband Paul Czinner and released in 1936, preserves the elements of this performance. A studio photograph from 1930 by an unknown photographer shows the costume she adopted, with minor variations, in all her performances. Shorts are worn over hose that reveal her legs up to mid-thigh, with a sleeveless jerkin laced at the front and a shirt with flowing sleeves and a loose collar. In the film, although not in this photograph, she has straight collar-length fair hair parted in a manner similar to that of Greta Garbo in many of her roles, the most notable in this context being the cross-dressed queen in *Queen Christina* (1933), directed for MGM by Rouben Mamoulian.

Bergner's footwear in some photographs of her as she appeared on stage suggests sandal-like, open-work leather uppers, but in the film she has ankle boots resembling those worn by Laurence Olivier's Orlando on the farm, in the court and in the woods. The woodland is elaborately 'realistic' in its vegetation and the abundant wildlife (including flocks of sheep) but has a distinctly 'studio' atmosphere – supported by the acoustic – and the architecture of the cottage recalls the stylized vernacular manner of late nineteenth- and early twentieth-century 'ideal homes'. Overall, the appeal of Bergner as Ganymede was consistent with her established (and very popular) gamine film and stage persona, and the athleticism of her performance – including a forward roll to express her delight in discovering Orlando is in the forest – suggests an affinity with the kind of exercise attire represented by the gymslip. In its time, this was strongly suggestive of the modern, physically active young woman. Her boots have none of the fetishistic quality found in Rehan and some other late nineteenth- and early twentieth-century examples: she is equipped for the outdoors, at least as represented in the studio, where even the weather is stylized. In an enraptured account of her performance at the Lessing Theater in Berlin in 1923, the critic Herbert Ihering had written that 'we were delighted as the words flowed through the relaxed body', and was especially impressed by the transitions in her performance of gender: 'Her voice broke, and one experienced the double transformation: from the girl into the boy into the girl he was playing. An exhilarating experience.'[19] In London, *The Times*' review of the film (4 September 1936) seems to strike a balance between relish and reservation:

> Miss Bergner, it is true, allows herself a freedom of movement and gesture which might be impossible on the stage, where her Rosalind would perhaps have kept more within the compass of the play. She overcomes the difficulty of her foreign accent and speaks her words with charm and relish, but she underlines them, as she underlines her conception of the character, with excessive emphasis and with a restless and mannered grace.

Advance publicity, in the shape of an article in *Screen Pictorial* (April 1936) touched on the cross-gender appeal of Bergner's appearance under an appreciative female gaze, with a significant hint of her kinship with performers in another kind of theatre:

Her hair is straight and soft and golden. Her face is the shape of an almond. Her body is incredibly small, yet exact in proportion: her limbs – in the short jerkin, breeches and tights she wears to disguise Rosalind as the youth, Ganymede – are at once the crazy envy and hopeless obsession of every chorus girl in London.

Comments like these, which recur in reviews and articles on Bergner in this and other roles, reflect the complexity and variety of performances that might be broadly defined as 'feminine'. More importantly, they suggest the kind of pleasingly equivocal appeal that – even if one finds her Rosalind over-energetic – corresponds to Virginia Woolf's enigmatic Orlando.

Two unequivocally 'feminine' Ganymedes: Katharine Hepburn in New York, 1950, and Niamh Cusack at Stratford-upon-Avon, 1996

Van Damm's much-reproduced photograph of Katharine Hepburn in the 1950 Theatre Guild production at the Cort Theatre in New York, posed on stage for a 'photo shoot', may not represent Hepburn's performance adequately, but the cut of the tunic (or doublet?) and the extent of elegant leg on display immediately disqualify the wearer as either a practical forest-dweller or a credible 'Ganymede'. (We have to assume the tights are coloured, but the suggestion of a hosiery advertisement is hard to resist.) Nor do hair and make-up contribute to anything other than confirming the unmistakable presence of Hepburn herself. But the delicate footwear and the scallop-edged cloak draped nonchalantly over her shoulders make no more than a creditable gesture to what may read as appropriate in an already stylized environment. Whether or not one might believe that this person would be any other than Hepburn is of course beside the point, an effect inevitable and indeed welcomed with many well-known actors – not to mention film stars. It might have been no obstacle to the degree of assent required by many of her fans for the play to be enjoyable. This raises the question that may shorten all discussion of several of these examples of female stardom: it's only a play after all, and if Hepburn is giving you your money's worth, do you really *mind* how credible Rosalind's disguise is? But that in turn raises the issue of what kind of theatre is being catered for and what this play can do for it. The *New Yorker* reviewer, Wolcott Gibbs, after confessing to a dislike of the play itself, considered Hepburn's 'physical equipment' for the role 'admirable, permitting her to impersonate a boy with the minimum of the absurdity generally attendant on such performances', although he found her delivery 'mannered' at times.[20] In the *New York Times* (19 February 1950), Brooks Atkinson declared that Michael Benthall's elaborate production of Shakespeare's comedy, with sets by James Bailey, had 'about as much taste as a Radio City Music Hall stage show' and put Shakespeare 'on the level of a colored postcard'. Hepburn did not 'capture the easy spontaneity of Shakespeare's mood in *As You Like It* nor the musical rapture of his poetry'. Her performance was 'intelligently planned in the head, but it does not flow from the heart'.

Four and a half decades later, Niamh Cusack, in Steven Pimlott's 1996 RSC production with a much less decorative design aesthetic, wore 'authentic' doublet and hose as Ganymede, but the Elizabethan costume, more credible in itself than Hepburn's display of dancer's legs, did little to disguise her gender. Michael Billington wrote that 'in her disguise of Ganymede she looks, with her honey-gold tresses, unequivocally feminine' (*Guardian*, 26 April 1996). In a review for *Shakespeare Quarterly*, I noted that in this outfit and once in the forest, Cusack seemed to become 'more conventionally girlish' than in the formality of the court dress of the earlier scenes. The physical representation of desire seemed likely to go further than usual, with her lips meeting Orlando's twice in 4.1, but in performances early in the run he did not seem to be more than momentarily puzzled to find himself kissing a boy, even when that boy was impersonating Rosalind. Later a 'take' was inserted to register his surprise when she pecked him on the cheek as she entered, and another was added when their lips met for a mutual kiss when he left to attend the duke. Here any mild hanky-panky between girl and boy/girl and Orlando was also qualified by the context of comparatively uninhibited behaviour from Phebe and Silvius, and the passionate kiss exchanged by Oliver and Celia over the prostrate form of the fainted Rosalind.[21]

Striking a balance: Peggy Ashcroft and Vanessa Redgrave at Stratford-upon-Avon, 1957, 1961

The 1957 production at the Shakespeare Memorial Theatre, directed by Glen Byam Shaw and designed by Motley, was the team's second production of the play there, the first being in 1952. The wintry setting for the first forest scenes, with almost skeletal trees and frosted twigs, gave way, with the advent of spring, to a sparse background of thin aspen-like branches with flattened leaves that resembles the kind of botanical pattern found in furnishing fabrics of the period. As Ganymede, Peggy Ashcroft wore very sensible trousers and boots, although with the coming of spring it was clearly warm enough for Celia to go barefoot. The breeches of Orlando (Richard Johnson) had a laced front flap – a vestigial codpiece – that the more restrained 'Ganymede' did without. In fact, his clothing, like that of other forest dwellers, seemed eminently comfortable and practical. The costumes of the court suggested the period of François I, with the attention to accurate line and mass, and economical use of the occasional telling detail, that are common to most of the designer team's work. The hair and make-up for Rosalind and Celia, and the hint of the New Look in the flare of Celia's skirt as Aliena, compromised charmingly between the late 1950s and a suggestion of the early 1500s. In a typically careful detail, Oliver's hair was longer (below the collar) than that of his brother, who has been denied access to courtly life: the young men, Orlando and Touchstone would have passed unremarked (at least so far as hairstyles go) in the street in 1957, although they would still have defied the short-cropped, sleekly brilliantined standard represented by photos of the cricketers and other sporting icons of masculinity in advertisements for Brylcreem.

In Michael Elliott's 1961 production with designs by Richard Negri, Vanessa Redgrave's Rosalind wore a loose short-sleeved shirt, her long fair hair caught up under a cap – its release was a notable effect in the moments when she could shed her disguise. Her breeches reached to the knee and she went barefoot as soon as weather permitted. This was a famously spirited and athletic performance, and Redgrave inspired extravagant language in the reviewers: in the *Daily Express* (5 July 1961) Bernard Levin described her as a 'creature of fire and light, her voice a golden gate opening on lapis-lazuli hinges, her body a slender supple reed rippling in the breeze of her love'.[22] J.C.Trewin in the *Illustrated London News* (14 July 1961) rhapsodized that 'this is noon in Arden, and this is the girl, impetuous, tender, gay, upon whom the forest airs attend . . . Rosalind is herself, and that is enough.' Orlando (Ian Bannen), wrote J.W. Lambert in *The Sunday Times* (9 July 1961), appeared 'to respond much more eagerly to the apparent boy than to the dream of the lost girl', a complication that seemed innovative at the time. Alan Brissenden remarks that in her 'pedal pushers', shirt and cap, Redgrave's Ganymede was an anticipation of what later became the 'swinging sixties': 'The women in the audience could respond to the lithe, lanky boy, the men to the lithe, slim girl beneath the disguise.'[23] In the later 'forest' acts, Celia's dirndl-like skirt and laced bodice had their counterpart in current late 1950s/early 1960s fashion, the general effect of both women being that of trendy bohemianism, a world of modern jazz (or folk), coffee bars and chianti in straw-wrapped flasks.

Redgrave's performance, and the Ganymede costume that seemed to take the play centuries away from the formal early Tudor (or François I) court of the production's first scenes, was symptomatic of a trend in many subsequent productions at Stratford-upon-Avon and elsewhere, in which a closer affinity with contemporary fashion has been achieved even when the overall design was not 'modern dress'. By the 1970s, one of the prime signifiers of liberated modernity had become the wearing of denim by men and women. In the 1973 Stratford production directed (exceptionally for the RSC at the time) by a woman, Buzz Goodbody, Eileen Atkins turned 'from a languorous lady in skirts to a recklessly androgynous Chelsea hippy in blue denims' (*Sunday Telegraph*, 17 June 1973), with immaculately tailored pantsuit and a bandanna to hold back her hair. Michael Billington could begin his notice of a 1974 production at the Shaw Theatre, London with the wry reflection that 'from the moment when Orlando appears in blue denim and sneakers, it is clear that John David's production. .. is going to be thoroughly and reassuringly conventional' (*Guardian*, 6 June 1974). Commenting on 'the revolutionary late Sixties' in *Sex and Suits*, Anne Hollander observes:

> mobility and palpability, replacing stasis and inviolability, became the desirable attributes of the clothed female body, not just of its garments or its secret nude state. A visible integration took place between the entire living, sentient woman and her costume. Like her male counterpart, she, too, could now suggest the self-possessed animal happy in its skin.[24]

Androgyny in an Arden of the mind: Juliet Stevenson at Stratford-upon-Avon, 1985, and Edith Evans at the Old Vic, 1936

For Adrian Noble's 1985 RSC production, with designs by Bob Crowley, the cast were able to have some say in their costuming. In this eclectic post-unisex if not postmodern world, with a set that was not in the least realistic, Rosalind's clothes for the 'spring' section of the play (white shirt and trousers, embroidered braces) were echoed by Orlando's, and even their hairstyles went some way towards a shared and fashionable androgyny. There was no footwear in the forest, at least for Rosalind, although there was a grandfather clock, painted green. Among the designer's references for costumes were the issues of *Vogue* current at the time of rehearsal (Spring 1985), although the principal beneficiary of this was Celia (Fiona Shaw). This may be one of the few productions in which at least a gesture was made to besmirching the face with umber, but once through the initial dangers of flight from the court, Celia's clothing was hardly 'poor and mean' (1.3.110–11). The most significant costuming strategy, however, was that devised for Hilton McRae as Orlando, which identified him as a rebel against the conservative dress suits of the usurper's court. (Frederick and his henchmen threw white sheets over their formal attire to become Duke Senior and the exiled court when the play moved into the forest.) In *Shakespeare Quarterly*, Roger Warren applauded the fact that 'for once, [Rosalind and Orlando] were matched. They were the same kind of people, warm, direct, impulsive'.

> With her contemporary unisex hairstyle and white suit, Miss Stevenson was equally convincing as boy and girl. Her baggy trousers followed the latest fashion but also suggested that she was in part a clown: she used a bowler hat and cane like a cabaret artiste to illustrate the 'divers paces' of Time.[25]

Psychologically, this Rosalind moved beyond play-acting: Irving Wardle wrote in *The Times* (24 April 1985) that she moved beyond the initial 'teasing routines' with Orlando to enter 'deeper waters where neither she, her lover, nor the audience, can tell truth from masquerade'.

Rather than allow the audience to remain fixated on the credibility of the Ganymede disguise, the performance allowed an exploration of the psychology of love in which the subterfuge was merely a means to an end. In the production's overall conceit, the darkness of the first act's 'palace' scenes was transformed by the draping of a white sheet over the stage and all its furniture as the escapees entered the 'forest'. Then, during the interval before the second act, 'spring', half of the play the stage was transformed to a literally green world, now with a brook running across the front, although the court's furniture, including the clock – now painted green – remained. The sense of doubling, as though one half of the play and one set of characters were the 'shadows' of their 'palace' counterparts, prompted some reviewers to invoke C.G. Jung. (In the *Guardian*, Billington labelled the production as 'Jung Ones in Arden', with a glance at the 1961 hit song 'The Young Ones', by Cliff Richard and the Shadows.) Whether or not this was understood or indeed accepted, the effect of mirroring was striking. In this context the Rosalind/Ganymede double was given a wider context, inclusive of but not limited to gender roles.

This aspect of Noble's *As You like It* suggests retrospective comparison with Esmé Church's Old Vic production in 1936, which transposed the play into an eighteenth-century pastoral world evoking the paintings of Watteau. In this environment, itself a fantasy from an earlier time rather than a representation of its realities, Edith Evans was able to explore the mercurial wit of Rosalind in a manner that many critics found appropriate to her own high (specifically, Restoration) comedy credentials. Reviewing the production's West End transfer to the New Theatre for the *Illustrated London News* (27 February 1936), Ivor Brown commented that 'her perfect exercises on the scales of mental bravery and amorous caprice belong rather to the formal comedy of manners than to the more natural high spirits of a Tudor sylvan lyric'. An anonymous reviewer in *The Times* (11 November 1936) reflected that 'her Rosalind, even if attired in doublet and hose, would have in her composition less of Elizabethan ardour than of the sentiment appropriate to knee breeches and waisted coat'.

> In a setting that was not at all inelegant the artificiality of her performance would seem more than a little odd. She is (shall we say?) not Rosalind, but Rosalind's sister, born a century later and born a trifle sophisticated. The humour is given with an air of wit, and this too often hinders emotional response to sayings which, when spoken differently, seem to dance on the edge of tears, and we miss that deep assurance of happiness which gives the Elizabethan sister freedom to tease and torment Orlando.

Although this may have seemed to this critic to be 'an entertainment which is pictorially poetic and always amusing, but somewhat lacking in the genuine high spirits and natural feeling of Shakespeare's comedy', the stylized costume itself served Evans well by focusing attention on her wit and mental vivacity, qualities for which she was prized rather than for any conventional glamour.

The cross-dresser cross-dressed: Rosalind in two all-male productions

The National Theatre's 1967 production at the Old Vic, directed by Clifford Williams and designed by Ralph Koltai, combined the latter's predilection for abstract decor using the newest materials with the radical notion of an all-male cast. The sets account for the headline of J.C.Trewin's review in the *Illustrated London News* (14 October 1967): 'Down in the

Forest, or Plastics in Arden'. Irving Wardle, surveying recent Shakespeare productions in *The Times* (14 October 1967), described 'an Arcadian dreamland of Perspex pyramids, plastic playsuits, and monster stalactites instead of trees' and suggested that they evoked another aspect of the zeitgeist: 'When the transvestite travellers arrive they seem less to be making a journey than taking a trip.' His earlier review ('Comic Result When Men Take Over from Actresses', 4 October) tried to reconcile the programme's inclusion of a lengthy quotation from Jan Kott's essay 'Shakespeare's bitter Arcadia', with what seemed like a disclaimer in the director's own note.[26] Williams appeared to be distancing himself from the label of experiment in the cross-dressing, and claimed to be seeking 'an atmosphere of spiritual parity which transcends sensuality in the search for poetic sexuality' – whatever that might be. The attempt, writes Laurence Senelick, 'was admirable but far too cautious'.[27] In any case, although Ronald Pickup as Rosalind and Anthony Hopkins as Audrey managed to steer clear of being camp, the same could not be said of Charles Kay's Celia. Wardle praised the restraint of Pickup's performance:

> A beaky, long-legged figure in a yachting suit, [Pickup's Rosalind] does conform to Kott's specification of the boy-girl – except that it is completely non-erotic. It begins demurely with a few well-observed feminine gestures, and takes on character only during the Ganymede scenes. It is a blank that comes to life under the stress of intense platonic feeling: and there is real excitement in seeing this Rosalind and Jeremy Brett's very masculine Orlando being taken unawares by serious emotion in the midst of their game.

In this realm of 'silver boots, plastic macs and tattered regimentals', the emphasis seemed to be on modernity rather than any exploration of androgyny or, indeed, any expression of passion. For all the brouhaha surrounding it, this was a cool production.

As You Like It, directed by Declan Donellan and designed by Nick Ormerod for their company Cheek by Jowl, was first seen at the Lyric, Hammersmith in 1991. The use of an all-male cast achieved a very different result. In part, this may have been a consequence of more than two decades of development in public attitudes to gender issues, but it is also a sign of a different kind of sensibility at work. As Peter Holland notes, Donellan began the play with the whole cast on stage, as Jacques spoke 'All the world's a stage' (2.7.140–67), and the men and women took their places on the opposite sides of the stage as he said 'all the men and women'. This initiated a process whereby 'the gender of character was . . . sometimes disconnected from the gender of actor and sometimes not'. Consequently 'a male actor performing a female role was not therefore more performative than a male actor playing a male role: instead the production allowed character to exist dissociated from performer'.[28]

This did not prevent Adrian Lester's Rosalind from being, in the words of Ian Dodd in *Tribune* (13 December 1991), 'an intensely female character whose femininity more importantly is an internal quality, not an external look'. His 'triumph [was] that, without attempting to look the part, his softly spoken six-foot male Rosalind exude[d] an utterly convincing sensual femininity (devoid of the camp clichés of a female impersonator) . . .' Laurence Senelick focuses on a vital element of the roleplay shared by the actor with both Rosalind and Ganymede:

> Once disguised in knickerbockers and country tweeds, Lester's Rosalind has difficulty in keeping her feminine nature in check; a high-strung anxiety exudes from every pore. She is girlishly sincere, radiantly in love, and distraught when Orlando fails to recognize her in her page's attire. At the same time, the dilemma of a young woman trying to act male and slightly missing the mark is also comically in play.[29]

Peter Holland, like other reviewers, found the emphasis on love rather than the specifics of sexuality and gender refreshing.

For once the epilogue, 'gibberish when spoken by a woman' made sense, its 'simple charm' resulting from 'Lester's natural easiness creating an exquisite engagement with the audience'.[30]

Conclusion: problems and opportunities

Peter Holland's account of Donellan's production concludes with an expression of satisfaction that cuts across the opposition between destabilization (implicitly serious, stern and radical) and pleasure:

> In such a production there were no problems unresolved and no problems avoided, the play's joyousness fully accepted and expressed by the company. Unproblematic comedy needed no stronger advocate.[31]

This points to a truth not quite universally acknowledged, that the play's cross-dressing in the pursuit of disguise, even without its original context, can afford as much pleasure – and in a great variety of ways – as it offers food for thought. Although a male actor as Rosalind will never have exactly the same significance as, in their own ways, either the original boy-actor or the post-Restoration actress, some degree of detachment from pictorial and sartorial realism and authenticity (whether of the period represented or the play's own time) can support attention to the wit that transcends gender even as it focuses on it. 'Do you not know I am a woman? When I think, I must speak,' says Rosalind (3.2.242–3), but as s/he voices a male cliché about women she is speaking to Celia, in one of the scenes where she is speaking as a woman (Rosalind no. 1) while still dressed as a boy. In Act 4, when Rosalind, in Celia's words, has 'simply misused our sex in [her] love-prate', she is threatened with what on any stage and in any regime of performance conventions would be an alarming double exposure: 'We must have your doublet and hose plucked over your head and show the world what the bird hath done to her own nest' (4.1.189–92).

Although its production history since the late nineteenth century has here been sketched in terms of the range of disguises, *As You Like It* does not depend solely on that element. Nor have the arrival of the professional actress after 1660 or the various ventures into all-male casting simply reversed, still less resolved, the polarities in play. Juliet Dusinberre, in the introduction to her edition, describes this richness concisely and eloquently: 'The complex performance of gender which the play requires may, as modern productions have shown, ultimately confound distinction between male and female, homoerotic and heterosexual, boy and girl, as Rosalind does in her epilogue.'[32] As for the boy-actor, and the effect of his own disguise, it is worth remembering that Edward Kynaston, the last great exponent of the calling, continued a distinguished career in male roles after the advent of the actress, and that as the actor and dramatist Colley Cibber recalled, in his later years Kynaston had 'something of a formal gravity in his Mien, which was attributed to the stately step he had been so early confin'd to, in a female Decency'.[33] In 1991 Adrian Lester, describing the work he did with the company's movement coach, compared the technical challenges of playing a woman to those of speaking French: 'You know you want to say something, so you think it in English and then speak it in French. Through Sue Lefton's movement we've been able to think about it in a detailed way as a woman.'[34] Taking the woman's part, wearing the farthingale and the stomacher, could provide the actor with what might now be termed 'transferable skills'.

How Designers Helped Juliet's Nurse Reclaim Her Bawdy

Patricia Lennox

Between 1922 and 1936, three major designers, Paul Shelving, Motley (Elizabeth Montgomery, Sophia Harris, Margaret Harris) and Oliver Messel, working independently on different productions of *Romeo and Juliet*, created a costume for Juliet's Nurse that contributed to an iconic image of her – a medieval woman swathed in a white wimple topped by a starched headdress, wide of girth, bawdy and warm-hearted. The costume makes the Nurse as instantly identifiable in *Shakespeare in Love* as in a ballet or opera based on Shakespeare's tragedy. This was a new style of costume that not only marked a major change in the way the Nurse was dressed but also the way she was performed. Throughout the nineteenth century she had appeared on stage dressed in rich dark fabrics with lace trimming, looking and behaving like a genteel lady's companion instead of Shakespeare's crafty realist. The Nurse's new style of costume, introduced in the

1920s and 1930s, also marked the reinstatement of her earthiness and of bawdy lines that had been cut since the mid-1700s. This chapter examines the evolution of that costume and its interconnection with the changes in scripting and performing the Nurse in the theatre between the wars. It focuses on three costume designers, two actresses (Edith Evans, Edna May Oliver), one director (John Gielgud), four stage productions (1922, 1924, 1932, 1935) and one film (MGM, 1936), and chronicles the development of the iconic costume. Central to the story is the way this twentieth-century wrapping up of the Nurse's head in wimple and coif was accompanied by an unwrapping of her tongue through the reinstatement of her ribaldry. Significantly, the costume serves as the marker of the early twentieth-century's move toward Shakespeare productions that gave primacy to original texts in versions presented with pared-down sets that accommodated the plays' swiftly shifting scenes. It serves also as a very clear example of the ways that a costume can shape and be shaped by theatrical conventions, the director's agenda and the actor who wears the costume.

After seeing actor-manager Johnston Forbes-Robertson's production of *Romeo and Juliet*, in 1895, George Bernard Shaw dismissed Dolores Drummond's Nurse as 'yet quite the worst impersonation I have ever seen of a not very difficult old woman's part'.[1] Even though this dismissal of the role was typical of Shaw's complaints about Shakespeare, he was seeing a performance with traditionally sanitized dialogue acted in the genteel style, favoured throughout the century, as epitomized by Mrs Davenport's Nurse in 1829, and by Mrs Stirling's Nurse in Henry Irving's production in 1882 and in actress-manager Mary Anderson's production in 1884. Following convention, Johnston Forbes-Robertson maintained cuts in most of the Nurse's lines, including all ribaldries and references to the body.[2] This garrulous lace-trimmed old lady propped up on her walking stick was foolish and fussy but, despite Shakespeare's original text, not particularly bawdy.[3] In contrast, when David Garrick had produced the play in 1744 at the Theatre Royal, Drury Lane, the only change he made to the Nurse's lines was to substitute 'breast' for 'dugs', although he famously added lines for Romeo and Juliet to speak before death in the tomb.[4]

It is reasonable to suppose that in Garrick's production, the Nurse's costume conformed to the usual eighteenth-century stage practice of having players, for the most part, wear conventional contemporary dress. This may even be the source of the nineteenth-century theatre's Nurse being dressed as a genteel upper servant. Productions of *Romeo and Juliet*, as with other classic scripts, have often been reshaped to meet the changing tastes of the public. Even Garrick by 1750 had reluctantly cut the Nurse's earthy lines and made other adjustments to the play in order to satisfy his audiences' preference for sentimentalized tragedy. The practice was continued by other actor-managers in productions throughout the nineteenth century and made this bawdy woman more suitable to refined tastes.[5] Maintaining a nineteenth-century Juliet's innocence was important, so Shakespeare's young woman, who imagines waking in the tomb to 'madly play with my forefathers' joints' and 'pluck the mangled Tybalt from his shroud' (4.3.51–2), became an ingénue with no thought of bashing her brains out with 'some great kinsman's bones'(4.3.53). Her Nurse did not speak of putting wormwood on her dugs (or breasts) or joke that on the wedding night 'you shall not rest but little' (4.5.7). Naturally, when the Nurse wished Mercutio 'good morrow' (2.4.105), she was spared his vulgar reply that 'the bawdy hand of the dial is now on the prick of noon' (2.4.108–9).

The nineteenth-century's delicate wisp of a Juliet, representing youthful 'tenderness and delicacy',[6] required a Nurse of equal sentimental sensibility. Leigh Hunt's complaint in 1831 about the Nurse, probably Mrs Gibbs, who 'with all her talent, will not do the Nurse at all. She has too much invincible life in the buxom person of hers and those round relishing tones, and cannot contrive to be broken down.'[7] The Nurse shown in nineteenth-century illustrations based on current stage productions is consistently a very old lady, usually thin, discreetly dressed in contemporary clothing appropriate for a genteel lady's companion and always with her walking stick, sometimes with her fan. She accompanies Juliets, including those of Harriet Smithson, Helen Faucit and Fanny Kemble, who wear versions of slender, currently fashionable dresses in styles closer to the Empire than the Renaissance. In an 1829 illustration, Fanny Kemble's Juliet typically wears a lightweight white dress with empire bust, but with the now popular puffed 'beret' sleeves.[8] At her side is Mrs Davenport[9] wearing the standard Nurse costume, a shawl wrapped up to her neck, a dark dress with a skirt of moderate width and an old lady's cap with lace flaps on either side that trail halfway down her chest. In later variations of this picture, a lace collar replaces her shawl. A sketch of Mrs W. Daly's Nurse in 1849 shows a thinnish old woman wearing a dress with modified hoop skirt, a decorated apron and the standard lace cap, leaning on the walking stick. In the Howard Staunton edition of 1863 with illustrations by Sir John Gilbert, the Nurse is similarly dressed.[10]

In 1830, Henry Perronet Briggs painted Kemble, now one of the most famous Juliets of the period, with her aunt the great tragedian Sarah Siddons cast in the painting as the Nurse, representing an ideal version of both roles. Juliet, dressed in the soft folds of the white gown of the earlier illustration, leans over Siddons, who as Nurse is seated in the centre of the painting. Siddons wears a cap of sheer, ruffled white organdie tied with lace under the chin. There is an open book on her lap and her finger points to a place on the page. Her plain black dress is absorbed into the dark background of her portion of the canvas, but her strikingly forceful face is highlighted by the dress's wide, rectangular white collar trimmed with lace. 'Siddons remains the focus of the artist's attention, her venerable presence lending dynastic authority and professional credibility to the pretension of her young niece.'[11] The paler Kemble, seen against a light background, looks more like a dream or memory by the intensely intelligent Siddons as Nurse.

The striking visual image is a reminder of how a specific style of costume can represent a Shakespeare character, but also of how young actresses can be upstaged by a more experienced one and Juliets are vulnerable to their Nurses – although obviously not the case in the 1895 production for Mrs Patrick Campbell's Juliet, who outshone Mrs Drummond as Nurse.

Influenced first by the Romantic movement in the early 1800s and by Victorian propriety from the mid-century onwards, Juliet's Nurse is dressed throughout the century as though she were following advice from *Etiquette of Good Society* (1889): 'The elder ladies should wear silks or some handsome material, richly trimmed with lace, a foreign shawl or lace mantle, and bonnets, not hats, whether in town or country.'[12] Towards the final decades of the nineteenth century, photographs of actors in costume provide an even more reliable and detailed record of the Nurse's appearance and confirm that the genteel family servant was still visible on the London stage. Mrs Stirling, renowned for a half-century on that stage, came out of retirement at seventy-one to give a performance of the Nurse which maintained this older tradition.

Stirling was a lovable Nurse, dressed as a sweet old lady both in Henry Irving's production at the Lyceum Theatre in London, with Ellen Terry as Juliet in 1882, and in the actress-manager Mary Anderson's production two years later at the same theatre, where Anderson showcased her own Juliet. Critics praised Mrs Stirling's performance in 1884: 'Mrs Stirling gives to the present representation as she did to that which Mr Irving directed – the immeasurable aid of her appearance as the nurse. Such a nurse our generation has not seen and no generation from Shakespeare's day to this can have seen better.'[13]

In 1882, rehearsing for the Irving production, Ellen Terry would have disagreed with the reviewer. She had strong ideas about new ways to play Juliet, had not been happy with her scenes with the Nurse and was frustrated by the older actress's insistence on a conventional performance. Terry remembers

FIGURE 12 *Mrs Stirling as a genteel Nurse in Henry Irving's production*. Illustrated Sporting and Dramatic News, *15 April 1882. Courtesy of Patricia Lennox.*

Mrs Stirling as 'a charming and ripe old actress' and in her memoir praises Mrs Stirling for not playing the part like 'a female pantaloon', for not assuming any 'great decrepitude' and for playing for emotion rather than laughs. 'Her parrot scream when she found me dead was horribly real and effective.'[14] But she also complains that Mrs Stirling insisted on keeping traditional 'stage business' in their scenes together. Terry asks, for example, why Juliet must 'go on coquetting and clucking over the Nurse when she returns from meeting Romeo to get the news out of her?' She especially objected to Stirling's insistence on Juliet's 'imitations of the Nurse on the line "Where's your mother?" [2.5.57]' and hated the "cheap reward" of the imitation's "safe laugh" '. She wanted her Juliet to grow angry with the Nurse's delaying tactics and to lose her temper with 'genuine rage', speaking with 'indignation' and 'tears'.[15] Eventually, Stirling reluctantly accepted some of the changes Terry wanted. Even so, Kate Terry Gielgud astutely observed in her memoir that 'the adorable Mrs Stirling at the Lyceum had shown us rather the pampered upper servant who had completely absorbed the manners of her betters'.[16]

Although Stirling's costume was similar to those in illustrations of Juliet's Nurse earlier in the nineteenth century, by the end of the century her costume for the Nurse reads as solidly Victorian.[17] In a photograph of Terry and Stirling, the slender Terry wears a Pre-Raphaelite version of a Renaissance dress, while the ample Nurse wears a full skirt with tucks and gathers adding detail, made of a dark-coloured silk with a woven damask pattern, accompanied by a dark jacket opened to show the blouse's froth of white lace. Wide lace cuffs emerge from the elbow-length puffed sleeves. On her head she wears a small black bonnet with a short black veil attached to the back and with the under-part of the brim lined with white lace ruffles that frame her dimpled face. The effect is dignified and even a bit grand. Surprisingly, she also wears a rosary as a necklace; the beads and cross are large enough to be seen from the back of the Lyceum's balconies. It hangs down to below her waist, with its slender cross, about five inches long, resting on her stomach. Two years later, in Mary Anderson's production, Mrs Stirling's costume is similar and, although not identical, has no significant differences.[18]

A photograph of another Nurse, Elinor Aickin, when she played the role in Frank Benson's 1911 production at Stratford-upon-Avon, suggests how the Nurse's widowed state became even more integrated into the costume. Aickin wears a slight variation on the costume seen on Stirling: the all-black widow's bonnet with veil at the back; the jacket is dark with wide lace cuffs, but there is no shawl or lace collar to lighten this with white, and the skirt is dark and full. Her expression exudes benign sweetness; this is an actress whose earlier portrayal in *King John* of the king's mother, Eleanor, was praised as having 'presented a milder and more lovable manner than is usual for this part'.[19] Aickin's Nurse's expression is full of benign sweetness – without the flicker of a bawdy thought.

The image and idea of the genteel Nurse was so entrenched that Tannehouser, an American film company, chose a similar portrayal for their one-reel silent version in 1911, one of a series of seven short Shakespeare films made by the company between 1910 and 1916.[20] Tannehouser films were low budget, done with a repertory group of actors who also helped build sets and make the costumes. Designs for costumes were often drawn from well-known illustrated editions of Shakespeare or from familiar theatrical performances. In the Tannehouser *Romeo and Juliet*, the Nurse remains the elderly, genteel upper servant. She wears a lace-trimmed dress, leans on a walking stick and carries a fan, all of which make her immediately recognizable as the Nurse.

Eight years later there was an intriguing production of *Romeo and Juliet* that linked the portrayals of the Nurse of the nineteenth and the twentieth centuries: Ellen Terry's last professional appearance on the London stage as the Nurse in the Basil Sidney/Doris Keane production at the Lyric Theatre in 1919. Although in her published lectures (1912), Terry refers to the Nurse as 'this depraved old party', whose only comfort is to tell Juliet to make the best of a bad business and marry Paris – 'which she insinuates is not such a bad choice after all'[21] – she now relished playing the role. Providing her own costume, she draped her Nurse in light layers of shawls and slim long skirt, and created a wimple effect through a bonnet-like head covering that expanded slightly on the sides so that some hair is visible to create a flattering shape around the still young face. Photographs show her with the Nurse's traditional walking stick, possibly a necessary prop since Terry's sight was failing. Biographer Christopher St John reports that in the ball scene, Terry topped her costume with a green and gold robe that Henry Irving had worn as Othello in 1881.[22] (The robe is in the collection of the Ellen Terry Memorial Museum.)

When she was planning on playing the Nurse, Terry had written to her family 'with glee' saying, 'I am keeping all the rude bits in!'[23] Her Nurse was 'a sly, coarse, old baggage, if an alluring one' that thrilled the audience with an 'exhibition of tragic force'.[24] On opening night the audience was calling out, cheering for Terry at the end of the second act. Her nephew John Gielgud remembered that 'though there was too much of her own sweetness and personal charm. . . now and again there were superb hints of [Shakespeare's] character'.[25] One such moment was the scene where the Nurse discovers the body of Juliet, which Terry turned into a tour de force. She moved from gaiety to a slightly bawdy laugh, to apprehension and a stronger fear before frantically shaking the girl, lifting her eyelids and finally giving 'a great agonized cry to heaven'. She did even more. After all the mourners had left the bedroom, her Nurse stood quietly by the bed and 'folded the girl's hands and knelt down beside her body as the curtain fell'.[26] No wonder Doris Keane, the producer whose own performance of Juliet was eclipsed by Terry in the reviews as well as the curtain calls, cut the scene after the first night. George Bernard Shaw felt Terry's talents were wasted on a role that he continued to think was not very difficult. He complained that Keane had cast 'a battleship for the part of a canal-barge'.[27]

Paul Shelving and the Birmingham Repertory Company 1922 and 1924

The original version of the iconic costume for the Nurse starts with Paul Shelving's designs for *Romeo and Juliet* in 1922 for the Birmingham Repertory Theatre. This is the first notable production to wrap the Nurse in a white wimple with her head completely covered with a wing-like white coif and to dress her to emphasize her bulk. This unique look for the Nurse, so unlike the nineteenth century's, was created by Shelving for Rep productions in Birmingham in 1922 and in London in 1924 as part of the Rep's season at the Regent, with nineteen-year-old John Gielgud as Romeo.[28] Shelving's imaginative costume design plays a major part in the transformation of the Nurse from genteel widow back to Shakespeare's boisterous servant, someone closer to Chaucer's lusty Wife of Bath than widowed Queen Victoria.

Shelving, whose designs for the Birmingham Repertory Theatre were highly influential though seldom seen in London, joined it in 1920. At this time the Rep, as it was (and is) affectionately called, was headed by Barry Jackson and flourished as an important regional theatre. Birmingham, England's second largest city and only a couple of hours by train from London and an hour from Stratford-upon-Avon, became known as the starting place for many successful actors. It was also noted for its innovative productions, particularly those directed by H.K. Ayliff, with sets and costumes designed by Shelving. The Rep was the first company in England to present Shakespeare in modern dress, starting with a Shelving-designed *Cymbeline* in 1923 and continuing through the 1930s and 1940s. But Shelving's Renaissance designs in 1922 for *Romeo and Juliet* were based on his extensive research into the paintings of fifteenth-century Italian artists, including Carpaccio, whose work he looked at for both the style of dress and the colours. Explaining his approach to historical design, Shelving wrote that the costume designer should be 'thoroughly familiar with the period dealt with, but his fancy should never become completely subordinate to archeological fact'. It should, instead, 'capture the spirit of the age rather than attempt a faithful reconstruction'.[29] This production directed by Ayliff at the Rep was a doublet-and-hose Shakespeare but daringly modern in its use of simple sets consisting of arches and painted curtains, and even more noteworthy for its inclusion of what was promoted as the full text of Shakespeare's play.

The *Birmingham Weekly* announced that the play would be 'given in its entirety, without any of the mutilation and excision which disfigure the usual productions of this play'.[30] One reviewer exclaimed that it was the 'first time we have really seen *Romeo and Juliet*'. When the Rep revived the production in London in 1924 with Gielgud as Romeo, the actor remembered the production being commendably 'free from cuts or extraneous business'.[31] Nevertheless, in the prompt book a number of the Nurse's lines are crossed through: her lengthy speeches are much cut, gone are the references to nursing, weaning and the husband's joke about falling backward.[32] Cuts are made not only to bowdlerize; some of the more innocuous lines are cut as well, including 'Sitting in the sun under the dovehouse wall' (1.3.28). Whether the Birmingham critics, many of whom were extremely Shakespeare-literate, did not miss the lines or gratefully chose to praise the relatively full text version as though it was complete, cannot be known. They welcomed the presence of all of the scenes, including the usually omitted musicians (4.5), and the 'complete' text. Less grateful London critics, two years later, noted the absence of many of the Nurse's lines – although there were also complaints that the play ran long at three and a half hours.

In her history of Shakespeare at the Birmingham Rep, Claire Cochrane points out that productions in Birmingham tended to be ignored by the London press[33] and, according to the archive's clipping book, this is true of the 1922 production. The local papers, however, gave it full attention and nearly consistently high praise for the actors and the design. Before opening night, local newspaper articles made it clear that Shelving's sets and costumes would be a major draw, as well as the cast featuring Gwen Ffrangcon-Davies as Juliet and Isabel Thornton as the Nurse. The reviews were full of praise. Under Ayliff's direction, Ffrangcon-Davies' impassioned Juliet was lovely but not overly romanticized, and Thornton's Nurse avoided being 'a nice, rather doddering old lady who ought to be an abbess instead of a nurse'.[34] This 'ideal conception of the Nurse'[35] was a performance that was 'stronger, perhaps in its roughish moments than [in] its maternal ones'.[36] Thornton's Nurse, 'incredibly fat and wheezy', was 'almost too good to be true', especially since 'all the whimsicabilities' of the servant Peter and the Nurse and the 'sparkling "padding" that almost invariably is dropped are retained'.[37]

FIGURE 13 *Isabel Thornton as Nurse with Gwen Ffrangcon-Davies as Juliet. Birmingham Repertory Company, design by Paul Shelving, 1922. By permission of the Sir Barry Jackson and Birmingham Repertory Theatre Archive, Library of Birmingham.*

As for her costume, the broad lines of the dress emphasizing her stoutness, its light colour, and the introduction of the wimple and coif signalled that this was a Nurse freed from the social constraints of silk and lace gentility. Much is made in the press, as it was in the publicity, of Shelving's set and costume designs placed in the fifteenth century, inspired by Carpaccio paintings. The reviews especially praised his use of colour, so it is frustrating that the existing photographs are in black and white. In the archives there is one tinted photo of Thornton as the Nurse. The wimple is startling white and the dress a soft beige with black trim – but as this is a tinted photo, it cannot be taken as definitive evidence in terms of colour. Gielgud's complaint about the London production two years later gives more information on the colours in Juliet's costumes. He felt that Shelving's designs for Juliet's 'dresses alone were most successful. . . she looked a vision' in 'high-waisted Botticelli dresses with flowing skirts, each one more becoming than the last'.[38] The pinks, greens and gold of her dresses provided a contrast to the subdued tone of the Nurse's dress. Even the black-and-white photographs make it clear that the Nurse is no longer dressed in dark colours. The skirt and jacket are pale, trimmed with dark bands, there are large dark buttons down the jacket front and diamond shapes on a belt hanging down her side, and a large square bag dangles from her belt – and there is definitely no rosary. This Nurse is a lively comic character and no longer the temperate Victorian widow of Mrs Aickins or the genteel upper servant of Mrs Davenport.

It is equally clear that this dress, wimple and coif are not taken from a Renaissance painting. The coif is shaped in smooth, curved wings, like small sails, on either side of the head. It might have been inspired by paintings from northern Germany or Flanders or by the peasant dress of Brittany – but it is not Renaissance Italy.[39] In late fifteenth-century Italian paintings, the women's headdress is a small cap or, as in the Madonnas by Filippo Lippi, Piero della Francesca and Giovanni Bellini, a scarf or veil draped over the head. Generally however, even when women in the paintings have a scarf or shawl over their head, no one is wrapped in a wimple; the bare neck is visible and the neckline a modified square. Shelving's wimple is wrapped so that it hides the Nurse's forehead and half of the sides of the face. Starting right below the jawbone, it drapes down over the neck in several soft folds – almost like double chins. The width of Shelving's original design for the Nurse's headdress fits Mercutio's exclamation on seeing her: 'A sail, a sail . . .' (2.4.94). In the London production the headdress becomes even larger, a full white circle echoing the lines of the costumes created for Diaghilev's *Ballets Russes* by Leon Bakst, whose very modern designs were much admired by Shelving. The historical disparity of the costume is never noted by any of the reviewers of either production.

The London production in 1924 replaced Thornton with Barbara Gott, whose Nurse the reviewers found timid. This was another character actress but one noted for her comic working-class 'Black Mammy' and Irish washerwomen roles. Critic Herbert Farjeon complained that she lacked a sense of 'touch and go'; in a rather sterile production (where 'Verona had no smell') she was no more than 'a clean Nurse, an efficient Nurse'.[40] The *Spectator* thought she was good 'without being completely good' and, suggesting that audiences were ready for a bawdier Nurse, complained it 'is a pity, too that her great speech in Act 1, Scene 3, was severely cut. Surely our stomachs are not nowadays too squeamish for its honest grossness through which so much character emerges.'[41] It is possible that Mrs Gott herself, for whatever reason, preferred not to say the lines, a not unusual hesitation on the part of a popular comedian feeling the cultural weight of Shakespeare. Although the Nurse's costume is nearly the same as in the 1922 production, one new detail is significant: Gott's Nurse wears a large string of rosary beads at the waist, which suggests a subtle link with Mrs Stirling's less boisterous Nurse.

Gielgud and Motley 1932 and 1935

John Gielgud's production of *Romeo and Juliet* had two incarnations: one a high-level version for the Oxford University Drama Society (OUDS)[42] in 1932 and the other in London at the New Theatre, where Gielgud was producing a season of plays in 1935. In 1932 the would-be actor and Oxford undergraduate George Devine invited Gielgud to stage the OUDS all-student production of *Romeo and Juliet*. Since Gielgud had wanted to direct for a long time, he accepted. The cast was Oxford students, but Gielgud brought in two professionals, both upcoming actresses[43] on the London stage: Peggy Ashcroft as Juliet and Edith Evans as the Nurse. Both women and several of the student actors would later be in the cast of Gielgud's 1935 London production.[44] OUDS productions usually hired a couple of professional actresses for major roles in the otherwise all-male cast of undergraduates. The director and actresses were usually the only professionals involved. Although productions were always designed by members of OUDS or by local artists, Gielgud insisted on bringing in costume designers from London: three recent art school graduates, Elizabeth Montgomery and the sisters Margaret and Sophia Harris, who worked collectively under the name of Motley. It was the team's first full-fledged design commission, and it began one of the outstanding director/designer relationships in modern theatre. Motley and Gielgud's thirty-year affiliation highlights the type of creative collaboration that became important for designers and directors in the twentieth century. Gielgud's Shakespeare productions were crucial to the gradual but effective shift towards performing the plays with (relatively) full text, flexible sets and natural styles of speaking, and Motley's designs played a major role. Gielgud claimed that 'any success I have as a director I gladly share with them for they are at all times the ideal collaborators'.[45]

Motley's style of elaborately beautiful costumes – when appropriate – and elegant but simple sets worked perfectly with Gielgud's style and his vision. Even with a very small budget they were able to create an 'exquisitely graded colour scheme, and simple but brilliantly suggestive scenery'.[46] Montgomery and the Harris sisters 'assumed that Shakespeare should be played in a contemporary theatre idiom, with as few scene changes as possible in a space that approximated the acting areas of the Globe theatre, even if it looked nothing like Shakespeare's Globe' and 'believed in expressing the values of the play, rather than pushing a concept'.[47] Even though Motley's career would include London's West End and New York's Broadway, many of their designs were done on minuscule budgets for companies like the Old Vic and the Shakespeare Memorial Theatre.[48] The designers became famous for their ability to produce grandeur on a small budget through inventive use of inexpensive materials: they made jewels out of bottle caps, covered medieval walls with burlap, dressed Shylock in a robe made of dish rags and transformed the humblest fabric into regal regalia with designs in gold paint.

For Oxford, they scavenged fabric and brought their sewing machines to the university, where they set up shop in their rooms and the student actors helped sew the costumes. As with Shelving, the costume designers described their research into Italian art, including Carpaccio, for inspiration for *Romeo and Juliet* designs, but then created their own version of the Renaissance. Their clothes were more wearable and less 'costumey' than Shelving's, and this time when Gielgud played Romeo in London, he did not complain about his costume as he had in 1924. For the 1935 London production, working with only a slightly larger budget than at Oxford, Motley designed sets as well as costumes, which gave them the control they wanted over the stage picture. With Peggy Ashcroft's acclaimed Juliet and Gielgud and Laurence Olivier sharing Romeo and Mercutio,[49] the 1935 production became London's longest-running *Romeo and Juliet*. For both productions, Motley designed a Nurse's costume that was a variation on the Shelving design familiar to Gielgud from the Birmingham Rep production in 1924. In London, Motley drew on Carpaccio's paintings for colours to create a stage picture based on shades of red, grey, brown and black. The play's families each had their own palette – sombre blacks, browns and greys for the Montagues, who the designers saw as old money, and an ostentatious palette of bright reds, blacks, white and greens for the nouveau riche Capulets. To 'enhance the impression of youth', Motley dressed the younger generation in greens, the 'shades of spring'. Michael Mullin records that 'With changing mood came costume changes, until, by the end of the play, the entire colour scheme had gone to black . . .', mourning all the tragedy's deaths.[50] For the ball, Peggy Ashcroft's passionate

Juliet wore a Capulet red dress painted with gold stars, but changed to a dress in the 'younger generation' colour of moss green in later scenes. Edith Evans, Nurse in both productions, wore a dress of heavy wool (dark red in the London production) and a white wimple and coif. Here the bulky dress was also necessary to pad out the slender Edith Evans, at this point noted for her elegant roles in Restoration comedy. The costume helped age and enlarge Evans and added volume to her body; the wimple confined her hair, and the shape of the coif rounded out and helped plump up her face. The coif was smaller and more realistic than the one Shelving designed, but functioned in a similar way – as did the bulky dress.[51] Rather charmingly, Motley also gave this otherwise plain-dressed Nurse a damask-patterned underskirt in a much richer fabric than the overskirt. This would be seen when she moved, also an indicator of her role as upper servant in the household.[52] It is a brilliant costume detail, one that suggests another layer of information about the Nurse, suggesting a touch of luxury, a bit of vanity, a love of colour and design. Nevertheless, in an elegant world of Carpaccio- and Bellini-inspired dresses, and men in jerkin and hose, the Nurse's simple dress and ample white headdress are more medieval than Renaissance. Since all of the costumes are interpreted for effectiveness on stage in an imagined period, it seems entirely appropriate.

Shelving had costumed a more roughly comic-servant Nurse than had been seen in a century, but it was the collaboration of Gielgud, Motley and Evans that gave back her bawdy and balanced the restored ribaldry with an almost abbess-like costume. The costume worked efficiently to transform a slender middle-aged woman into a broad old woman, a buxom person with much invincible life, the type Leigh Hunt deplored as inappropriate in 1831[53] but who now seemed exactly right for Shakespeare's Nurse. Most importantly, the costume also desexualized her so that when she chattered on imagining Juliet's wedding night (4.5.3–11) she remained comic rather than prurient. In Gielgud's full-text productions, Ashcroft's Juliet had passion and strength, and Evans' Nurse was

Shakespeare's outspoken woman, fond, foolish, garrulous, 'as earthy as a potato, as slow as a cart horse and as cunning as a badger'.[54]

The OUDS *Romeo and Juliet* was Motley's first production to be viewed, reviewed and acclaimed by London critics. Many of the reviewers acknowledged the creative collaboration between the director and the designers whose minimal sets in London allowed the movement necessary for Gielgud's full-text, straightforward staging.[55] Reviewers responded to the combination of Evans' performance and the costume, a manner of dressing the Nurse that few had seen before. She was 'a magnificent creation who might have stepped out of a Dutch painting: vulgar and voluminous and with the solidity of the earth in her blunt realism'.[56] Evans' portrayal of the Nurse was completely in accordance with the costume. At Oxford she was 'unwieldy, slow, heavy, and pale as lead . . . resigned to the faithlessness of man and made old by the griefs, woes and sorrows of life'.[57] One reviewer summarized: 'She has the walk of an old woman; the hands of a sly one, and all the nurses' experience of ribaldry and affection are in the curious tortoise-like movement of her head.'[58] With her lines and bawdy jokes restored in this full-text production, 'The nurse was also more human than in a truncated version'.[59] Evans' Nurse 'is not satisfied to merely speak the jokes, but shows a quick, glowing apprehension of the personality to which the jokes belong [she is] alive on the realistic plane'.[60]

Between the OUDS production and Gielgud's of 1935, discussed above, Evans went to New York and played the Nurse to Katharine Cornell's Juliet in a prestigious Broadway production directed by Guthrie McClintic in 1934.[61] Her costume in this American production, designed by Jo Mielziner who also did the sets, was very similar to the one created for her by Motley. Evans' Nurse continued to wear a wimple and coif and to be praised in reviews. The *New York Times* called her performance 'a masterpiece', while the *New York Post* found her a 'loving, high colored, wrinkle-less and magnificently comic Nurse', and *Theatre Arts Monthly* praised her for avoiding the 'low comedy tricks which lesser players bring to the part'.[62] After the play's run of eighty-nine performances, Evans returned to London to continue her star turns in Shakespeare, Shaw and Restoration comedies, and once again to be the Nurse in the Gielgud production designed by Motley. Evans, having first played the Nurse in her twenties when a student and then as a fledgling actress specializing in playing old women, would remain associated with the role throughout her long career. When Hignett's cigarettes added her to their series of collectable cigarette cards featuring actors in the best-known roles, Edith Evans was pictured in her Motley-designed Nurse's wimple and coif, an indication of how closely she was associated with the role and how identifiable the costume had become.

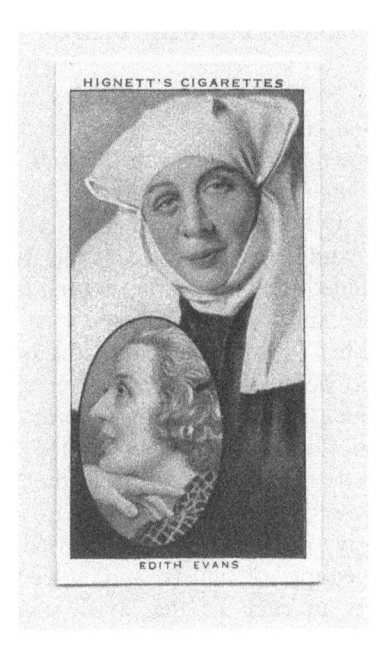

FIGURE 14 *Edith Evans as Nurse, costume design by Motley. Hignett's cigarette card, c.1933–9, by permission of George Arendts Collection, the New York Public Library, Aston, Lenox and Tilden Foundation.*

Evans would return to the role in 1961 at Stratford-upon-Avon for the Royal Shakespeare Company production there, directed by Peter Hall and designed by Desmond Heeley. Her Nurse's costume was similar to Motley's design: a voluminous heavy dark dress and a white wimple wrapped snugly around the head and throat. The white headdress, designed by Heeley in accordance with the director's request for real clothes for real people, was not quite so high, so wide or so starched as Motley's, but it still framed Evans' now age-lined face in pristine white. Her Nurse remained naïve and just a bit crafty – still the old turtle.

MGM, Hollywood, Oliver Messel and Adrian 1936

Although Evans' Nurse dressed in Motley's wimple and coif had become a well-known image, as the cigarette card testifies, the costume gained wider currency through MGM's lavish 1936 film of *Romeo and Juliet*,[63] directed by George Cukor and designed by Oliver Messel. The film starred the mature Norma Shearer and Leslie Howard as the teenaged lovers and the cast included similarly mature actors; John Barrymore played Mercutio and Basil Rathbone was Tybalt. Forty-eight-year-old Edna May Oliver played the Nurse as a very old woman who hobbled about using her cane. Messel, a fashionable young British designer, was imported to Hollywood, as all the studio publicity pointed out, specifically for the film and designed the majority of the film's hundreds of costumes. Messel's long theatre career as a designer was still in its early days.[64] He had devised scenery and costumes for a couple of ballets, and, since 1926, for one or two numbers in each of the lavish annual revues of impresario C.B.Cochran. Messel's first significant success had come in 1932 with the long-running production of *The Miracle*, a wordless spectacle with music, conceived and directed by Max Reinhardt and performed in a theatre transformed by Messel into a medieval cathedral. Before coming to Hollywood for *Romeo and Juliet*, he had also designed costumes for two prestigious historical films made in England, *The Private Life of Don Juan* (Korda, 1931) and *The Scarlet Pimpernel* with Leslie Howard (1934).

MGM's powerful producer Irving Thalberg insisted on hiring Messel despite the fact that the studio already had the brilliant set designer Cedric Gibbons and Adrian who designed gowns for its stars. In the film's opening credits, Messel shares costume credits with Adrian and set credits with Gibbons.[65] Messel also has a separate screen credit as Artistic Consultant. The result, especially with the sets, is a curious mix of the delicately refined romanticism of Messel and the ornate furnishing style favoured by Gibbons.[66] Of the costumes, the cut and drape of some of Juliet's dresses closely resemble the glamorous 1930s gowns designed by Adrian for Hollywood stars like Shearer.[67] Otherwise, looking at Messel's later work, as well as his costume designs for the film, it is clear that in the film his vision and design dominate, a vision based as much on ballet design as it is on Renaissance art.

As part of the prestige packaging of the film, Messel's knowledge of Renaissance art is always emphasized in publicity, along with the information that the film had been over a year in the making. The publicity inflated Messel's credentials, so that when *Variety*[68] praised his designs it identified him as an expert in fifteenth-century costuming, which was not the case – at least when he began the film. One publicity article describes how Messel devised a method to raise the hairline on the women's foreheads to match those of Renaissance portraits – all based on his research into fifteenth-century beauty techniques. Clearly, the elegant British designer was part of promoting the film advertised as having 'more stars than there are in heaven'. As Russell Jackson points out, the film was, in fact, 'a vision of the Italian Renaissance superimposed on an idealized version of Shakespeare's tragedy – and MGM's vision of itself'.[69]

In the files of the Messel collection at the Victoria & Albert Museum there are photographs of over a hundred designs for the costumes in *Romeo and Juliet*, male and female, leads and extras. Messel and the MGM design team spent a much-publicized three months in Italy, filming, photographing – and buying postcards – as research preparing for this upscale, cultural extravaganza of Renaissance Italy.[70] In order to understand the visual impact on screen of the Nurse's plain dress, the wimple and white coif and how it sets this character apart, it is important to picture the contrast with the elaborate clothing on everyone else. Messel's drawings and the film are full of dresses and jackets of dramatically patterned fabrics. MGM's publicity emphasized how the studio bought rare pieces of cloth and embroidery in Italy as well as commissioning the weaving of historically authentic fabrics. Both Messel's drawings and the actual garments play fast and loose with period details, combining authenticity with Messel's own flights of fancy. He favoured the nearly historically correct design for men's tights with a stripe around the upper thigh of one leg, but a more fanciful style for the heavily embroidered bead and metal work on doublets. For example, one worn by Romeo features slanted pockets across the upper breast, shoulder embroidery like slender epaulettes, laced sleeves with white chemise showing through and, on another of his doublet-jackets, two large golden embroidered birds. The overall effect is more bullfighter than Renaissance lover. Mercutio is dressed with similar over-decoration, but his costume includes remarkable footed tights in shiny black material. The women's dresses are similarly overwrought with arabesques, curlicues, sunbursts, flowers, stripes and layering, although always with a slender silhouette. Juliet's costumes are much influenced by a combination of Bellini's Renaissance paintings and the 1930s elegance of Adrian's gowns.

Among the many Messel costume sketches for the film in the V&A archives are two small drawings of a seated woman, head wrapped in a white cloth and wearing an ample dress. It is the closest thing in the collection that looks like the Nurse.

Among the sketches for elaborate clothes for men and women this seems a comparatively unimportant sketch, more suitable for a woman in the marketplace scene, but it matches what appears on the Nurse on screen. Edna May Oliver's Nurse is dressed in almost a copy of what Motley had put on Edith Evans, as though there was no other way to dress her – the costume had become the signifier of Shakespeare's Nurse.

In the ballet *Sleeping Beauty* designed by Messel a decade later, the woman rocking the baby princess's cradle is instantly identifiable – she is wearing the same costume as Juliet's Nurse.[71]

In the 1936 film, the performance of the Nurse was still the product of collaboration between actress and costume. As with Motley's designs for Evans, Oliver's Nurse has a white coif that covers her head, is tight across the forehead and at the sides of the face, spreads out across the back, and hangs below her

FIGURE 15 *Edna May Oliver as Nurse looking for Romeo. MGM film, design by Oliver Messel, 1936, screen capture.*

shoulders. It joins the wimple that drapes across her neck and the top of her chest. The dress is padded out to more or less the same width as the headdress. Again the costume works to make a middle-aged woman into an old one. The yards of fabric help to slow her movements as she trudges about (the published film script describes her 'waddling' twice).[72] As with Evans in Gielgud's productions, it was necessary to bulk out the otherwise angular body of Edna May Oliver. She needed a maternal shape, something not usually associated with her film roles. Oliver had a reputation for playing starchy but energetic and determinedly outspoken spinsters like Betsy Trotwood in *David Copperfield*, Aunt March in *Little Women* and Miss Pross in *A Tale of Two Cities*. Unlike Evans, who although not beautiful knew she could 'act beauty',[73] Oliver said, 'When you have a face like a horse, what else can you do but play comedy?'[74]

Casting Edna May Oliver, the studio's leading character actress and comedienne, was an obvious choice in some ways, but not in others. She specialized in redoubtable maiden ladies – not bawdy comedy. *Film Journal* thought her not comfortable as the Nurse. There is something starchy about this gravel-voiced Nurse, especially in her scenes with Shearer's over-refined Juliet. In general, Oliver's Nurse seems more at home in her scenes away from Juliet. One charming moment occurs when the old Nurse is teased by the Capulets' very pretty maids during preparations for the wedding feast. The screenplay describes them entering with 'baskets of flowers and wreaths and chains of flowers. The flower girls catch sight of the Nurse and dance about her, putting a wreath on her head and winding chains of flowers about her.'[75] She falls back smiling happily on a pile of flowers.

She is at her best in the encounter with Romeo and Mercutio, where some of her ribaldry is retained. Talbot Jennings, the film's adapter, speculated to the *New York Times* that the moral watchdogs at the Hayes Office and the Legion of Decency would be censoring Shakespeare: 'They'll never let us use that bit about the nurse'.[76] Talbot's adaptation kept an almost Victorian degree of propriety and removed most of the Nurse's coarser comments – but not the exchange with Mercutio about the time of day. As predicted, the censors *looked* closely – they asked that the bedroom scene be reshot so that when Romeo sits on the bed he keeps both feet on the floor – but they did not *listen* quite as closely. Perhaps it was the unfamiliar language, or Edna May Oliver's reputation for straight-laced spinsters, but the censors heard nothing wrong in the Nurse's repeating that 'merry man' her husband's double-meaning comment that Juliet 'wilt fall backward' when she 'hast more wit'.[77] Even more unexpected is the survival in the script and on-screen of Mercutio's observation that 'the bawdy hand of the dial is now upon the prick of noon' and the Nurse's knowing response as she nudges him and slaps his wrist with her fan saying, 'Out upon you! – What a man you are.'[78] A reporter on the set during filming of this segment described the actors 'engaged in a bawdy comedy scene, with many broad gestures and winkings and knowing looks'.[79] The Nurse's hat ends up in the fountain, knocked off by Barrymore's very boisterous Mercutio, much to the amusement of the courtesans watching from a balcony overlooking the piazza.[80] Even on the censored Hollywood screen, the Nurse's bawdy had been returned to her.

Shelving, Motley and Messel

The Nurse in a wimple and coif is the invention of three British designers. They made Shakespeare's Nurse clearly English, robust, warm, loving, comic and bawdy. These costumes for the Nurse designed by Paul Shelving, Motley and Oliver Messel work in a number of ways, starting with the designers' use of the costume as a short cut to the director's and actress's interpretations of the character.[81] Their Nurse is an old woman in a wide skirt of heavy material, topped by a jacket designed to emphasize a bulky figure. The yards of fabric in her voluminous garments are balanced by the equally wide coif. The result is an enclosed body, a solid figure of fabric, with skin visible only at the hands and part of the face. In contrast, each of the designers imagines an ethereal Juliet – Botticelli's Flora in the *Primavera*, for example – a slender, fashionable Lady Capulet and ladies at the Capulet ball in costumes inspired by a Carpaccio or Bellini painting. In a Renaissance world where bodies are clearly seen, with men in tights and form-fitting jackets and women in flowing wisps of dresses, the Nurse is bulky. There among the striped hose, embroidered bodices, gilded patterns on intricately decorated fabric and the rich colours, she and Friar Laurence are the only ones dressed in solid blocks of neutral colour. Shelving's Nurse does have a few stripes and large, almost clown-like, buttons punctuating her costume, but compared to the gold-sprayed fabric, the elaborately arranged hair and the jewelled ornaments on everyone else on stage, her dress remains very basic.

If, as J.C.Flugle claims in *The Psychology of Clothing*, accessorizing is the most persistent and basic of all clothing 'instincts', then the elaborately folded white coif is the accessory that proclaims the importance of the Nurse's unique position in the Capulet household. Her rank among the servants is high enough to give her the means to maintain this sculptured headdress with at least a yard of fabric, which requires starching and ironing, and whose whiteness could only be kept up to standard by a steady supply of new cloth to replace the old. When all three of the designers talk of their research into Renaissance art for the *Romeo and Juliet* costumes, they always mention the works of Carpaccio as the most prominent of their influences. However, there is no nurse in those paintings whose dress resembles their costume. The painter's *Birth of the Virgin* (1508) does include a nurse, but she wears a plain cloth veil over the head and certainly not a wimple. The Italian film directors Franco Zeffirelli in *Romeo and Juliet* (1968) and Renato Castellani in *Giulietta e Romeo* (1954) were far more accurate in historicizing the costumes. Their films really do look like Italian Renaissance paintings – but Zeffirelli still puts the Nurse in a wimple and elaborate coif.

Size matters here. The costume helps present a figure of solid bulk, a substantial woman. For Thornton the corpulence was there already, but Edith Evans and Edna May Oliver were younger and of much slighter build, and needed dresses with voluminous folds to give them the appearance of a (somewhat) maternal old servant. Flugel also talks about the way clothing elongates and enhances the body movements. The heavy layers of fabric above and below the neck encouraged the more laborious movements of the 'lame' (2.5.4) old(er) Nurse in contrast to the supple, youthful Juliet. The wide skirt also provides the comfort of a maternal lap that the fourteen-year-old girl can sit on or lean against.[82] The wide hips and an ample bosom stuffed into the top – or the top stuffed in order to create an ample bosom – present a character fully gendered as female. The crisp control of the headdress belies the laxity of the Nurse's speech. Her talk is scattered, full of innuendos, and comes pouring out in a stream of reminiscences. In her wimple and coif, and even more so in the flat circle of the broad-brimmed black hat placed on top of this when she goes out, she is visually and verbally a close kin of *The Canterbury Tales'* (c.1400) lusty Wife of Bath whose linen 'headkerchiefs were of the finest weave / Ten pounds and more they weighed'.[83] All that is missing is the Wife's red petticoat. Shelving, Motley and Messel had created a costume that signalled the return in performance of a franker, ribald and comic Nurse. When Gielgud in 1932, like his aunt Ellen Terry earlier, refused to censor the Nurse's language, this costume helped make her reminiscences about weaning and jokes about Juliet's wedding night seem earthy rather than prurient. This is important because when Mercutio sees her in the piazza and calls out 'a bawd, a bawd, a bawd' (2.4.126), it must not seem true, even though we know she is there to arrange a lovers' assignation.

In the decades that followed, in myriad productions of *Romeo and Juliet*[84] the Nurse has worn any number of styles of headscarves, wrapped turbans, little caps – but the starched headdress introduced by Paul Shelving in 1922, created anew by Motley in 1932 and 1935, and adapted by Oliver Messel in Hollywood in 1936, has remained the icon. The image is immediately recognized in a Shakespeare context as Juliet's

Nurse: the broad-bodied woman, with a cane and a fan, wearing a starched white headdress.[85] It was the directors – H.K.Ayliff with the Birmingham Rep, John Gielgud with his own productions and George Cukor in Hollywood – who rescued Shakespeare's Nurse from nineteenth-century gentility. But it was their designers – Shelving, Motley and Messel – whose costumes are the signifier of that change.

Shakespeare Stripped: Costuming Prisoner-of-war Entertainments and Cabaret

Kate Dorney

When Ben Jonson described Shakespeare as 'not of an age but for all time',[1] he probably did not foresee a period, four centuries later, when *Hamlet* was reimagined as a Hollywood detective story and performed by emaciated servicemen in a Japanese prisoner-of-war (PoW) camp. Nor, it seems safe to assume, did Jonson imagine that Shakespeare's work might inspire a floorshow featuring scantily clad showgirls. But these are not imaginary incidents; they are two very specific instances of the myriad ways in which Shakespeare's work has pervaded Anglophone language and culture, and I want to use them to think about the ways in which Shakespeare's work is essentialized, stripped down, reduced to the bare necessities. The design and clothing of Shakespeare productions has long occupied scholars and practitioners. From Henry Peacham's drawings for *Titus Andronicus* to Charles Macklin's *Macbeth*, and on into the twenty-first century, theatre and fashion historians have dissected the way these characters are presented on this stage. This chapter will look instead at costuming in shows inspired by Shakespeare's work, examining two instances in which the rich visual images conjured in the plays are stripped down to the bare essentials.

Artist Ronald Searle (1920–2011) was a PoW in Thailand and Singapore during the Second World War and designed costumes and sets for several shows produced for the prisoners' entertainment and temporary distraction. We have a number of these designs in the Victoria & Albert Museum, including some for a 1944 revue sketch called *Hamlet Goes Hollywood*. The designs for the show are crowded together on a tiny, much-folded piece of paper and the notes suggest, unsurprisingly, a make-do and mend attitude to costuming. Ronald Cobb (active 1948–79) was presenting Shakespeare with a rather different emphasis on the bare necessities: designing skimpy showgirl costumes as part of a literary themed revue at a nightclub called Eve in London in the late 1960s/early 1970s. Each of Cobb's designs reduces the play to components displayable on a headdress and very brief costume, typically comprising a c-string (known at the time as an invisible g string), a breast-baring or revealing bra-top and separated sleeves along with the occasional prop. *Hamlet* becomes a dagger, a ghost and a dead king. *Antony and Cleopatra* is reduced to Rome and Egypt represented by a centurion's helmet and an asp respectively.

In these examples, Shakespeare, clothes and costumes interact in complex ways. For the showgirls, the scanty costumes are their uniform, a bizarre confection of plastic, gauze and body paint that draws attention to their bodies, but also to their roles as performers. No club patron could mistake them for a guest or hostess in their costume; they are not dressed up in their best clothes as a hostess or guest might be, but clearly costumed and part of the show. For the PoWs, uniform provided an identity, a community, a means of protecting their bodies from the elements, particularly for those working in the jungle. As their captivity and forced labour continued, their uniforms became tattered, endlessly patched, repaired and replaced by items from their dead colleagues, or even fashioned from salvaged materials.[2] The costumes they wore in the camp entertainments were cobbled together or borrowed in the same way, offering curious parallels with the use and appearance of clothing in Shakespeare's own period. In both cases, fabric is a precious commodity that must be reused, and occupation and status are clearly signalled by apparel.

Searle enlisted in the army in April 1939, aged nineteen, 'a somewhat weedy scholarship student at the Cambridge School of Art, unconvinced by Neville Chamberlain's piece of paper' promising 'peace in our time'.[3] After the Second World War he became one of Britain's most celebrated cartoonists whose work captured the defiance and bravado of Britain's post-war youth: the children of the Atomic Age. The anarchic, angular girls of St Trinian's were his creations and, along with his illustrations for *Molesworth*, portrayed a cynical, witty sharp-eyed youth in opposition to a bloated, bumbling and ridiculous older generation and establishment. He also worked for the satirical magazine *Punch* and, after his move to France at the beginning of the 1960s, for *Le Monde* and *Le Figaro*.

In October 1941, Searle's brigade embarked for North Africa. En route they were directed to the Far East and arrived in Singapore just in time to witness the Japanese invasion and be taken prisoner. Searle later expressed contempt for films like *Bridge On the River Kwai* (1957), which he claimed falsified the experiences of PoWs working on the Burma–Thailand railway (he was one of them) and his account of his own experiences *To the Kwai and Back* is a stark testimony to the suffering that the PoWs endured.

The costume designs discussed here are for a revue sketch called *Hamlet Goes Hollywood*, and were made by Searle during his time in Changi Jail towards the end of his captivity. In both the First and Second World Wars, PoWs in many camps wrote and performed revues (collections of sketches) and put on plays to boost morale, create a distraction from their misery and torment, and introduce a degree of normality or familiarity into their existence. These were not Searle's primary distraction; instead, as he wrote in his memoirs, he preferred to record his surroundings having 'convinced myself that my mission was to emerge from the various camps, the jungle and finally prison, with a "significant" pictorial record that would reveal to the world something of what happened during those lost and more or less unphotographed years'.[4] He covertly sketched prisoners, guards, civilians and landscapes, secreting his sketch books and drawings in different locations, and sometimes even in the beds of cholera patients, to keep them safe from the Japanese. In the 1980s he gave these sketches to the Imperial War Museum (IWM) which published the sketches, along with Searle's account of their creation, in *To the Kwai and Back* (1986). He also donated a sketchbook of notes, stage and costumes designs for the Barn Theatre at Sime Road Prison Camp to the IWM, and this sketchbook is a key source of information both for the production of *Hamlet Goes Hollywood* and for British involvement in the theatrical activities in Changi. The sketchbook, along with the collection of material in the V&A, gives an insight into the resourcefulness and ingenuity of PoWs in the creation of theatrical entertainment.

As Michael Dobson and Richard Fawkes have both noted, the burgeoning of the Little Theatre movement in Britain in the early part of the twentieth century led to an increase in talented and knowledgeable amateur performers and technicians.[5] As a result of this, the British Services engaged in the Second World War contained many talented amateurs as well as professionals. Theatre was an important element in morale-boosting across the European and Far Eastern fronts. Entertainment was recognized as a key element in bonding fighting units as well as staving off boredom and keeping up morale. Britain and the USA employed a number of civilian professionals to provide entertainments to troops awaiting deployment but also formed concert parties of professionals and talented amateurs within the armed forces to entertain servicemen in the field. Although the average serviceman's idea of entertainment was formed by their experiences at the cinema, war-time entertainments introduced them all to variety shows composed of comic sketches, songs, dancing and 'acts' or 'turns' (which might include conjuring, acrobatics, imitation, etc). In captivity the PoWs created their own entertainments along these lines. They turned to forms that were familiar, like popular shows and classic, but also to concert party/revue because it was inclusive and did not require any prior knowledge of the classics, extensive learning of lines or complex plots for untried actors.[6]

In Europe, PoW companies had a large repertoire, performing everything from Shakespeare and George Bernard Shaw to Ben Travers and Noël Coward.[7] PoWs in Germany were often encouraged, and in some cases indulged, by their guards, receiving loans of costume from professional theatres, make-up and items of civilian clothing that made their way to them via parcels from home as well as contributions from the YMCA.[8] PoWs in the Far East received little encouragement and even smaller provision. Their Red Cross parcels were frequently withheld; the heat, damp and insects destroyed books and clothing, and so their repertoire tended more towards revue and shows that could be recreated from memory.

Searle is eloquent about the privations that he and his comrades faced, but he refers to the camp entertainments only in passing, despite his input into them as a writer, performer, costume and set designer and programme illustrator. The V&A's remarkable collection of programmes and designs for Changi theatricals was passed to the museum by Searle's fellow PoW John Beckerley, who assisted him with the sets. Beckerley recalls that 'at Sime Road we had a flourishing theatre which later merged with the Changi Theatre group'.[9] This was just one of many theatres in the vast PoW complex that had once been a British garrison. Alongside the Sime Road and Changi Theatre groups was the thirty-strong 'Changi Concert Party' formed by Australian PoWs at Selarang Barracks (also part of the compound), and various other local amateur shows.[10] The PoWs and civilian prisoners were moved around various parts of the complex leading to changes in the formation of groups. Unlike in Germany, where officers and other ranks were separated into different camps, prisoners in Singapore were kept together. The camps maintained military discipline and chains of command so the entertainments were organized and sanctioned by officers but drew on performers and technicians from across the ranks. Beckerley's drawings of the Barn Theatre, where *Hamlet Goes Hollywood* was staged, show an extraordinarily well-equipped space – presumably, along with many other theatre spaces, sets and wardrobe items, a legacy of the British administration added to by the ingenuity of the PoWs (one of the many remarkable items to survive is a dress fashioned from mosquito netting worn by a serviceman performing in a revue).[11] If the sketches by Beckerley, Searle and other PoWs are accurate reflections of the shows, then production standards were much higher than one might expect given their living conditions. Various accounts of life in Changi suggest the inmates were incredibly, ingeniously resourceful, but not miracle workers.[12] In Searle's Barn sketchbook in the IWM, there is a cartoon among the costume designs for *Cinderella* (1944) asking for contributions to the wardrobe for the Cathay Concert Party. Alongside a sketch of a naked woman and a man in a military cap covering his modesty with a sword is a notice in block capitals:

WANTED – <u>DESPERATELY!</u>
~~ARTIC~~ COSTUMES!
IF YOU HAVE ANY ARTICLES OF CLOTHING OR SMALL PROPS WHICH
YOU ARE PREPARED TO GIVE OR LOAN WILL YOU PLEASE CONTACT:
    LT ARCHER HUT 11
    LT MACKLEOD HUT 11
OR: CAPT WHELON HUT 44
    CAPT WELLBURY HUT 10
    CAPT HORNER HUT 8[13]

The *Hamlet Goes Hollywood* sketch was performed at the 'Rag Bag Revue' on 21 March 1944. In Searle's sketchbook, the revue is described as 'dippings from previous revues' while the programme describes it as containing 'excerpts from many previous Changi successes', suggesting a very mixed bag.[14] From a portion of the script written out in the sketchbook (Searle played the Ghost so this is probably his 'part'), it seems the governing conceit of the sketch was exactly as the title suggests: *Hamlet* gets the Hollywood treatment. Searle was the right age to have grown up under the influence of Hollywood films with their swashbuckling and hard-bitten heroes, although the sketch may equally well have been a satire on the spread of American culture. Either way, the disjuncture between the high tragedy of the original, and the Hollywood remake is still funny:

HAMLET Gee! Look my lord, it comes (*loud clanking of chains*)

[*Enter Ghost*]

GHOST OH HAMLET, HEAR THY FATHER'S GHOST. I COULD A TALE UNFOLD WHOSE LIGHTEST WORD WOULD HARROW UP THY SOUL. LIST, OH LIST, T'WAS GIVEN OUT THAT SLEEPING ONE DAY IN MY ORCHARD, A SERPENT STUNG ME. That was no serpent. It was your uncle. The snake!

HAMLET No kidding! So it was moider, huh? Well, what do you know about that!

GHOST YEAH. WHILE SLEEPIN' YOUR UNCLE STOLE UPON ME AND WITH JUICE OF CURSED HEBENON IN A VIAL, POURED IT IN THE PORCHES OF MINE EAR – and gave me de woiks.

HAMLET The dirty double crosser.

GHOST MURDER MOST FOUL. AVENGE ME HAMLET. ADIEU, ADIEU, ADIEU. [*EXIT*]

[*Pops out*] – I'll be seein' you![15]

For all its comedy, there is something poignant about the scene when one reflects on the actors and audience. Searle weighed around six stone (eighty-four pounds) at this time, so would have made an effective though insubstantial ghost, if not quite the Ghost Shakespeare describes. Having been disarmed on capture and forced to wear an armband advertising his shameful cowardice (Japanese soldiers were trained to believe that suicide was the only honourable course when captured and so had no respect for the Allied soldiers they guarded), he could hardly appear 'Armed at point exactly' (1.2.200), or looking in any way martial. But he would have had one thing in common with Hamlet's Ghost: he and his fellow prisoners would have been able to relate only too well to the idea of being in purgatory and being imprisoned without knowing how long their incarceration would last. When Searle's Ghost announced: 'I could a tale unfold whose lightest word would harrow up thy soul', there is a significant elision from Shakespeare's text which reads: 'But that I am forbid / To tell the secrets of my prison-house, I could a tale unfold' (1.5.13–15). Searle could not have known that he would survive his prison-house but he was, as I have already noted, determined to provide evidence of his experience if he did. His sketchbooks in the IWM and the designs and programmes in the V&A are a small part of the material that unveiled the secrets of Changi.[16]

How did the audience of *Hamlet Goes Hollywood* relate to the original text, I wonder? If the sketch followed the plot, what did they make of Hamlet's inaction – would it have seemed like a luxury? If they weren't familiar with the text, and took Searle's Ghost at his word, would the tale he unfolded have seemed laughable or ironic? His tale is one of him being poisoned in his sleep. It would not have been difficult for the performers or audience to think of tales considerably more harrowing than that; their lives were a living hell. By this point, Searle, for example, had witnessed the bombing of half a million refugees who had fled to Singapore and were under siege with the retreating Allied forces, the displaying of the severed heads of 'uncooperative' Chinese and Malay civilians, the random beatings of civilians and prisoners, and the deaths of comrades through tropical fever, cholera, exhaustion and starvation. He had been marched through the jungle to build the Burma–Thailand railway (known as the Death Railway) where emaciated, malnourished prisoners hacked at the rockface to create a cutting, and then transported to Changi Jail where 10,000 men were squeezed into a prison built to hold 600 and were crammed six or seven to a cell, subsisting on fewer than 500 calories a day. As Searle commented:

> the pangs of hunger were frequently more demoralising than the combined miseries of beri-beri, dysentery and the clammy hand of malaria. We talked ceaselessly about food, we dreamed about food and, after we had eaten our miserable allowance for the day, tried to take our minds off it with any handy diversion.[17]

Was *Hamlet Goes Hollywood* a handy diversion? An opportunity for reflection? Or both? Given that the PoWs lived in daily contact with death and disease, were malnourished and suffering from the effects of heat, mosquitoes and depression, it is difficult to speculate on what might have moved them. David Piper, a PoW in Taiwan during the same period that Searle was in Changi, found himself 'extraordinarily moved' during the interval of the 1944 pantomime *Dick Whittington* when one of the Dutch hospital orderlies sang a lyric Piper had written to Handel's Largo. The pantomime itself he found 'a very good show indeed, was warm and drowsy and amused for 2½ hours'.[18]

Did *Hamlet Goes Hollywood* engender similar feelings? Beneath Searle's lines for the Ghost part in the IWM sketchbook is a rough ink drawing of the characters similar to the design in the V&A, but much less detailed. The V&A drawing is in colour (colour is one of the fluctuating elements among Searle's sketches, presumably depending on his access to colouring materials) and gives notes on costume composition. Hamlet looks more like a schoolmaster than a student in his long black gown, cap and knee britches, but the notes suggest the actor will actually be wearing a beret with a feather in it, a green army shirt and pyjama trousers under his khaki shorts, tied at the knee and tucked into his socks under the gown. Not too difficult to achieve. But what about the gown, where would that come from? He also has a ruff – did they knock it up for him in the wardrobe department, perhaps out of mosquito netting? Or perhaps, as is the case with so many other costume designs, the realized costume was less exciting than the design. Horatio is dressed like a hard-boiled Hollywood detective in a trench-coat and trilby and we must hope he has some of the gumshoe dialogue to match the outfit. The King (Claudius) looks more like Macbeth than a Dane in his kilt (perhaps borrowed from a fellow prisoner from the Gordon Highlanders who had been stationed in the barracks earlier in the war), woollen jerkin and short red socks.[19] The real challenge here is that Searle has also drawn the King wearing a shirt with huge puffed sleeves and has put a question mark next to them, as if querying how it can be done. The sketch and notes also suggest he will have a sword which seems unlikely, unless it is a wooden one, but again, it is by no means the only time a sword appears in his sketches for the theatre shows. The Queen (Gertrude) seems to be in full Tudor dress while Ophelia is wearing something more like an eighteenth-century evening gown. Searle's notes reveal that they plundered the theatre wardrobe, perhaps left behind by the garrison theatre or war-time entertainers, or created for earlier shows. The Queen is wearing a jacket from *Cinderella* with a 'dressing-gown skirt with wire hoop';[20] Ophelia is wearing a 'lady's dress from *Man of Destiny*' with a Tudor headdress and there are several drawings for this, so we might assume that this would be manufactured somehow. Both *Cinderella* and *Man of Destiny* are shows that Searle worked on and his designs for them are in the IWM Barn Theatre notebook. As Ghost, he gave himself the simplest costume of all – 'two sheets'. Perhaps, as I speculated before, he decided less was more, given that it was probably too much to ask wardrobe to run up a suit of armour.

Changi's 'Ragbag Revue' is a world away from the revues of Paris, New York and London that brought the scantily clad beautiful showgirl into popular culture and inspired nightclubs like the Eve, the site of our next bare necessity Shakespeare. Along with prison and garrison theatre, nudity is a long-established part of Britain's theatre ecology. In the Regency period, *tableaux vivants* had carefully contrived the impression of nudity with fleshings (tight, flesh-coloured clothes and stockings); these had carried through into the Victorian and Edwardian eras in music-halls and emerged in nightclubs in the 1920s and 1930s. The Windmill Theatre developed its renowned non-stop variety show *Revuedeville* in 1932, combining nude tableaux with song, dance and comic routines. Judith Walkowitz points out that the Windmill somehow managed to reduce nude shows to a safe, middle-class diversion where there was very little interaction between the audience and performers.[21] Even the infamous 'Windmill commandos' who raced for the front two rows and sat with their coats over their laps were essentially passive, quietly watching the show and clapping at the end. When US servicemen poured into London in the 1940s they livened up the place no end, clapping and cheering and loudly exhorting the dancers to strip. As striptease arrived in London in the 1950s, the Windmill kept its audiences by introducing fan dances and the dance of the seven veils. Shows designed to titillate but never reveal all could maintain their pretension to art rather than commerce.[22] The Eve club, where Ronald Cobb and Helen Archer conceived their elaborate revues, was a continuation of that tradition.

Established in 1953, the club was a latecomer to the cabaret scene. Unlike the shady nightclubs of Soho, the Eve was located on Regent Street and designed to attract a wealthy clientele. Owners Helen Archer (née Elena Constantinescu) and Jimmy O'Brien had worked in other clubs before establishing their own and appreciated the importance of having unique selling points: an impressive menu and wine list, original and exciting floorshows, and beautiful showgirls and dancers. In a letter to the V&A Museum outlining the club's history, Archer wrote that their aim was:

> to break the pattern of late-night entertainment as it then was. We aspired to a more happy, relaxed and cheerful atmosphere than that which existed in the post-war years . . .
>
> Floorshows, such as they were, in the early 50s, were cheap (and not always cheerful) and they were based without imagination on the music of the Twenties or on Latin American or on 'Gay Paree' . . .
>
> We decided to present a totally new concept of floorshow to include only the most beautiful showgirls and the most talented dancers and to present them in costumes which were original and inventive and designed by an inspired Cobb who created his costumes in our own workshops. At the same time we challenged Cobb to come up with designs on themes which had not heretofore been associated with floorshows. He successfully met our various requests and consequently we came up with numbers based on themes such as Huxley's Brave New World to the music of Stravinsky, cleverly arranged and orchestrated for six musicians. The Mind of Goya might also have been considered as being somewhat bizarre. Likewise 'Astronomical Sorcery' based on the constellations to the music of the Sorcerer's Apprentice.[23]

The club's ten-year anniversary prospectus is an ABC of attractions and facts that captures the light-hearted and tongue-in-cheek tone of the place: 'our puns are misplaced – possibly – but our heart's in the right place. And so is our club. In Regent Street.'[24] The location is critical in distinguishing Eve as a place of entertainment and leisure from Soho establishments like Raymond's Revuebar which opened its doors in 1958 and Murray's, where Archer, O'Brien and Cobb had worked before establishing the Eve. Murray's was a cabaret club with a strict admissions policy and a clientele that included politicians, criminals and film stars who could entertain guests or be entertained in a safe environment. It was rumoured that the performers made themselves available to select clients 'after hours' and Murray's reputation for risqué glamour was boosted further when the club achieved notoriety as the venue where Christine Keeler and Mandy Rice Davies (working as showgirls) met MP John Profumo (whose affair with Keeler brought down Harold Macmillan's government). Raymond's Revuebar, also in Soho, mixed the attractions of a private members' club with that of a variety theatre like the Windmill with one important difference: it guaranteed mobile nudity through the medium of striptease. It had membership rules and boasted about its restaurant and wine list, but its outstanding attraction was a 240-seat cabaret-style auditorium in which one could see a succession of striptease shows. Owner Paul Raymond described the opening of the Revuebar in 1958 as 'the start of the stampede into sensuality'.[25]

The Eve club, in contrast, promised floorshows that were the high point of the 'journey into fantasy' that O'Brien envisaged for her clients.[26] It had a clientele presumably looking for something more than naked women, perhaps nudity disguised as art, or something redolent of the more genteel days before the war. Information on the club is scant, other than the letter from Archer giving the history of the club, some programmes she donated to the V&A, and the obituaries of O'Brien and Archer (later O'Brien). The club never appears in histories of London in the 1960s and 1970s, in accounts of cabaret, revue or striptease; yet it was, according to the obituaries, 'a honeypot for espionage',[27] as O'Brien was employed by MI5 and MI6 to pass on the information that guests shared with the hostesses.

The Shakespeare sequence appeared as part of the Bibliotheque floorshow which covered a range of literary genres including Science Fiction, the Crime Novel and Drama, which was represented by six Shakespeare plays reduced to their bare essentials to form the basis of the costumes. The wit of the costumes is that they do not merely dress the girls as a character from one of the plays; they present an accretion of objects or references from the plays as a puzzle for the audience to unpick. The bijou dimensions of the club – the stage was around twelve feet square and made of illuminated glass – were perfect for this development of intimate revue. The club numbered politicians, legal professionals, royalty, celebrities and other establishment figures among its members, and they would have been able to see the individual elements of the costumes quite clearly and appreciate the wit inherent in the design. To reinforce the element of a parlour game, the patrons were also encouraged to spot different points each time they returned (which was, of course, also good for business).

The mechanics of Eve showgirl costumes insist on stately, slow deportment: heavy headdresses, 'invisible g strings' or c-strings as they are now called[28] – designed by Cobb – that were essentially a c-shaped piece of wire with a bar at the back (to hold the wire in place) and a moulded concealing panel for the pubis. The focal points of the costume are always head, breasts and pubis, drawing the eye down the body to the long shapely legs. Cobb had long experience of designing revue costumes having worked for the Entertainments National Service Association (ENSA) during the Second World War, and at Murray's before moving with Archer and O'Brien to Eve. These costumes are probably the pinnacle of Cobb's career: an environment in which nothing competed with his creations for the attention of the audience, in which supplies were plentiful, costumes were made under his supervision in the club's workshop and in which he had an imaginative collaborator and choreographer in Archer.

Macbeth (Figure 16) is one of the best and most easily identifiable of the designs. The c-string is a horned skull – the horns are presumably a contemporary reference to witchcraft, the headdress continues the horned theme, adding a crown and a very stylized tree (perhaps representing the blasted heath where Macbeth encounters the witches). One sleeve ends in a red (bloodied) hand clutching a dagger, while the other hand holds a shield with the Wyrd sisters' heads attached.

FIGURE 16 *Design by Ronald Cobb for Macbeth showgirl in Bibliotheque floorshow at the Eve club (1960–70), S.716-1996, Theatre & Performance Department, Victoria & Albert Museum.* © V&A Images.

The Merchant of Venice is perhaps the most shocking. The c-string is shaped like the head of a Jewish man complete with yarmulke and peyots; the headdress is Venetian in style topped with a pair of scales supporting a bleeding heart (the pound of flesh) on one side and ducats on the other. On one arm is a striped and puffed sleeve for a male costume denoting Venice and supporting the three caskets used to test Portia's suitors. The other sleeve is scarlet silk with a long black triangle of ragged cloth emblazoned with a star. The cloth is presumably a reference to Shylock's 'Jewish gaberdine' and the star another reference to Judaism even though it is, in fact, a pentacle rather than a six-pointed Star of David.

Romeo and Juliet shows a headdress supporting the heraldic shields of the Montagues and Capulets while a cloud obscures the sun and moon (to which the lovers constantly refer); their colours are carried on down each side of the costume: one sleeve puffed and slashed to denote Romeo, the other a hanging sleeve denoting Juliet. On Juliet's side the showgirl's hand holds a phial of the sleeping draught while on Romeo's side she clutches a spade – an allusion to their grave. This time the c-string is in the shape of a star, presumably a reference to the star-crossed lovers for those in the audience unable to decode the larger clues.

Hamlet (Figure 17) is particularly interesting because the V&A has a part of the costume (the headdress) as well as the design, and we are able to compare intent and execution. The headdress can almost carry the story alone. The black crenellated tower of Elsinore rises from a crown flagged by a skull wearing a jester's cap (Yorick) on one side and a ghostly bearded figure wearing a crown on the other (old Hamlet), whose white costume trails down and over the showgirl's arm. On one side the showgirl wears a sleeve of a puffed, slashed, black doublet (Hamlet's mourning), on the other a black hanging sleeve spotted with blood. Around her neck she wears chains, perhaps a reference to Denmark being a prison, and this time the c-string shows the face of the drowned Ophelia surrounded by flowers.

Antony and Cleopatra is less easy to guess. The dominant motif is that of a Roman soldier's armour, so we have a stylized truncated tunic that exposes the breasts with a trailing cape representing Rome. The asp and gold jewellery winding round one of the showgirl's arm symbolize Cleopatra, as does the Egyptian motif on the c-string. Again, the c-string provides an additional clue in that Cleopatra's Needle (or at any rate, an obelisk) seems to be rising from the motif. The headdress is particularly elaborate comprising a Roman helmet surmounted by Cleopatra's barge 'a burnish'd throne' with a poop of 'beaten gold' (2.2.195–6), surmounted by a tower. At this point in the show, if the audience had guessed the first few

FIGURE 17 *Design by Ronald Cobb for Hamlet showgirl in Bibliotheque floorshow at the Eve club (1960–70), S.713-1996, Theatre & Performance Department, Victoria & Albert Museum.* © V&A Images.

plays, the asp would presumably be enough to identify *Antony and Cleopatra*, so the other details are for real connoisseurs, and maybe even only for Shakespeare and ancient history enthusiasts.

The last design in this sequence is the weakest – by which I mean it most resembles a standard showgirl costume and has none of the wit of the others discussed here. And it is almost tasteful. The headdress for *A Midsummer Night's Dream* has Bottom's ass's ears combined with Titania's fairy crown and wings. The costume comprises a breast and hip girdle and stockings representing the fairy bower of flowers. The sleeves are made of spangled fabric, suggesting the midsummer night sky and in one hand the showgirl holds 'Love-in-idleness', the 'little western flower' (2.1.166) whose juice changes the lovers' vision. Where are Pyramus and Thisbe? The Lion? The Wall? These are elements that Cobb could have had fun with, as Nick Ormerod did in Cheek by Jowl's 1985 production, where the costume was a short wall on top of a long tunic. It is as if Cobb has been taken over by the spirit of Herbert Beerbohm Tree. It seems odd to insert a comedy at this point anyway, but as far as our records show, the Drama section of Bibliotheque began with the bang of the Scottish Play and ended with this whimper.

As spectacle, these costume designs are amusing and impressive, but also discomforting in every sense of the word. The physical discomfort the performers would have experienced wearing a heavy headdress, a wire c-string and a number of props on each arm is one element; then there is the liminal status of the performers who are by no means off-limits to club patrons. The floorshow took place in two halves each night at 10.30pm and 1am. But for the rest of the evening, the girls were available as dancing partners. For the uninitiated the brochure explains: 'your hostess may excuse herself in time to change into her costume and repair her make-up. She is loath to go – but duty calls. Having seen her dance you will be even prouder to welcome her back.'[29]

Unlike the Windmill and a number of other venues, there is no proscenium arch to separate the performers from the audience, and it is difficult to determine to what extent these performers had a character to inhabit. Recent scholarly attention to costume design focuses on the extent to which design is the main tool through which an actor can establish and inhabit their character, but other than the generic character of showgirl, the Eve girls have no stable character. Their costume changes on a regular basis and they embody concepts rather than characters. They are literally, in the crudest possible sense, carriers of meaning. Although the Eve girls are not part of a huge ensemble like Ziegfeld Follies, or the Alfred Jackson Girls whom Siegfried Kracauer described as a distanced, dehumanized, mechanized production line, they are nearly naked women (probably at the pinnacle of their career) moving slowly and smiling graciously, but effectively devoid of personality.[30] The showgirls were on the lowest rung in the nightclub talentocracy; they were moving scenery, providing a backdrop to the dancers and singers.

Searle's Ghost is also a liminal figure: the performer hovering on the threshold between life and death, the character between the living world and the afterlife. The discomfort or disquiet the audience might have experienced watching the sketch is not recorded, but it is interesting to think about to what extent the show dwelt on death. The one common signifier of *Hamlet* that we might expect to see – a skull – is present, but not commented on in the notes. Did the skull appear in *Hamlet Goes Hollywood*? And if so, in what form? The V&A has at least two human skulls that have gone on for Yorick; what did they use in Changi – a human skull, a plastic or plaster prop? To what effect? In Eve's club, particularly in the Shakespeare sequence, skulls and other dead heads are very much in vogue – a convenient and effective signifier in the intellectual game of guessing the work of art. A bare necessity.

PART THREE

Interviews with Contemporary Designers

The Designers

Jane Greenwood and Robert Morgan

The two award-winning designers interviewed for *Shakespeare and Costume* represent an impressive range of work in theatre, film, television, dance and opera as well as in productions of Shakespeare's plays. Jane Greenwood's design career began in England but soon moved to Canada and then the United States. Her work includes more than five decades of film and theatre design for American regional theatres, Broadway and Off-Broadway, including the Public Theater's New York Shakespeare Festival. Robert Morgan has been deeply involved with designing Shakespeare productions for a wide range of American regional theatres, including the American Players Theater and San Diego's Old Globe, for more than three decades, which has given him the unique opportunity to design multiple versions of Shakespeare's plays.

Jane Greenwood

How did you get started?

I studied at the Liverpool Art School and then the theatre arts programme at Central School of Arts and Crafts in London. During the three-year programme there, I studied period costume, the style and cut of clothes, and set and costume design. My fellow students also enjoyed working with the actors at the Royal Academy of Dramatic Art for their yearly shows. I had wonderful teachers: Norah Waugh, Jeanetta Cochrane and Margaret Woodward. Desmond Heeley taught a class in prop making – all the students loved his class. My teacher Norah Waugh's books *Corsets and Crinolines*, *The Cut of Women's Clothes* and *The Cut of Men's Clothes* became bibles in costume making and an integral part of every costume designer's personal library. I will always remember Norah's words: 'You can make a dress out of anything, and if it is the correct silhouette for the period, it will look wonderful.' Norah hammered into us that the silhouette is paramount for correct period clothes – very often it is the underpinnings of a period that, while not discernible when one is fully dressed, create the correct shape.

As a student I worked part-time for Frank Winter, a theatrical milliner. We were finishing hats for a pantomime on ice of *Aladdin*. The pagoda hats had many bells that I had to sew onto each point. After the noise deafened the director when the dancers skated out on the ice, the bells had to go. I should have learned then that the theatre would be an unusual and sometimes rocky ride!

After graduation, Frank Hauser, the artistic director of Oxford Playhouse, offered me a Wardrobe/Design job. It meant being chief cook and bottle-washer for the Costume Department – but looking back, I learned a great deal about how to actually design, make and keep clothes on the actors! Desmond Heeley came to the theatre to design for Peter Brook's production of *Prince Genji*. I remember the layers of kimonos in beautiful colours and being introduced to the designer Tanya Moiseiwitsch on opening night. Because of that introduction, I ended up in the Shakespeare Theatre at Stratford, Ontario for two seasons, working as a draper in the costume shop with Tyrone Guthrie directing and the costumer Ivan Alderman who came over for each season from England to Ontario.[1]

Ivan was brilliant but quite terrifying to a beginning draper. I worked in the men's department with him, and I remember how my scissors shook when he came to check the garments I was cutting! Eventually we became great friends – I kept in touch with Ivan always through his years working with Laurence Olivier, first at the Chichester Theatre and then the National Theatre, where Ivan created a fabulous costume shop – it was 'state of the art' before we used that phrase!

When we came back to New York to travel to England by boat, Ivan introduced me to Ray Diffen in 1962 and changed my life. Ray offered me a position as a draper and later that year, I came to New York and began work in his costume shop as a draper. Ray and I designed *The Importance of Being Earnest* together. After this production I met and subsequently married the designer Ben Edwards, and he asked me to design *The Ballad of a Sad Café*, adapted by Edward Albee from Carson McCullers' novella. That was my first Broadway production. Ben, my husband and mentor, served as one of the producers as well as the set designer. When designers ask me how I got my start in New York, I tell them I married the producer!

Ben and I went on to design *Hamlet*, directed by John Gielgud and starring Richard Burton. It was decided *Hamlet* would be done as a rehearsal, with actors wearing contemporary clothes – this was a big change from the elaborate period clothes expected in the 1960s. It was not an easy assignment since everyone had an opinion as to what they should wear.

In addition to designing in New York and for regional theatres like the Guthrie in Minneapolis, I taught at Yale School of Drama and designed for the movies, including *Can't*

Stop the Music, Arthur, The Four Seasons and *Glengarry Glen Ross*. Eventually, I had to make a choice because it was too hectic flying back to my classes from movie sets all over the country. So I chose New York and to teach at Yale.

Who were the early influences?

My early influences were my art teacher Miss Ashworth, and the International Ballet with Robert Helpmann and Margot Fonteyn, especially the production of the ballet *Comus*. The Motley sisters were also a great inspiration to me. They were working in the 1930s and 1940s in England and they were innovative in the way they realized their designs; they were a great example of the 'bottle top' school of decoration.[2]

What were the influences in using historical periods in Shakespeare productions?

Janet Arnold was an important influence; she wrote extraordinary pattern books for all periods, but especially the Elizabethan and Tudor periods. For a while I shared a room with her at the students' hostel in Tavistock Square, London. Although our personalities were quite different and she was neat and I messy, we remained firm friends until sadly she died. Janet's work formed the basis of the 'original practice' costume designs that Jennie Tiramani does for the reconstructed Globe Theatre in London.

But you can design for Shakespeare in any period. You work with a director and their ideas. There was an *Othello* (1991) at the Public Theater with Raul Julia in the lead. Joe Dowling directed and Christopher Walken was Iago. Dowling did not want them in tights, so we looked at Carpaccio with a modern motorbike look! There were lots of leather jackets that were quasi-Renaissance and tight trousers. The girls wore the fashion of the moment with the Italian Renaissance in mind.

Actually some of the most interesting productions of Shakespeare I have designed have been in the park. For example, the 2012 New York Shakespeare Festival's *As You Like It* in Central Park was set in 1840 in the backwoods of Kentucky. Wealthy folk like the duke wore good clothes of the period. The men at court wore frock coats and everyone at court was more 'pulled together'. Jaques was a bit of a fop, a dandy. For Celia I found a bodice from a costume probably from the 1920s. All the women's dresses were simple country styles with reproduction patterned cottons of the early nineteenth century. Phoebe was more country and Audrey's top was very low cut, showing lots of bosom. Touchstone wore an old cut-away coat and baggy trousers, and his hair stood up on end. Period buttons were carefully searched for and chosen. Old quilts were even used for some of the women's skirts.

For period productions I typically look at paintings, photographs and actual clothing – and refer back to them in my design and construction. Right now I am excited about a costume I designed for a show at Manhattan Theatre Club, which is set in upstate New York in 1917. I had a photograph of a dress I wanted to use as an example and remembered I had seen a picture of the dress as part of a museum collection, so I tracked it down. In these instances this is a designer making a definitive choice to use a period dress that is right for the character and copying it. There is no need to make it up, if you want it to be a dress of the period.

For several years beginning in the mid-1960s I worked at the American Shakespeare Festival Theatre in Stratford, Connecticut. One of the first shows I did there was *Much Ado About Nothing* with Peter Gill directing. I had the costumes made at Ray Diffen's shop, all traditional Elizabethan clothes. Bill Cunningham was just beginning as a photographer in New York and he brought Antonio Lopez, a fashion illustrator, to look at the clothes. They were very interested in the corsets and farthingales, and took photographs of a model wearing the pieces. It intrigued me that the fashion world found this interest in taking period shapes and making them new again.

The photographs were excellent, and the costumes are on display at the Florence Griswold museum in Old Lyme, Connecticut.

I designed for *Love's Labour's Lost* as the first of a long string of shows directed by Michael Kahn, who would later become the artistic director at the American Shakespeare Festival Theatre. In Shakespeare's *Love's Labour's Lost*, the King and three lords swear off women in favour of studying and fasting. Michael Kahn had the idea for the 1968 production in Stratford that the four of them were a bit like the Beatles going to visit the Maharishi in India earlier the same year. I looked at pictures of the Fab Four in India and used them as inspiration for the costumes of the four principal actors. The girls were in colourful jumpsuits and riding Vespas. It was a very trendy and of-the-moment production, and the audience loved it. We just had a hard time keeping the girls on the Vespas: at one rehearsal, one girl rode straight into the orchestra pit but was miraculously unhurt. It was certainly a fun production.

For *The Merry Wives of Windsor* in 1971, also directed by Kahn, I looked at Elizabethan woodcut prints and copied the distinct lines of the woodcuts in all the costumes using velvet appliquéd onto homespun cotton as well as the black-and-white palette of the woodcuts. The only colours added were in certain accessories such as hats and aprons. It was a very arduous construction, and the only show at Stratford that I remember when all the clothes were late for the first dress rehearsal. Everyone had to come onstage in their tights and hats, which upset Michael Kahn, but they were all dressed by opening night – just barely!

What about your modern-dress *Hamlet*?

Here is the story of the 1964 Richard Burton *Hamlet* in rehearsal clothes: John Gielgud and Burton were making a period movie together – probably *Beckett*. As they were riding along on horseback, Gielgud asked Burton if he had considered playing Hamlet. The answer was, 'Yes, of course, but not in these clothes.'

FIGURE 18 *Jane Greenwood dresses Jan Miner for* The Merry Wives of Windsor *(1971) at the American Shakespeare Festival, Stratford, CT. Courtesy of Jane Greenwood.*

The production planning took place with John Gielgud, Ben Edwards and myself at Noël Coward's compound, Firefly, in the Caribbean. John had been invited to stay and asked us to join him for design meetings there, while at the same time enjoying the luxury of Jamaica in the winter! There were a number of little cottages on the estate and we had meetings around the swimming pool. Other actors were also there working on other productions. Then we rehearsed in Canada.

At one point during rehearsals, Gielgud became concerned about the simplicity of the costumes, which were muslin rehearsal skirts and sweaters for the women, although Gertrude does enter wearing a fur coat (her own). The men were in

FIGURE 19 *Sketch by Jane Greenwood for* The Merry Wives of Windsor *(1971), Stratford, CT. Courtesy of Jane Greenwood.*

trousers and tops. Hamlet wore a turtleneck sweater, and Polonius wore a suit with a vest. Only the Players wore medievalish costumes in bright colours, with large appliqués. They were all very bold with strong cut-outs – all very 'handmade'. The idea for this came from a set of Renaissance playing cards.

So when someone questioned Gielgud about the wisdom of the design, he thought that maybe for the play scene the court should all be wearing capes. My assistant Jack Edwards and I went back to the tailor shop and between all of us, we had a set of capes for the following day. When Gielgud saw them the next evening he admitted, 'Jane, we really don't need the capes!'

When you design, how much input do the actors have?

A designer has chosen a certain style for each production. I enjoy the process of how that can grow with the action and the actors, but also make sure that I do not lose sight of the goal! When you are designing, observing clothes being made, seeing them on the hanger, they are still yours. You can move things around; you have a licence to change. But once the actor has them on, you have to let go. They belong to the character, the actor. You move on to the next project. Sometimes the actors' requirements can upset the apple cart, but they have to make the costumes theirs – or at least their characters'. For example, in the summer of 2012 when Rosalind, played by Lily Rabe, tried on her first dress, she felt the sleeves were too fancy, so we took some of the trim off. It looked fine and in no way changed the silhouette of the dress.

What would you tell an aspiring designer?

With over fifty-odd years of designing, here are some thoughts. A costume designer has to have a strong eye muscle. It is not enough to look: you have to look hard. The difference between designing for film rather than stage is that the camera can choose what it wants to see. You can focus in on the detail of a collar or shoe. But on stage you have to remember that the audience sees the whole person all the time they are onstage. Even in the shadows, the silhouette is there. The camera can influence how the viewer sees a character, but on stage it is so much about the silhouette.

Always serve the play as clearly as possible – read and look carefully and truthfully at the piece, and know who everyone is or is pretending to be.

Teaching at Yale since 1976 has been a pleasure and a great learning experience for me. Over the years there have been many interesting students, and some have gone on to great careers, which is satisfying to see. I am grateful to all of them for helping me to accept changes in style, and not lie back on proven solutions, but rather keep looking in fresh ways.

Robert Morgan

How did you get started designing for Shakespeare productions?

After graduating from Stanford in 1969, I began designing at the Colorado Shakespeare Festival. As many of my generation were, I was enthralled by Desmond Heeley's work, and much of my early design work in Colorado was heavily influenced by him. It was a great time for young designers; the regional theatre movement was expanding rapidly, and there was an open market for young designers to step into. Bill Ball, who founded ACT (American Conservatory Theater) in San Francisco, saw my work in Colorado, and persuaded me to leave my teaching position at the University of California at Santa Barbara to join the staff of young designers at ACT. Among them were Bob Blackman and Ralph Funicello, with whom I have since happily designed dozens of productions, many of them Shakespeare. Ben Moore, who has been the Managing Director of Seattle Rep for probably twenty-five years now and was an undergraduate schoolmate of mine at Dartmouth, was the production manager.

Those were heady times. Bill was at his most brilliant with spectacular productions of *Taming of the Shrew* and *Cyrano de Bergerac*, but we young designers had to wait in line behind old hands like Ann Roth and Bob Fletcher when it came to Bill's Shakespeare and Chekhov productions. We longed to be doing those big shows, but we had the much more valuable experience of being apprenticed to great, mature designers. We perforce learned all the practical stuff, and the higher levels of our craft that were far beyond our graduate school educations.

I worked at the Oregon Shakespeare Festival in one of those early years, too, then went to the Guthrie in Minneapolis to do *Dr Faustus* with Ralph while Desmond was in residence designing a brilliant Michael Langham production of *The Matchmaker*. Ralph Funicello and I hung out with Des and watched him like hawks. We absorbed a lifetime's worth of inspiration as well as having the great honour of becoming friends with an extraordinary human being. Several times I flew back to the Guthrie to see a production Des had designed.

Specifically, I remember the Michael Langham productions of *Measure for Measure* and *The Winter's Tale*. They were exquisitely designed. Des did set design and costumes for both. I also remember that *Measure for Measure* was set in an early 1800s Vienna of wet, black brick – oh so grim – and Terry Sateren, the technical director, managed to get a misting agent piped through the theatre duct so that the whole thing was set in a miasma of smoggy, dim locales minimally lit by Duane Schuler. At one point out of this fog stepped Barbara Bryne as the old prostitute in a panniered gown of lame rags. It was pretty spectacular, and I can see it in my mind's eye, even to this day.

After my initial five-year residency at ACT, still waiting impatiently and indignantly to design Shakespeare, I went to the Old Globe in San Diego with the young and flash director Jack O'Brien to do *Hamlet*, featuring a young Mark Lamos, who had at that time made a formidable name for himself as an actor. Every costume was made from cotton velour in different shades of grey, all wet dyed. We then sewed on miles of gold and silver soutache trim, and after that the garments were sprayed with FEV (French Enamel Varnish, now outlawed) and spattered with metallic paint. It was very beautiful onstage under light, although when I occasionally run across those garments in stock I shudder at how awful they look, especially up close and under fluorescent light. The amount of labour that the shop committed in fabric prep and trim was enormous, prohibitive in this day and age. And that is when my real immersion in Shakespeare began – designing for the incomparable Jack. We did a fondly remembered 1790s production of *Midsummer Night's Dream* to a haunting Conrad Susa (American composer 1935–2013) score to open the new outdoor theatre, and years of Shakespeare followed for me at the Globe. When Jack finally left San Diego to pursue an international career, I was lucky enough to do a season of summer Shakespeare there with the director Darko Tresnjak.

For the past twelve years, I've worked at the American Players Theater in Spring Green, Wisconsin – my artistic home now – primarily with Artistic Director David Frank. In summer 2013 I got a chance to revisit *Antony and Cleopatra* in a seven-actor chamber version of the play, directed by Kate Buckley in the American Players Theater's small indoor theatre. The set was very simple, as were the clothes. I suppose the audience thought of it as modern dress, but it was in fact an abstraction that judiciously used very simple modern clothing with almost no detail. The women – Cleopatra and Charmian – wore strapless sheaths of four-ply silk crêpe that looked remarkably Egyptian one moment and like modern evening dresses the next. The men, in battle dress, wore safari wear. Their mufti was like resort wear – linen trousers, cotton sweaters. It sounds awful when I describe it, but it was remarkably effective.

Are there special challenges in designing Shakespeare productions?

Well, reading and understanding the plays, for starters. They are so fiendishly complex and yet simple, at the same time. The first time with each of the plays, you are lucky if you get even a gloss on the play that does it justice. However, you can always rely on your director and dramaturge for detailed explanations and inspiration, but then you are not bringing all of yourself to the project or in fact being very responsible. So I read and read. And I love to read Shakespeare criticism, too. I want to understand how each play works.

FIGURE 20 *Robert Morgan sketch for Maria in* Twelfth Night. *Courtesy of Robert Morgan.*

Has your process changed from when you began designing for Shakespeare and now after more experience?

I have actually thought quite a bit about this over the years. When I was young and stupid, I thought I could intuit these plays. Can you imagine? There is the presumption of youth and inexperience. I thought that I could bring something inexplicably fresh and original, and I was an incorrigible show-off. It makes me wince now to think of some of the work I put onstage. This was back in the days of high-concept productions; they were all the rage then, but not so much now. In the 1970s there was Nagel Jackson's *The Taming of the Shrew* set in the American Wild West. I remember, too, that Jack O'Brien staged *As You Like It* set in the Pacific Northwest. Ellis Rabb did a celebrated 1960s St Tropez version of *The Merchant of Venice* that featured bronzed muscle men and toy poodles. And I worked on a modern-dress Euro-punk version of *Measure for Measure* in which Lucio wore a snakeskin jump suit alongside Venice Beach types on rollerblades. It seems a tired idea now; at the time we thought we were cutting edge. I like to think that the director John Barton and Royal Shakespeare voice director Cecily Berry created a much-needed aesthetic revolution in American Shakespearean production by simply bringing us back to the words – that is, how to understand them, use them and make them paramount. The words are quicksilver, and the thoughts and emotions they evoke in a listener are more active and powerful than any static, exotic picture I can help bring to the stage.

So now I just try to play a supportive, second fiddle in the ensemble. I try to stay behind the actors now, not get out ahead of them and not overtly define character so that they cannot work their own magic and move the audience with multiple and complex perceptions. I need to be clear and supportive, but not noticed. I think, now, I mostly design social status, which requires restraint, and a pulling back from the instinct to design interior character and subtext. My job, it seems to me now, is to make clear a character's social status. Is he a Capulet or a Montague? Is he a gravedigger or a prince? It sounds like a plebeian task, and perhaps it is so, but I still find it an interesting exercise. That is where I can be helpful to the director. And designers are there to provide a service. I do not like talking about the possible art of it. That may turn up, if you are lucky and/or talented. But there is not much use in dwelling on art or analysing it or hoping for it. You just have to do the work and see what happens.

How do you usually work with the director and/or production designer?

The process varies with the individual. Some directors need to talk out loud and have extensive dialogue, in order to clarify their own thinking. Some directors read the play to you, acting out all the characters. Some come to the first meeting knowing exactly what they want design to do for their production down to the colour on the leading lady in Act 3. Some leave it all to you and really do not want to talk at all, believing that remaining indirect throws responsibility back on the designer to envision the project totally. I love working every way. If it were always the same, I would be bored stiff. Directors have the toughest job: the responsibility for everything but no control over anything. They really need you to be very good at what you do and for you to do your best. I love being able to deliver that, whenever I can. This is something I can take pride in.

I must say, I hate doing what are called 'roughs'. I don't want directors to see them, actually, because they are so undeveloped. I prefer to refine these original ideas into final colour renderings and then show them. It is only when I can get through that stage of design that I know for sure that what I have drawn and painted is what I actually mean it to be. So I would rather do colour plates and throw them away if they are wrong. At least the director is confident that they are looking at a fully considered design.

How would you describe your design process for a Shakespeare play and does this differ from your approach to other plays?

I would say that the process for a Shakespeare play is the same, inasmuch as it can ever be given the reality of different directors, texts, production and approaches. However, a Shakespearean production takes more time: time with the text, time to think, time to sketch the large casts of characters. I cannot imagine it taking less than six weeks.

Are there special problems with designing for historical periods?

I would have to say no. Designing a production in a period earlier than the last century is far easier than modern or contemporary dress, in my opinion. In earlier periods, the designer is the expert and a certain amount of abstraction of period accuracy is usually the norm, at least in theatre as opposed to film. As director Nicky Martin once trenchantly observed to me, 'Period accuracy is not a theatrical value'. The social nuance of distant past clothing is, by and large, unrecognizable to most others, so most choices fall to the designer alone. And there is greater freedom for the designer to clarify character using such basic design tools as colour, mass, texture and rhythm, without regard to the real and often incomprehensible dictates of dress at the time in question.

Designing contemporary dress is fascinating, but it can be absolute hell to get right. Nuance of social expression and supposed historical accuracy is not just the designer's province: everyone has a legitimate opinion as to what constitutes the 'rightness' of a design. This includes not just the director and the actors, but also their husbands, wives, boyfriends and girlfriends, their agents and the producer's mother.

Every time I design a play, I do research, even if I have designed in the period many times before. If I go back to the primary source material, there is always something new of interest. This keeps me from getting sloppy and designing what Maryann Verheyen (Professor of Costume Design) always calls 'oldie-timey' costumes. The best research is a museum visit to view the actual portraiture. Reproductions are second best.

Do you have a favourite period to work in when designing for Shakespeare?

No. Having said that, I love to work in the nineteenth century. It is 'ago', so you get the necessary remove for fable and myth, but you also have at hand a recognizable social dress with all of the detail necessary to flesh out character when necessary. For instance, I have always wanted to do *Love's Labour's Lost* in the 1830s. I did *Winter's Tale* in Vienna that spanned from Edwardian to the 1920s very successfully, an Edwardian *Measure for Measure*, and a *Midsummer Night's Dream* that shifted from the 1790s at the beginning to the 1810s at the end. Sometimes these elisions can theatrically enhance the arc of the story.

I actually love the transitional periods, such as Stuart costume as the bridge from Elizabethan to Cavalier; 1795 is a weird and wonderful in-between, separating mid-eighteenth-century dress and the Napoleonic period; 1914–18 between Edwardian and the 1920s. These eras are marvellously uneasy and expressive, and using them as a base for a play's design allows for great differences in clothing between the generations represented by the cast. Of course, you cannot just choose to design in these periods willy-nilly. However, when I have the opportunity, I always choose to go to these transitional periods, because they are so fresh to the eye.

I also very much enjoy working in an abstraction of the present, just as Ralph Fiennes did in the recent *Coriolanus*. The *Antony and Cleopatra* I am working on now is in that vein, and I am excited about it. It is very tough to find modern equivalents to traditional historical dress that you can mute so as not to appear merely clever. The audience always needs some help in placing the story, but really do not need too much.

You have done so many Shakespeare productions over the years, but do you have any favourites?

Oh, that *Midsummer Night's Dream* that I did with Jack O'Brien – it was an overwhelmingly magical experience due to a cosmic nexus of circumstances. We revived that production five years later, and it was stillborn. We had the form and intent of the thing, but not the particular flashes of inspiration that fired the original. It was a sobering lesson about what it takes to birth a successful production.

In conclusion, is there a Shakespearean character that you have not designed for, but that you would like to – and what would you want their look to be?

I have no idea, because I would need a director and some time to read and think. But I have always wanted to do *Troilus and Cressida*, just to understand it better. And so far I have missed out on *Much Ado*, one of my favourites. But all in all, I have had a phenomenal streak, often revisiting the biggies three or four times. It is like going to church. You know the liturgy, but it resonates differently each time.

NOTES

Introduction

1. Aoife Monks, *The Actor in Costume* (London, 2010), 142.
2. Michael Blakemore, *Next Season* (New York, 1968), 121.
3. *Rehearsing* Hamlet, dir. Joseph Papp, New York Public Theater, 1982, costumes designed by Theoni V. Aldredge. See 'Joseph Papp and Diane Venora Rehearse *Hamlet*: A Television Documentary', *Shakespeare on Screen: Hamlet*, Sara Hatchuel ed. (Montpelier, France, 2011), 117–42.
4. M.Channing Linthicum, *Costume in the Drama of Shakespeare and his Contemporaries* (New York, 1963).
5. Jean MacIntyre, *Costumes and Scripts in the Elizabethan Theatres* (Alberta, 1992), 2.
6. See Bridget Escolme, 'Costume' in *Shakespeare and the Making of Theatre* (London, 2012), 128–45; Barbara Hodgdon, 'Brideing the Shrew: Costumes That Matter' in *Shakespeare Survey 60* (Cambridge, 2007), 84–101; Barbara Hodgdon, 'Shopping in the Archives: Material Memories' and Carol Chillington Rutter, ' "Her First Remembrance of the Moor': Actors and the Materials of Memory' in *Shakespeare, Memory and Performance*, Peter Holland ed. (Cambridge, 2006), 135–67, 168–20. Jenny Tiramani, 'Exploring the Early Modern Stage and Costume Design', in *Shakespeare's Globe: A Theatrical Experiment*, Christie Carson and Farah Karim-Cooper eds (Cambridge, 2008), 57–65; Sarah Werner's introduction to *New Directions in Renaissance Drama and Performance Studies*, Sarah Werner ed. (London, 2010), 1–14. For twentieth-century costume designers, see Lynn Pecktal, *Costume Design: Techniques of Modern Masters* (New York, 1993). See also Janet Arnold, *Patterns of Fashion*, vols 1–4 (London, 1964, 1977,

1985, 2008), for the detailed information instrumental to designers recreating period dress for 1600 to 1940.

7 Ann Rosalind Jones and Peter Stallybrass, *Renaissance Clothing in the Materials of Memory* (Cambridge, 2000); Ann Rosalind Jones and Margaret Rosenthal, *Habiti Antichi et Moderni, The Clothing of the Renaissance World* (London, 2008); Susan Vincent, *Dressing the Elite* (London, 2003); Catherine Richardson, *Shakespeare and Material Culture* (Oxford, 2011); Natasha Korda, *Labor's Lost: Women's Work and the Early Modern English Stage* (Philadelphia, PA, 2011). For further texts on clothing, dress and theatre, see also Natasha Korda and Jonathan Gil Harris, *Staged Properties in Early Modern English Drama* (Cambridge, 2002); Maria Hayward, *Dress at the Court of King Henry VIII* (2007); Andrew Sofer, *The Stage Life of Props* (Ann Arbor, MI, 2003); Bella Mirabella, *Ornamentalism: the Art of Renaissance Accessories* (Ann Arbor, MI, 2011), Robert I. Lublin's *Costuming the Shakespearean Stage* (Aldershot, 2011), as well as Ulinka Rublack's *Dressing Up: Cultural Identity in Renaissance Europe* (2011), and Eugenia Paulicelli, *Writing Fashion in Early Modern Italy from Sprezzatura to Satire* (Burlington, VT, 2014), both of which further expand our understanding of attire and dress practice beyond England.

Brief Overview: A Stage History of Shakespeare and Costume

1 Valuable accounts of post-Restoration performances with an emphasis on decor and costume include: Dennis Kennedy, *Looking at Shakespeare. A Visual History of Twentieth-century Performance* (Cambridge, 1996) and Stuart Sillars, *Shakespeare, Time and the Victorians. A Pictorial Exploration* (Cambridge, 2012). Aspects of design figure prominently in the accounts of individual directors in *The Routledge Companion to Directors' Shakespeare*, John Russell Brown ed. (London and New York, 2008). Diane de Marley, *Costume on the Stage, 1600–1940* (London, 1992) and Michael Dobson and Stanley Wells, *The Oxford Companion to Shakespeare* (Oxford, 2001)

are convenient sources for illustrations of actors in Shakespearean roles.

2 For example, Kenneth Macgowan's *The Theatre of Tomorrow* (New York and London, 1923), and his collaboration with Robert Edmond Jones on *Continental Stagecraft* (New York, 1922); books in English on the great Austrian director Max Reinhardt, including Oliver Sayler's *Max Reinhardt and His Theatre* (New York, 1924).

3 Keir Elam, *The Semiotics of Theatre and Drama* (London and New York, 1980), 57.

4 David Edgar, *How Plays Work* (London, 2009), 182.

5 Roland Barthes, 'Les maladies du costume de théâtre' (*Théâtre Populaire*, March–April 1955), in *Écrits sur le théâtre*, Jean-Loup Rivière ed. (Paris, 2002), 137–41, 137.

6 The terms are drawn from Richard Marienstras, *Le proche et le lointain: Sur Shakespeare, le drame élisabéthain et l'idéologie anglaise aux XVIe et XVIIe siècles* (Paris, 1981).

7 Claire Cochrane, *Shakespeare at the Birmingham Repertory Theatre, 1913–1929* (London, 1993), chs 6 and 7, gives a detailed account of these influential productions and their reception.

8 See R.A.Foakes, *Illustrations of the English Stage, 1580–1642* (London, 1985), 49–51.

9 Jean MacIntyre, *Costumes and Scripts in the Elizabethan Theatres* (Edmonton, 1992), ch. 1, 'Conventions of Costume and Costume Change', emphasizes the dramaturgical significance of apparel.

10 Kalman A. Burnim, *David Garrick, Director* (Pittsburgh, PA, 1961), 76.

11 On Macklin's decision to attempt appropriately Scottish dress, see William W. Appleton, *Charles Macklin. An Actor's Life* (Cambridge, MA, 1961), 172–5.

12 Burnim, *David Garrick*, 77.

13 Two notable images of Garrick in this costume, including an engraving of Hogarth's painting, are illustrated and discussed in the catalogue of an exhibition at the Courtauld Gallery, London: *Theatre in the Age of Garrick. English Mezzotints from the Collection of the Hon. Christopher Lennox-Boyd*, Christopher

Lennox-Boyd, Guy Shaw and Sarah Halliwell eds (London, 1994), 67–8.

14 Sybil Rosenfeld, *A Short History of Scene Design in Great Britain* (Oxford, 1973), 97, quoting James Boaden's *Memoirs of the Life of John Philip Kemble* (Philadelphia, PA, 1825).

15 Wilde's remark is quoted by W. Graham Robertson, *Time Was* (London, 1931), 151.

16 Sally Beauman, *The Royal Shakespeare Company. A History of Ten Decades* (Oxford, 1982), 60.

17 On Barker's productions, see Dennis Kennedy, *Granville Barker and the Dream of Theatre* (Cambridge, 1985) (Barker did not hyphenate his name until later in his career).

18 J.L.Styan, *The Shakespeare Revolution* (Cambridge, 1977).

19 See Michael Mullin, *Design by Motley* (Cranbury, NJ, 1996).

20 On Moiseiwitsch's career, see the lavishly illustrated exhibition catalogue *The Stage is All the World* (Chicago, IL, 1994).

21 The permutations on the *Dream* are described by Gary Jay Williams, *Our Moonlight Revels: 'A Midsummer Night's Dream' in the Theatre* (Iowa City, IA, 1997).

22 Jenny Tiramani, 'Janet Arnold and the Globe Wardrobe: Handmade Clothes for Shakespeare's Actors', *Costume: The Journal of the Costume Society* 34 (2000), 118–22.

23 Doris Zinkeisen, *Designing for the Stage* (London and New York, [1938]), 5, 54.

'The Compass of a Lie'? Royal Clothing at Court and in the Plays of Shakespeare, 1598–1613

I am most grateful to Bella Mirabella and Patricia Lennox for their help in bringing this chapter to fruition. I would also like to thank Mark Stoyle and Catherine Richardson for their comments on earlier drafts. All references to Shakespeare plays are from *The Arden Complete Works*, Third series, Richard Proudfoot, Ann Thompson and Daniel Scott Kastan, eds (London, 2011).

1 Stephen Gosson, *Playes confuted in fiue actions* (London, 1582), C5r.
2 Thomas Dekker, *The Magnificent Entertainment* (London, 1604), I2v.
3 Quoted by Gerard H. Cox, ' "Like a Prince Indeed": Hal's triumph on Honor in 1 Henry IV', in *Pageantry in the Shakespearean Theater*, David M. Bergeron ed. (Athens, OH, 1985), 135. Shakespeare's references to 'a fair vestal, throned by the west' (2.1.158) and 'the imperial votress' (2.1.163) in *A Midsummer Night's Dream* have been seen as acknowledging Elizabeth's love of the theatre.
4 James Craigie ed., *Basilicon Doron of King James VI* (Edinburgh, 1944), 1, 163. For the wider context see Susan Vincent, *Dressing the Elite: Clothes in Early Modern England* (London, 2003).
5 Ann Rosalind Jones and Peter Stallybrass, *Renaissance Clothing and the Materials of Memory* (Cambridge, 2000), 2; Catherine Richardson, *Shakespeare and Material Culture* (Oxford, 2011), 5–14.
6 The will of the actor Simon Jewell, who died in 1592, is a good example. His assets included his share of the company's 'horses waggen and apparel newe boughte', 'a blacke veluet purse imbrodered with golde and siluer' and 'all my playenge thinges in a box and my veluet shewes', the latter being left to another actor, Robert Nichols, The National Archive, Kew (TNA) PCC 63 Harrington; published as Mary Edmonds, 'Pembroke's men', *Review of English Studies*, ns 25 (1974), 129–36. Scott McMillin and Sally-Beth MacLean, *The Queen's Men and their Plays* (Cambridge, 1998), 61.
7 For Elizabeth's craftsmen and women, see Janet Arnold, *Queen Elizabeth's Wardrobe Unlock'd* (Leeds, 1988), ch. 8. For the broader London context see Jane Ashelford, *Dress in the Age of Elizabeth I* (London, 1988).
8 TNA LC9/93, f. 55r.
9 Analysis of TNA LC9/52 (1557–8) to LC9/93 (1602–3).
10 Figures derived from British Library (BL) Stowe MS 557. For a glossary of textile and clothing terms see *Queen Elizabeth's Wardrobe*, 359–76.

11 TNA, AO3/1115 and LC9/96.

12 Analysis of the accounts in TNA LC5/37.

13 Analysis of the accounts in TNA LC5/37.

14 Analysis of the accounts in TNA LC5/37.

15 Analysis of the four gift rolls: TNA C47/3/40 (1598), Folger Shakespeare Library MS.Z.d.17 (1599), Musée Fondation Martin Bodmer, Bodmer MS (BL MS RP 294) Geneva (1600); from *The Elizabethan New Year's Gift Exchanges 1559–1603*, Jane A. Lawson ed., 482–99 and TNA C47/3/41 (1603).

16 TNA, C47/3/40.

17 Figures derived from TNA, C47/3/41.

18 TNA, C47/3/41.

19 Or, as Shepherd observed about Autolycus' clothes in *The Winter's Tale*, 'His garments are rich, but he wears them not handsomely' (4.4.751–2).

20 TNA 31/3/29, f. 204v. The latter were styled in a variety of ways, as seen in her portraits and descriptions such as that of de Maisse from 1597 'on either side of her ears hung two great curls of hair, almost down to her shoulders'.

21 TNA LC5/37, 212, 257. These royal wigs may have inspired Shakespeare's description of 'crisped, snaky golden locks' in *The Merchant of Venice* (3.2.92), which were 'often known to be the dowry of a second head' (3.2.94–5).

22 According to Sir John Fortescue in *The Governance of England*, a king was expected to buy 'riche clothes, riche furres, other than be wonned to fall vndre theyerely charges off his wardrober, rich stones . . . and other juels and ornamentes conuenyent to his estate roiall . . . and do other such nobell and grete costes, as bi sitith is roiall mageste', in *Sir John Fortescue on The Governance of England*, C.Plummer ed. (Oxford, 1885), 125.

23 Paul Hentzner, *Travels in England During the Reign of Queen Elizabeth . . . to which is now added Sir Robert Naunton's Fragmenta Regalia* (London, 1797), 26.

24 Lisa Jardine, ' "Maketh thy doublet of changeable taffeta": Dress codes, sumptuary law and "natural orders" ', in *Still*

Harping On: Women and Drama in the Age of Shakespeare, L.Jardine ed. (Sussex, 1983), 141–68.

25 There is an extensive literature on sumptuary legislation. See Winifred Hooper, 'The Tudor Sumptuary Laws', *English Historical Review* 30 (1915), 433–49; F.E.Baldwin, *Sumptuary Legislation and Personal Regulation in England* (Baltimore, MD, 1926); Negley B. Harte, 'State Control over Dress and Social Change in Pre-industrial England', in *Trade, Government and Economy in Pre-Industrial England: Essays Presented to F. J. Fisher*, D.C.Coleman and A.H.Johns eds (London, 1976), 132–65. Alan Hunt, *Governance of the Consuming Passions: A History of Sumptuary Law* (New York, 1996); Maria Hayward, *Rich Apparel: Clothing and the Law in Henry VIII's England* (Aldershot, 2009), 17–39.

26 Judith H. Hofenk de Graaff, Wilma G. Roelofs and Maarten van Bommel, *The Colourful Past: The Origins, Chemistry and Identification of Natural Dyestuffs* (London, 2004), 264–83. It is telling that there is no entry for purple in M.Channing Linthicum, *Costume in the Drama of Shakespeare and his Contemporaries* (Oxford, 1936).

27 Jane Lawson, 'Rainbow for a Reign: The Colours of a Queen's Wardrobe', *Costume* 31 (2007), 26–44. The link between purple and royalty is demonstrated by a sequence of entertainments held over the Christmas period in the winter of 1594–5 when Gray's Inn held a procession on horseback through the city by the 'Prince of Purpoole' and observers thought he must be 'some great prince, in very deed, passing through the City', *Gesta Grayorum or the History of the High and Mighty Prince Henry of Purpoole*, D.Bland ed. (Liverpool, 1968), 57.

28 R.A.Foakes ed., *Henslowe's Diary* (Cambridge, 1961, 2002), 294.

29 Shakespeare drew on a range of sources including Hall's Chronicle and Holinshed's Chronicle. See Annabel Patterson, *Reading Holinshed's Chronicles* (Chicago, 1994), Peter Saccio, *Shakespeare's English Kings: History, Chronicle and Drama* (Oxford, 1977) and Geoffrey Bullough, *Narrative and Dramatic Sources of Shakespeare*, 8 volumes (London, 1957–75), especially volumes 3 and 4.

30 Maria Hayward, *Dress at the Court of King Henry VIII* (Leeds, 2007), 134–5.

31 David R. Starkey, 'Henry VI's Old Blue Gown', *The Court Historian* 4(1) (1999), 2–3.

32 Horatio Brown ed., *Calendar of State Papers, Venetian, 1603–07* (London, 1900), 66. For a wider discussion on the significance of diamonds see Marcia Pointon, *Brilliant Effects: A Cultural History of Gem Stones and Jewellery* (New Haven, CT and London, 2010).

33 Diana Scarisbrick, *Jewellery in Britain 1066–1837* (London, 1994), ch. 3 and more specifically, Diana Scarisbrick, *Tudor and Jacobean Jewellery, 1508–1625* (London, 1996).

34 Mary Sullivan, *Court Masques of James I: Their Influence on Shakespeare and the Public Theatres* (New York, 1913), 113. See Karen Raper, 'Chains of Pearls: Gender, Property, Identity', in *Ornamentalism: The Art of Renaissance Accessories*, Bella Mirabella ed. (Ann Arbor, MI, 2011), 159–81.

35 Foakes, *Henslowe's Diary*, 317–18.

36 John Harington, *Nugae Antiquae*, I (London, 1804), 170–1.

37 Coronation conferred the ability to heal by touch on the monarch and consequently, anything touching the monarch's skin was by implication felt to be special. For more on this topic, see Marc Bloch, *Royal Touch: Sacred Monarchy and Scrofula in England and France*, trans. J.E.Anderson (London, 1973).

38 For a fuller discussion, see Ernst Kantorowicz, *The King's Two Bodies: A Study in Medieval Political Theology* (Princeton, NJ, 1957), 24.

39 Jenny Tiramani, 'Pins and Aglets', in *Everyday Objects: Medieval and Early Modern Material Culture and its Meanings*, T.Hamling and C.Richardson eds (Farnham, 2010), 85–94.

40 For example, the queen was painted wearing her parliament robes in *Elizabeth I with the Cardinal and Theological Virtues*, unknown artist, *c.*1598, Dover Museum and Bronze Age Boat Gallery, see Tarnya Cooper and Jane Eade, *Elizabeth and Her People* (London, 2013), 72–3.

41 B.L.Stowe MS 557, ff.5r, 8r, 11r. For a wider discussion of Elizabeth's robes, see Arnold, *Queen Elizabeth's Wardrobe*, 52–69; Anne F. Sutton, 'The Coronation Robes of Richard III and Anne Neville', *Costume* 13 (1979), 8–16.

42 B.L.Stowe MS 557, f.11r.

43 Foakes, *Henslowe's Diary*, 292.

44 Other indicators of rank were the amount of fur used on the robes, and the pattern and placement of the ermine tails; see Hayward, *Dress*, 222–3.

45 Ann Pasternak Slater, *Shakespeare the Director* (Sussex, 1982), 157–64. King Lear, Goneril, Regan, Kent and Edgar all make references to mantles, whether real or as a metaphor for concealment. Some of the references are a play on words as in the case of Cordelia's reference to her having had 'to dismantle / So many folds of favour' (*KL*, 1.1.238–9).

46 Janet Dillon, *Shakespeare and the Staging of English History* (Oxford, 2012), especially ch. 5.

47 A.Jefferies Collins ed., *Jewels and Plate of Queen Elizabeth I: The Inventory of 1574* (London, 1955), 264, 266.

48 For example, see John Donne's satire 'Well; I may now receive':

As fresh, and sweet their apparels be, as be
The fields they sold to buy them; 'For a king
Those hose are', cry the flatterers; and bring
Them next week to the theatre to sell.

(*Satire IV*, 180–4)

49 Foakes, *Henslowe's Diary*, 323.

50 Arnold, *Queen Elizabeth*, 7. Other aspects of this source are problematic – in particular the ambassador's reference to seeing the queen's breasts and belly.

51 TNA, AO1/2048/1, f.6r. Also see Arnold, *Queen Elizabeth*, 139–41.

52 Alan C. Dessen and Leslie Thomson, *A Dictionary of Stage Directions in English Drama, 1580–1642* (Cambridge, 1999), 150.

53 For example, Julius Caesar was described as wearing a doublet (*JC*, 1.2.264).

54 See Alexander Leggatt, *Shakespare's Political Drama: The History Plays and the Roman Plays* (London, 1988). For similar parallels in the use of ceremony in plays set in classical Rome and England's medieval past, see Michael Neill,' "Exeunt with a Dead March": Funeral Pageantry on the Shakespearean Stage', in *Pageantry in the Shakespearean Theater*, David M. Bergeron ed. (Athens, GA, 1981), 169–70.

55 For example, *Hamlet*, 2.2.453–4; Pasternak Slater, *Shakespeare the Director*, 141–2.

56 See 'Journey through England and Scotland made by Lupold von Wedel in the years 1584 and 1585', *Transactions of the Royal Historical Society*, New Series, 9 (1895), 250.

57 For a fuller discussion of how need is represented in *King Lear*, see Pasternak Slater, *Shakespeare and the Director*, 157–64.

58 Ian Archer, 'City and Court Connected: The Material Dimensions of Royal Ceremonial', *Huntington Library Quarterly* 71(1) (2008), 157–79. For the significance of red for coronations, see Maria Hayward, 'Crimson, Scarlet, Murrey and Carnation: Red at the Court of Henry VIII', *Textile History* 38(2) (2007), 135–50.

59 TNA, LC2/4/5, f.78.

60 The stage directions for the coronation procession of Anne Boleyn, after 4.1.37:

> 'The order of the coronation. 1. A lively flourish of trumpets. 2. Then, two Judges. 3. Lord CHANCELLOR, with purse and mace before him. 4. Choristers singing. Music. 5. Mayor of London, bearing the mace. Then GARTER, in his coat of arms, and on his head he wears a gilt copper crown. 6. Marquess Dorset, bearing a sceptre of gold, on his head a demi-coronal of gold. With him the Earl of SURREY, bearing the rod of silver with the dove, crowned with an earl's coronet. Collars of esses. 7. Duke of SUFFOLK, in his robe of estate, his coronet on his head, bearing a long white wand, as High Steward. With him, the Duke of NORFOLK, with the rod of marshalship, a coronet on his head. Collars of esses. 8. A canopy, borne by four of the Cinque Ports; under it, the Queen [ANNE] in her robe, in her hair, richly adorned with pearl; crowned. On each side of her, the Bishops of London

and Winchester. 9. The old Duchess of Norfolk, in a coronal of gold wrought with flowers, bearing the Queen's train. 10. Certain Ladies or Countesses, with plain circlets of gold without flowers. Exeunt, first passing over the stage in order and state, and then a great flourish of trumpets.

The stage directions for the christening of princess Elizabeth, at the beginning of 5.4:

Enter trumpets sounding; then two Aldermen, Lord Mayor, GARTER, CRANMER, Duke of NORFOLK with his marshal's staff, Duke of SUFFOLK, two Noblemen bearing great standing bowls for the christening gifts; then four Noblemen bearing a canopy, under which the Duchess of Norfolk, godmother, bearing the child richly habited in a mantle, etc., train borne by a Lady; then follows the Marchioness Dorset, the other godmother, and Ladies. The troop pass once about the stage, and Garter speaks.

William Shakespeare and John Fletcher, *King Henry VIII (All is True)*, Gordon McMullan ed. (London, 2000).

61 Jonathan Bate and Dora Thornton, *Shakespeare: Staging the World* (London, 2012), 211, 213. For the differences in James's style of rule in Scotland and England, see Jenny Wormald, 'James VI and I: Two Kings or One?', *History* 68 (1983), 187–209.

62 Cox, 'Like a Prince Indeed', 130–49.

63 Foakes, *Henslowe's Diary*, 217, 323.

64 Albert Feuillerat, *Documents Relating to the Office of the Revels in the Time of Queen Elizabeth* (Louvain, 1908), 142.

65 Tobias Capwell, *The Noble Art of the Sword: Fashion and Fencing in Renaissance Europe 1520–1630* (London, 2012), 82–111.

66 Foakes, *Henslowe's Diary*, 61.

67 See Judith Richards, ' "To Promote a Woman to Beare Rule": Talking of Queens in Mid-Tudor England', *Sixteenth Century Journal* 28(1) (1997), 101–21. Roy Strong, *The Cult of Elizabeth: Elizabethan Portraiture and Pageantry* (London, 1977), 50–2, 154, 156, and Karen Hearn, *Dynasties: Painting in Tudor and Jacobean England, 1530–1630* (London, 1995), 89–90.

68 Arnold, *Queen Elizabeth's Wardrobe*, ch. 6; Maria Hayward, 'Dressed to Impress', in *Tudor Queenship: The Reigns of Mary and Elizabeth*, A.Hunt and A.Whitelock eds (Basingstoke, 2010), 88–90. Janet Arnold, 'The Pair of Straight Bodies and a Pair of Drawers Dating from 1603 which Clothe the Effigy of Queen Elizabeth I in Westminster Abbey', *Costume* 41 (2007), 1–10.

69 Hayward, *Dress and Kingship* (forthcoming). James ordered suits in significant numbers including sixty-five in 1603–4 and fifty-one in 1613–14. In contrast he ordered far fewer cloaks, but these were often flamboyant in style and decoration as was the case with a cloak of black uncut velvet cut in flowers, the skirts lined with peach cloth of silver cut in flowers and bordered with silk lace.

70 Shakespeare did not create his strongest royal queen, Cleopatra, until after Elizabeth's death. While Cleopatra compared herself to Isis, goddess of fertility, and Elizabeth promoted herself as the virgin queen, both women ruled in a male world, both exploited their position to play the game of courtly love, and both dressed to impress; Bate and Thornton, *Shakespeare: Staging the World*, 140–2.

71 Hayward, *Dress*, 111. Also see David Bevington, *Action is Eloquence: Shakespeare's Language of Gesture* (Cambridge, MA, 1984), 49.

72 See Dillon, *Shakespeare and the Staging*, 70–2.

73 And when offered the chance to remove the sheet, Cobham observed:

> My shame will not be shifted with my sheet:
> No, it will hang upon my richest robes
> And show itself, attire me how I can.
>
> (*2H6*, 2.4.107–9)

74 For more on disguisings see W.R.Streitberger, *Court Revels 1485–1559* (Toronto, 1994), 3–4.

75 For the Elizabethan revels see E.K. Chambers, *The Elizabethan Stage*, I (Oxford, 1923), 71–105. Also Streitberger, *Court Revels*, 225–30.

76 Dillon, *Early English Theatre*, 127.

77 Feuillerat, *Documents*, 320.

78 Feuillerat, *Documents*, 27.

79 'of hys lyvynge herbye who havynge apparell to lett & cannot so cheplye lett the same as hyr hyghnes maskes be lett', Albert Feuillerat, *Documents Relating to the Office of the Revels in the Time of Queen Elizabeth* (Louvain, 1908), 409.

80 David R. Starkey, *Rivals in Power: Lives and Letters of the Great Tudor Dynasties* (London, 1990), 266.

81 Thomas Churchyard who devised the entertainments for Elizabeth's visit to Norwich in 1578 complained that rain had damaged 'Veluets, Silkes, Tinsels, and some cloth of golde, being cutte out for these purposes', in *A Discourse of the Queenes Maiesties entertainement* (London, 1578), E4v, quoted in David M. Bergeron, 'The "I" of the Beholder: Thomas Churchyard and the 1578 Norwich Pageant', in *The Progresses, Pageants and Entertainments of Queen Elizabeth I*, Jayne E. Archer, Elizabeth Goldring and Sarah Knight eds (Oxford, 2007), 156.

82 Anne Somerset, *Elizabeth I* (London, 1977), 471–2.

83 Feuillerat, *Documents*, 392.

84 For progresses in general see Archer, Goldring and Knight eds, *Progresses*. For the 1573 progress to Kent see ibid, 35, 55. For more detail relating to the 1573 progress, see James Gibson ed., *Kent: Diocese of Canterbury*, 3 volumes, Record of Early English Drama (2003), 1.95, 201–2; 2.549–51, 857–8.

85 Feuillerat, *Documents*, 185.

86 E.K.Chambers, *William Shakespeare: Facts and Problems* (Oxford, 1930), 1, 372.

87 Arthur F. Kinney ed., *Elizabethan and Jacobean England: Sources and Documents of the English Renaissance* (Chichester, 2010), 366.

88 For clothing being used as security for loans, see Foakes, *Henslowe's Diary*, xxv–xxvii. For clothing listed in wills and inventories see Susan North, 'What the Elizabethans Wore: Evidence from Wills and Inventories of the "Middling Sort" ', in *Elizabeth I and her People*, Tarnya Cooper and Jade Eade eds (London, 2013), 34–41.

89 L.Pearsall Smith ed., *Life and Letters of Henry Wotton* (London, 1907), 2, 32.

90 Janet Dillon, *The Cambridge Introduction to Early English Theatre* (Cambridge, 2006), 122.

91 Dillon, *Shakespeare and the Staging*, 63–5; Kevin A. Quarmby, *The Disguised Ruler in Shakespeare and His Contemporaries* (Farnham, 2012), 46–56.

92 G.Chambers, *The Life of Mary Queen of Scots: Drawn from the State Papers* (London, 1818), 1, 275.

93 Antonia Fraser, *Mary Queen of Scots* (London, 2002), 445–6.

94 Blair Worden, 'Which Play was Performed at the Globe Theatre on 7 February 1601?', *London Review of Books* 25, 10 July 2003.

95 Chambers, *William Shakespeare*, 2, 326. Bate and Thornton, *Shakespeare: Staging the World*, 97–8. For a detailed discussion of the clothes depicted in the coronation portrait and their significance, see Janet Arnold, 'The Coronation Portrait of Queen Elizabeth I', *Burlington Magazine* 120 (1978), 727–41. The figure of Tamora, in the sketch attributed to Henry Peacham and thought to depict a scene from *Titus Andronicus*, is important in this context. Tamora is shown kneeling, wearing a crown, with her hair hanging down her back. The significance of this can be read in various ways. While potentially a symbol of her pleading, or her paganism as queen of the Goths, English queens went to their coronations with their hair loose over their shoulders; see S.P.Cerasano,' "Borrowed Robes", Costume Prices, and the Drawing of *Titus Andronicus*', *Shakespeare Studies* 22 (1994), 47.

96 Philip Sidney, *Apology for Poetry*, 1595; Dillon, *Early English Theatre*, 155.

97 Jenny Tiramani, 'The Sanders Portrait', *Costume*, 39 (2005), 43–52.

98 Gosson, *Playes*, C5r.

Suits of Green: Festive Livery on Shakespeare's Stage

1 Quotations from Shakespeare's plays are from *The Merchant of Venice*, John Drakakis ed., The Arden Shakespeare, Third Series (London, 2010). Portions of this essay originally appeared

in Erika T. Lin, 'Popular Festivity and the Early Modern Stage: The Case of *George a Greene*', *Theatre Journal* 61 (2009), 271–97, © 2009 The Johns Hopkins University Press. Revised and reprinted with permission of Johns Hopkins University Press.

2 Livery was also used in a variety of other contexts, including the battlefield, the court and London's profession-based livery companies. On late medieval courtly livery practices during the May holidays, see Susan Crane, *The Performance of Self: Ritual, Clothing, and Identity During the Hundred Years War* (Philadelphia, PA, 2002), 39–72. On the livery companies, see Steve Rappaport, *Worlds Within Worlds: Structures of Life in Sixteenth-Century London* (Cambridge, 1989).

3 For issues related to the play's authorship and date as well as other versions of the tale and its hero, see Lin, 'Popular Festivity', 272 n.3, 274 n.5, 274 n.7, 275 n.8, 276–7.

4 Quotations from the play are taken from *A Pleasant Conceyted Comedie of George a Greene, the Pinner of Wakefield* (London, 1599).

5 The giving of livery and a fee in exchange for service can also be found in all of the ballads related to the play. For more details, see Lin, 'Popular Festivity', 291 n.74.

6 Ann Rosalind Jones and Peter Stallybrass, *Renaissance Clothing and the Materials of Memory* (Cambridge, 2000), 20.

7 Alexandra F. Johnston, 'The Robin Hood of the Records', in *Playing Robin Hood: The Legend as Performance in Five Centuries*, Lois Potter ed. (Newark, DE, 1998), 27–44, especially 33, 40. In *The Early Plays of Robin Hood* (Cambridge, 1981), David Wiles argues that Robin Hood and the May Lord, or Summer King, were the same figure. However, see Alexandra F. Johnston and Sally-Beth MacLean, 'Reformation and Resistance in Thames/Severn Parishes: The Dramatic Witness', in *The Parish in English Life, 1400–1600*, Katherine L. French, Gary G. Gibbs, and Beat A. Kümin eds (Manchester, 1997), 178–200, 183 n.15; and Johnston, 'Robin Hood of the Records', 29–30, 33, 36, for compelling arguments against Wiles's assertion. For a view somewhere in between, see Paul Whitfield White's introduction to the texts of the late

sixteenth-century Robin Hood games in *Robin Hood and Other Outlaw Tales* (2nd ed.), Stephen Knight and Thomas Ohlgren eds (Kalamazoo, MI, 2000), 281–2.

8 Wiles, *Early Plays of Robin Hood*, 13; Sally-Beth MacLean, 'King Games and Robin Hood: Play and Profit at Kingston upon Thames', *Research Opportunities in Renaissance Drama* 29 (1986–7), 85–93, 89; James D. Stokes, 'Robin Hood and the Churchwardens in Yeovil', *Medieval and Renaissance Drama in England* 3 (1986), 1–25, 5; and John Wasson, 'The St. George and Robin Hood Plays in Devon', *Medieval English Theatre* 2 (1980), 67–8, 67. The anonymous poem *A Gest of Robyn Hode*, first published early in the sixteenth century, also mentions green clothing, although it refers to 'Lyncolne grene'. *A Gest of Robyn Hode*, in Knight and Ohlgren, *Robin Hood and Other Outlaw Tales*, line 1685. All subsequent quotations from *A Gest* will be from this edition.

9 These include 'j hatte for Robin Hoode', a 'Roben Hoodes sewtte' and 'the fryers trusse in Roben Hoode'. *Henslowe's Diary* (2nd ed.), R.A.Foakes ed. (Cambridge, 2002), 317–18, 322–3. Given the obvious connection with George a Greene's name as well as the livery he gives to Jenkin, it seems likely that green costumes would have been worn in this play not only by the outlaw and his men but also by the pinder and his servant. For more on green, see Bruce R. Smith, *The Key of Green: Passion and Perception in Renaissance Culture* (Chicago, IL, 2009), especially ch. 6, 'The Curtain between the Theatre and the Globe', which briefly addresses questions of costume and livery.

10 Indeed, the practice of a single player taking on multiple roles became an increasingly essential component of early modern performance. The fifteenth-century Croxton *Play of the Sacrament* included twelve characters divided among nine different performers. By the early years of Elizabeth's reign, each actor took, on average, three to four parts in a single play. By the end of the sixteenth century, we find that, in *The Seven Deadly Sins, Part Two* (*c.*1590), John Sincler played five different roles and Richard Cowley played seven. W.R. Streitberger, 'Personnel and Professionalization', in *A New History of Early English Drama*, John D. Cox and David Scott

Kastan eds (New York, 1997), 337–55, 340; and Andrew Gurr, *The Shakespearean Stage, 1574–1642* (3rd ed.) (Cambridge, 1992), 105.

11 Quotations are taken from Philip Stubbes, *The Anatomie of Abuses: Contayning a Discouerie, or Briefe Summarie of Such Notable Vices and Imperfections, as Now Raigne in Many Christian Countreyes of the Worlde: but (Especiallie) in a Verie Famous Ilande Called Ailgna* (London, 1583). The popular pamphlet was subsequently reprinted in 1584, 1585 and 1595. For more recent editions, see Arthur Freeman ed., *The Anatomie of Abuses* (New York, 1973) and *The Second Part of the Anatomie of Abuses* (New York, 1973), as well as Margaret Jane Kidnie ed., *Philip Stubbes, The Anatomie of Abuses* (Tempe, AZ, 2002).

12 Wiles, *Early Plays of Robin Hood*, 9, 13–14; MacLean, 'King Games and Robin Hood', 86–7. For further accounts of Robin Hood activities, see Lin, 'Popular Festivity', 284–91; Wiles, *Early Plays of Robin Hood*; Ronald Hutton, *The Stations of the Sun: A History of the Ritual Year in Britain* (Oxford, 1996), 270–4; and John Forrest, *The History of Morris Dancing, 1458–1750* (Toronto, 1999).

13 Jones and Stallybrass, *Renaissance Clothing*, 181–93. On 'cast clothing', see Urvashi Chakravarty, 'Livery, Liberty, and Legal Fictions', *English Literary Renaissance* 42 (2012), 365–90, especially 369, 386–9. Cast livery functioned as material currency, allowing for the transfer of wealth from master to servant, though such transactions were never purely economic, of course. For more on the second-hand clothing trade and its ties to theatre as well as to thievery, see also Natasha Korda, 'The Case of Moll Frith: Women's Work and the "All-Male Stage" ', in *Women Players in England, 1500–1660: Beyond the All-Male Stage*, Pamela Allen Brown and Peter Parolin eds (Aldershot, 2005), 71–87.

14 As Andrew Gurr notes, 'The Earl of Leicester paid £543 for seven doublets and two cloaks, at an average cost for each item rather higher than the price Shakespeare paid for a house in Stratford'; and as Jones and Stallybrass so aptly put it, 'Whatever we might think about the price of an Armani suit, we could not equate its cost with the price of a house'. Gurr,

Shakespearean Stage, 13; Jones and Stallybrass, *Renaissance Clothing*, 178.

15 *Oxford English Dictionary (OED) Online*, 2nd ed. (1989), s.v. 'guarded, *adj.*' (def. 3a), published online June 2013, http://www.oed.com.mutex.gmu.edu/view/Entry/82143.

16 *OED Online*. On livery and servants working against their masters' interests, see Amanda Bailey, *Flaunting: Style and the Subversive Male Body in Renaissance England* (Toronto, 2007), 51–76. Bailey notes, for instance, one account that specifically inveighs against servants once 'wont to wear blue Coates' who now 'most commonly weare cloakes garded with laces' (55). Chakravarty offers a different reading here, arguing that 'guarded' implies Bassanio's generosity as a master ('Livery', 375). This interpretation is convincing insofar as it affirms the play's general sense that Bassanio is, like Lancelot, an 'unthrifty knave' (1.3.172) and thus becomes dependent on Shylock as a result of his extravagance. However, Chakravarty's excellent article also draws attention to contradictions in livery's function as a mark not only of servitude but also of freedom – a view that complements my sense of 'guarded' livery's association with upstart servants and, thus, with notions of festive inversion, which I discuss further on pp. 53–58.

17 *OED Online*, 2nd ed., s.v. 'guard, *n.*' (def. 11c), published online June 2013, http://www.oed.com.mutex.gmu.edu/view/Entry/82132.

18 For more on references to servants as 'bluecoats', see Chakravarty, 'Livery', 369, 376–85; and G.K.Hunter, 'Flatcaps and Bluecoats: Visual Signals on the Elizabethan Stage', *Essays and Studies* n.s. 33 (1980), 16–47.

19 I refer to his father throughout as 'Gobbo' (instead of 'Giobbe' or 'Iobbe', which, as many scholars have noted, was the Italian form of 'Job') specifically because of the name's festive implications. As Arden editor John Drakakis records, John Florio defined 'Gobbo' in 1611 as meaning, among other things, 'crooke backe'. This definition, I would argue, underscores the contrast between age and youth, an issue I have written about elsewhere in relation to early modern cross-dressing and that here plays into subsequent stage business about Lancelot's beard as well. See Erika T. Lin, 'A Witch in the Morris: Hobbyhorse

Tricks and Early Modern Erotic Transformations', in *The Oxford Handbook of Dance and Theater*, Nadine George-Graves ed. (Oxford, forthcoming); and Drakakis, *Merchant*, 166–7.

20 On 'fortune' as a concept having both economic and religious overtones, see Jane Hwang Degenhardt, 'The Meta-theatrical Mediterranean: Theatrical Contrivance and Miraculous Reunion in *The Travels of The Three English Brothers*, *The Four Prentices of London*, and *Pericles*', in *Rivalry and Rhetoric in the Early Modern Mediterranean*, Barbara Fuchs and Emily Weissbourd eds (Toronto, forthcoming).

21 According to Knight and Ohlgren, '[t]he phrase *cloth and fee*' in *A Gest* 'echoes the Latin formula *cum robis et foedis*, used to designate payment of legal services with both money and gifts of clothing' (line 416n).

22 Adrienne Williams Boyarin, *Miracles of the Virgin in Medieval England: Law and Jewishness in Marian Legends* (Cambridge, 2010), 32 (italics in original). The miracle tale exists in Latin as well as in two Middle English versions from *c*.1390 to *c*.1450. For the text of the English miracle tale, see Beverly Boyd, *The Middle English Miracles of the Virgin* (San Marino, CA, 1964), 44–9; and Carl Horstmann ed., *The Minor Poems of the Vernon MS*, Early English Text Society, o.s. 98 (London, 1892), 157–61. For the connection between this tale and Robin Hood, see Knight and Ohlgren's comments in *A Gest*, introduction (82) and also line 255n; and William H. Clawson, *The Gest of Robin Hood* (Toronto, 1909), 25–41. On Robin Hood's traditional association with the Virgin Mary, see Paul Whitfield White, *Drama and Religion in English Provincial Society, 1485–1660* (Cambridge, 2008), 59–62.

23 On early modern stage make-up, see Farah Karim-Cooper, *Cosmetics in Shakespearean and Renaissance Drama* (Edinburgh, 2006); and Andrea Ria Stevens, *Inventions of the Skin: The Painted Body in Early English Drama, 1400–1642* (Edinburgh, 2013).

24 On early modern notions of beards as situated in the interstices between the categories of costume, prop, and body part, see Will Fisher, *Materializing Gender in Early Modern English Literature and Culture* (Cambridge, 2006), 83–128.

25 See, for example, Drakakis, *Merchant*, 2.2.76–7n.

26 On the mobility of sartorial signifiers used to represent Jews, see Peter Berek, ' "Looking Jewish" on the Early Modern Stage', in *Religion and Drama in Early Modern England: The Performance of Religion on the Renaissance Stage*, Jane Hwang Degenhardt and Elizabeth Williamson eds (Farnham, 2011), 55–70.

27 See, for example, Claire Sponsler, *Drama and Resistance: Bodies, Goods, and Theatricality in Late Medieval England* (Minneapolis, MN, 1997), 24–49; and Margo Todd, 'Profane Pastimes and the Reformed Community: The Persistence of Popular Festivities in Early Modern Scotland', *Journal of British Studies* 39 (2000), 123–56.

28 Chakravarty reads this line as underscoring Bassanio's power and wealth ('Livery', 375). Arden editor John Drakakis glosses it as putting the 'servants to their work (i.e. the preparations for supper); *liveries* is a metonymy for servingmen' (2.2.109n).

29 Meg Twycross and Sarah Carpenter, *Masks and Masking in Medieval and Early Tudor England* (Aldershot, 2002), 169–88.

30 On English anxiety about this lack of physical differentiation, see Ania Loomba, 'Outsiders in Shakespeare's England', in *The Cambridge Companion to Shakespeare*, Margreta de Grazia and Stanley Wells eds (Cambridge, 2001), 147–66, 156. Portia and Nerissa's cross-dressing might be read in a similar vein, as a practice whose associations with holiday pastimes might have enabled early modern spectators to view Shakespeare's play as itself a form of festivity.

31 See Gurr, *Shakespearean Stage*, 33–49, for a brief account of the 'precarious and changeable' (34) state of the commercial acting companies. A more detailed history may be found in Andrew Gurr, *The Shakespearian Playing Companies* (Oxford, 1996).

'Honest Clothes' in *The Merry Wives of Windsor*

1 References are to Giorgio Melchiori ed., *The Merry Wives of Windsor* The Arden Shakespeare, Third Series (London, 1999).

2 Giorgio Melchiori, picking up on another instance of the dense repetition of words, points out that Shakespeare uses the word 'cozen' and its derivatives ten times in *Merry Wives*, 'Introduction', Melchiori ed., 1999, 12.

3 Caius begins this refrain when he finds Simple in his closet: 'What shall de honest man do in my closet? Dere is no honest man dat shall come in my closet' (1.4.67–8), and it grows in volume in the buck-basket scene: 'Your wife is as honest a 'omans as I will desires among five thousand' (3.3.204–5), Evans assures Ford; 'I see 'tis an honest woman' (207), and Caius agrees.

4 On early modern credit and its links to reputation, see Craig Muldrew, *The Economy of Obligation, the Culture of Credit and Social Relations in Early Modern England* (Basingstoke, 1998).

5 Melchiori, 51.

6 For a list of these references see p. 70.

7 Graham Holderness, 'Cleaning House: the Courtly and the Popular in *The Merry Wives of Windsor*', *Critical Survey* 22(1) (Spring 2010), 26–40.

8 Oxfordshire Record Office, Oxford. MS Oxf. Dioc. Papers c 25, ff. 189r–v, available on 'An Electronic Text Edition of Depositions 1560–1760 (ETED)', CD-ROM with *Testifying to Language and Life in Early Modern England*, Merja Kytö, Peter Grund and Terry Walker (Amsterdam, 2011).

9 Worcestershire Archive and Archaeology Service (WAAS), 794.052, vol. 7, f.285v.

10 Ingram, *Church Courts, Sex and Marriage*, 13–15, sees an increase beginning after 1570.

11 Pamela Allen Brown, *Better a Shrew than a Sheep: Women, Drama, and the Culture of Jest in Early Modern England* (Ithaca, NY, 2002), 44.

12 Henry Smith, *A Preparative to Marriage* (London, 1591), 27, 29, 31. My thanks to Bella Mirabella for this formulation of the contribution made by ornament.

13 KALC PRC 17/22, f167, 1542.

14 Canterbury Cathedral Archive and Library (CCAL), X.10.5, f.79–80.

15 This is a discourse of particular significance to the middling sort – women like the merry wives of Windsor – whose financial and social situation enabled a particular kind of female identity, honesty and housework, and the threat to reputation caused by slander. For a fuller discussion of women's work in the play see Natasha Korda, in ' "Judicious Oeillades": Supervising Marital Property in *The Merry Wives of Windsor*', in *Marxist Shakespeares*, Jean E. Howard ed. (London 2001), and Wendy Wall, 'Why does Puck Sweep?: Fairylore, Merry Wives, and Social Struggle', *Shakespeare Quarterly* 52 (2001), 67–106.

16 The National Archives, London, Assizes, Northern Circuit, MS ASSI45/3/1, f. 145r, available on ETED.

17 Evidence for the moral valence of other items of clothing includes William Sawell's proof of his assertion that Margaret Gold is 'an unquiet woman': 'this deponent saw her so dronke in Canterbury that she was not able to goo astand but did fall and divers times in thee stretes . . . and at that time she lost her apron also', CCAL, X.10.7, f.114v.

18 WAAS, 794.052, vol. 7, ff.3v–4v (my italics). One of her husband's workers, with whom he had been forced to stay in the past when he had fallen out with his wife, states explicitly that Cleveley had 'tould pretely his greiffes unto this deponent sayeinge my wyfe is some what unrulye'.

19 Janet Arnold with Jenny Tiramani and Santina Levey, *Patterns of Fashion 4* (Basingstoke, 2008), 12.

20 See for instance 'An Homily Against Excess of Apparel', where it is stated that the prophet warned the people of Sion that 'In that day . . . shall the Lord take away the ornament of the slippers, and the caules, and the round attires, and the sweet balls, and the bracelets, and the attires of the head . . .' and many other things besides. *Certain Homilies Appointed to be Read in Churches in the Time of Queen Elizabeth of Famous Memory* (London, 1851), 328.

21 For the Italian veil's movement from a sign of chastity to one of 'sin and seduction', see Eugenia Paulicelli, 'From the Sacred to the Secular: The Gendered Geography of Veils in Italian

Cinquecento Fashion', in *Ornamentalism*, Mirabella ed. (Ann Arbor, MI, 2011).

22 Susan Vincent, *Dressing the Elite* (Oxford and New York, 2003), 52. On the complexities of linen's engagement with cleanliness, status and chastity on a smaller scale, see Bella Mirabella, 'Embellishing Herself with a Cloth: The Contradictory Life of the Handkerchief', in *Ornamentalism*, Mirabella ed.

23 Thomas Bentley, *The monument of Matrones* (London, 1582), 369–71.

24 For an interesting reading of them see Richard Helgerson, in 'The Buck Basket, the Witch, and the Queen of Fairies, The Women's World of Shakespeare's Windsor', in *Renaissance Culture and the Everyday*, Fumerton and Hunt eds (Philadelphia, PA, 1999).

25 For further analysis of this image see Catherine Richardson, ' "Havying Nothing upon Hym Saving Onely His Sherte": Event, Narrative and Material Culture in Early Modern England', in *Clothing Culture 1350–1650*, Richardson ed. (Aldershot, 2004), 209–21.

26 *OED*, 3c.

27 Somerset Quarter Sessions, MS Q/SR 75, f. 75r, available on ETED.

28 For more on women's discussion of sexual crime see Laura Gowing, *Common Bodies* (New Haven, CT, 2003), esp. ch. 3.

29 CCAL, X.10.14 f.167.

30 See Natasha Korda, 'Froes, Rebatoes and Other "Outlandish Comodityes" ', in *Everyday Objects, Medieval and Early Modern Material Culture and its Meanings*, Hamling and Richardson eds (Aldershot, 2010), 95–106.

31 Harriet Phillips, 'Late Falstaff, the Merry World, and The Merry Wives of Windsor', *Shakespeare* (2013), 1–27.

32 He summarizes the 'civil qualities' of urban citizenship as 'discretion, discourse, wisdom, self-knowledge, and honesty'. Withington, 'Putting the City into Shakespeare's City Comedy', in *Shakespeare and Early Modern Political Thought*, David Armitage, Carol Condren and Andrew Fitzmaurice eds (Cambridge, 2009), 211, 207. The analysis offered here suggests

that in the play, as in early modern towns, male civil qualities
and female sexuality were inseparable, forming a tight pair that
represented familial probity.

How to Do Things with Shoes

1   Julian Bowsher and Pat Miller, *The Rose and the Globe:
    Playhouses of Shakespeare's Bankside, Southwark, Excavations
    1988–90* (London, 2009), 138–57, 191–2, 200–8; Julian
    Bowsher, *Shakespeare's London Theatreland: Archaeology,
    History and Drama* (London, 2012), 184–6. On early modern
    shoe-sizes, see Olaf Goubitz, Carol van Driel-Murray and
    Willy Groenman-van Waateringe, *Stepping Through Time:
    Archaeological Footwear from Prehistoric Times until 1800*
    (Zwolle, Netherlands, 2001), 11. See also Natasha Korda,
    ' "The Sign of the Last": Gender, Material Culture, and
    Artisanal Nostalgia in *The Shoemaker's Holiday*', *Journal of
    Medieval and Early Modern Studies* 43(3) (2013), 573–97.
    I am grateful to Julian Bowsher for generously sharing his
    expertise and data on MoLA's footwear finds.

2   William Shakespeare, *The Arden Shakespeare Complete Works*,
    Third Series, Richard Proudfoot, Ann Thompson and David
    Scott Kastan eds (London, 2011). All further references are to
    this edition.

3   The *Oxford English Dictionary* dates the earliest usage of
    'treads the Stage' to 1691 and of 'trod the boards' to 1858,
    citing Gerard Langbaine, *An Account of the English Dramatic
    Poets*, and Edward G. E. Bulwer-Lytton, *What Will He Do
    with It?*, respectively ('tread, *v.*' 1.b). Yet as Jonson's dedicatory
    poem in the First Folio attests, 'to tread the stage' was in usage
    in Shakespeare's time ('To live again, to heare thy Buskin tread, /
    And shake a stage'); Jonson, 'To the Memory of My Beloved,
    the Author, Mr. William Shakespeare, and What He Hath Left
    Us' in William Shakespeare, *Mr. William Shakespeares
    Comedies, Histories, & Tragedies* (London, 1623), sig. A4r.
    Milton refers to 'the well-trod stage' in 'L'Allegro' in *Poems of
    Mr. John Milton* (London, 1645 [1646]), 36. The reliance of
    acting upon footwork is likewise suggested by the superstitious

catchphrase 'break a leg!', of uncertain origin, but apparently not in common usage until the early twentieth century. Eric Partridge, *A Dictionary of Catch Phrases from the Sixteenth Century to the Present Day* (New York, 1977), 56.

4 See John Bulwer, *Chirologia, or, The Naturall Language of the Hand Composed of the Speaking Motions, and Discoursing Gestures Thereof: Whereunto is Added Chironomia, or, The Art of Manuall Rhetoricke, Consisting of the Naturall Expressions, Digested by Art in the Hand, as the Chiefest Instrument of Eloquence, by Historicall Manifesto's Exemplified out of the Authentique Registers of Common Life and Civill Conversation: with Types, or Chyrograms, a Long-Wish'd for Illustration of this Argument* (London, 1644). On hand-gesture in early modern theatre, see, for example, Alfred Harbage, 'Elizabethan Acting', *PMLA* 54 (1939), 685–708; B.L. Joseph, *Elizabethan Acting* (London, 1951); Andrew Gurr, 'Elizabethan Action', *Studies in Philology* 63(2) (1966), 144–56; David M. Bevington, *Action is Eloquence: Shakespeare's Language of Gesture* (Cambridge, MA, 1984); John H. Astington, 'Eye and Hand on Shakespeare's Stage', *Renaissance and Reformation* 22(1) (1986), 109–21.

5 Tim Ingold, 'Culture on the Ground: The World Perceived Through the Feet', *Journal of Material Culture* 9(3) (2000), 315–40.

6 Ingold, 'Culture on the Ground', 317–18.

7 Ingold, 'Culture on the Ground', 321, 330.

8 Richard Brome, *The Court Begger. A Comedie Acted at the Cock-pit by His Majesties Servants, Anno 1632* (London, 1653), sig. S3r; Alan C. Dessen and Leslie Thomson, *A Dictionary of Stage Directions in English Drama, 1580–1642* (Cambridge, 1999), 96; see also 64–5. Unless otherwise indicated, all references to stage directions in this essay cite page numbers in Dessen and Thomson parenthetically. I am grateful to Leslie Thomson for sharing expertise and unpublished data in private correspondence.

9 Richard Brome, *The Court Begger*, sig. S3r.

10 On Renaissance dancing, see Charles Baskerville, *The Elizabethan Jig and Related Song Drama* (Chicago, IL, 1929);

Mark Franko, *The Dancing Body in Renaissance Choreography (c.1416–1589)* (Birmingham, AL, 1986); John Forrest, *The History of Morris Dancing, 1458–1750* (Toronto, 1999); Skiles Howard, *The Politics of Courtly Dancing in Early Modern England* (Amherst, MA, 1998); Barbara Ravelhofer, *The Early Stuart Masque: Dance, Costume, and Music* (Oxford and New York, 2006); Lynn Matluck Brooks, *Women's Work: Making Dance in Europe before 1800* (Madison, WI, 2007); Margaret M. McGowan, *Dance in the Renaissance: European Fashion, French Obsession* (New Haven, CT, 2008).

11 Post-play jigs were the specialty of stage-clowns like Richard Tarlton and William Kemp, and functioned to galvanize audiences through rousing footwork. In his description of 'Play-houses', Donald Lupton says: '[W]hen the play is done, you shall have a jigge or dance ... they mean to put their legs to it, as well as their tongs.' Lupton, *London and the Countrey Carbonadoed and Quartred into Severall Characters* (London, 1632), 81. Thomas Platter observes of a performance of *Julius Caesar* in 1599: 'when the play was over, they danced very marvellously and gracefully together as is their wont, two dressed as men and two as women.' Platter, *Travels in England*, trans. Clare Williams, 166.

12 On the 'wooden O' as sounding-board, see Bruce R. Smith, *The Acoustic World of Early Modern England: Attending to the O-factor* (Chicago, IL, 1999).

13 Bulwer, *Chirologia*, A5v.

14 See Henry Chettle and Anthony Munday, *The Death of Robert, Earle of Huntington. Otherwise Called Robin Hood of Merrie Sherwodde: with the Lamentable Tragedie of Chaste Matilda, His Faire Maid Marian, Poysoned at Dunmowe by King John* (London, 1601), sig. K3v, and Ben Jonson, *Catiline His Conspiracy. A Tragoedie* in *The Workes of Benjamin Jonson* (London, 1616), 727, respectively. Dessen and Thompson's *Dictionary of Stage Directions* does not include 'quaking' in its index of 'actions'.

15 In Massinger's *The Picture*, the clown Hilario 'leape[s] ... caper[s] / And frisk[s] 'ith ayre for joy'. Philip Massinger, *The Picture. A Tragecomedie, As It Was Often Presented with*

Good Allowance, at the Globe, and Black-Friers Play-houses, by the Kings Majesties Servants (London, 1630), sigs. G1r–G1v.

16 All further references to the plays of Ben Jonson are to *The Cambridge Edition of the Works of Ben Jonson Online* (Cambridge, 2014).

17 Baldassarre Castiglione, *The Courtyer of Count Baldessar Castlio Divided into Foure Bookes. Very Necessary and Profitable for Yonge Gentilmen and Gentilwomen Abiding in Court, Palaice or Place, Done into English by Thomas Hoby* (London, 1561), sig. Zz1r. Brathwaite similarly advises the gentleman-dancer to 'come off bravely and sprightly, rather than with an affected curiositie'. Richard Brathwaite, *The English Gentleman. Containing Sundry Excellent Rules or Exquisite Observations, Tending to Direction of Every Gentleman, of Selecter Ranke and Qualitie; How to Demeane or Accommodate Himselfe in the Manage of Publike or Private Affaires* (London, 1630), 204–5.

18 Brome, *Court Begger*, sig. S3v.

19 Brome, *Court Begger*, sig. S3r.

20 Brome, *Court Begger*, sig. S4r.

21 Brome, *Court Begger*, sig. R1r.

22 Brome, *Court Begger*, sig. R1r.

23 Quintilian, *The Orator's Education, Books 11–12*, Donald A. Russell ed. and trans., Loeb Classical Library (Cambridge, MA, 2001), 149–52 (11.3.125–9).

24 Quintilian, *The Orator's Education*, 131 (11.3.88).

25 A funeral elegy for Richard Burbage published in 1619 finds this gesture particularly memorable, recalling 'oft have I seene him, leap into the Grave'. Cited in *A Dictionary of Actors and of Other Persons Associated with the Public Representation of Plays in England before 1642*, Edwin Nungezer (New Haven, CT, 1929), 74.

26 Stephen Gosson, *Plays Confuted in Five Actions* (London, 1582), sigs. C6r, G5v.

27 Gosson, *Plays Confuted in Five Actions*, sig. E7v.

NOTES

28 Gosson, *Plays Confuted in Five Actions*, sig. E1r.

29 Thomas Dekker, *The Guls Horne-booke* (London, 1609), 28–9.

30 Henry Fitzgeffrey, *Satyres: and Satyricall Epigrams with Certaine Observations at Black-Fryers* (London, 1617), sigs. F1v, F2r–F2v, F5v, F7v.

31 Barnabe Rich, *Faultes Faults, and Nothing Else but Faultes* (London, 1606), C4v–D1r.

32 Henry Chettle, *Kind-harts Dreame* (London, [1593?]), sig. B2v.

33 Samuel Rowlands, *Humors Ordinarie Where a Man May be Very Merrie, and Exceeding Well Used for his Sixe-pence* (London, 1605), sig. C4r.

34 Peter Thomson, 'Richard Tarlton (d.1588)', *Oxford Dictionary of National Biography*, Oxford, 2004); online ed., Lawrence Goldman ed., http://www.oxforddnb.com/view/article/26971 (accessed 30 June 2013). On slops, see OED, 'slop, *n*.1', 4.a. Slops are described in Act 2, scene 2 of Thomas Middleton and Thomas Dekker's *The Roaring Girl*, Paul Mulholland ed., The Revels Plays (Manchester, 1987), where Moll is fitted for a pair by her tailor, and also wears them on the title page woodcut of the 1611 edition.

35 R.A.Foakes ed., *Henslowe's Diary*, 2nd edition (Cambridge, 2002), fol. 115r.

36 William Kemp, *Kemps Nine Daies Wonder Performed in a Daunce from London to Norwich*, Alexander Dyce ed. (London, 1840 [1600]). See also Martin Butler, 'Kemp, William (d. in or after 1610?)', *Oxford Dictionary of National Biography* (Oxford, 2004); online ed., Lawrence Goldman ed., http://www.oxforddnb.com/view/article/15334 (accessed 30 June 2013).

37 Kemp, *Nine Daies Wonder*, 3, 9, 12.

38 Kemp, *Nine Daies Wonder*, 18.

39 Thomas Heywood, *An Apology for Actors. Containing Three Briefe Treatises. 1. Their Antiquity. 2. Their Ancient Dignity. 3. The True Use of Their Quality* (London, 1612), sig. B2r.

40 Heywood, *An Apology for Actors*, sigs. B1v–B2r.

41 Heywood, *An Apology for Actors*, sig. B2r.

42 Foakes ed., *Henslowe's Diary*, fol. 37v.

43 I.e. 'lent wm birde ales [i.e. alias] borne the 27 of novemb[er] [1598] to bye a payer of sylke stockens to playe the gwisse [i.e. the Duc de Guise] in xxs'; 'Lent unto my sonne [i.e. Edward Alleyn] & wm Jube [i.e. Juby] the 31 of Septemb[er] 1601 to bye divers thinges & sewttes & stockenes for the playe of the weaste enges [i.e. *Conquest of the West Indies*] the some of xli xs.' Foakes, *Henslowe's Diary*, fols. 38v, 94r.

44 Foakes, *Henslowe's Diary*, fol. 41v.

45 See the many pairs of silk stockings in Henslowe's pawn accounts (which, if unredeemed, might be sold to actors); Foakes, *Henslowe's Diary*, fols. 74v–75r, 77r–78v.

46 John Stow, *The Annales, or a Generall Chronicle of England, Begun First by Maister John Stow, and after Him Continued and Augmented with Matters Forreyne, and Domestique, Auncient and Moderne, unto the Ende of This Present Yeere 1614 by Edmond Howes, Gentleman* (London, 1615), 867. The inventories of the Wardrobe of Robes show that Howes' account is exaggerated, as the queen's hosier continued to provide her with an average of twenty pairs of cloth stockings (cut on the bias and seamed at the back) per year until 1577, when they were eventually supplanted by knitted silk or worsted stockings. Janet Arnold, *Queen Elizabeth's Wardrobe Unlock'd* (Leeds, 1988), 208–9.

47 I.e. 'An ornamental pattern in silk thread worked on the side of a stocking' (*OED*, 'clock, *n*.2', 1).

48 Philip Stubbes, *The Anatomie of Abuses Contayning a Discoverie, or Briefe Summarie of Such Notable Vices and Imperfections, as Now Raigne in Many Christian Countreyes of the World: but (Especiallie) in a Verie Famous Ilande Called Ailgna* (London, 1583), sig. E3v.

49 Robert Greene, *A Quip for an Upstart Courtier: Or, A Quaint Dispute between Velvet Breeches and Cloth-breeches, Wherein is Plainely Set Downe the Disorders in All Estates and Trades* (London, 1592), sigs. F3r–F3v.

50 Dekker, *Guls Horne-booke*, 28. In the Induction to Jonson's *The Staple of News* (1625), Lady Censure comes to the playhouse to see 'which Actor has the best legge and foote' (Ind. 41).

51 On the symbolic significance of the colour yellow in relation to Malvolio's stockings, see Linthicum, *Costume*, 48–50. See also Loreen L. Giese, 'Malvolio's Yellow Stockings: Coding Illicit Sexuality in Early Modern London', *Medieval and Renaissance Drama in England* 19 (2006), 235–46.

52 Andrea Vianello, 'Courtly Lady or Courtesan? The Venetian Chopine in the Renaissance', in *Shoes: A History from Sandals to Sneakers*, Giorgio Riello and Peter McNeil eds (Oxford and New York, 2006), 76–93; Lucy Pratt and Linda Woolley, *Shoes* (London, 1999), 18–20.

53 Thomas Dekker, *The Dramatic Works of Thomas Dekker*, Fredson Bowers ed., 4 vols (Cambridge, 1953–61).

54 In *Bartholomew Fair*, Win wears 'fine high shoes, like the Spanish lady!' and Littlewit asks her to 'go a little; I would fain see thee pace, pretty Win!' (1.1.18–19).

55 The phrase 'to tread the shoe awry', like the French faux pas, referred to a 'fall from virtue' or 'chastity' (OED, 'awry, *adv.*, *adj.*, and *v.*' 2.c). In Henry Porter's *Two Angry Women of Abingdon*, Mall says: 'maides that weares Corke shooes, may step awry'; in Marston's *Sophonisba* (*c.*1605), when Sophonisba asks Zanthia to remove her shoe, the latter says: ' 'Tis wonder Madam you treade not awry . . . You goe very high', suggesting that she is wearing chopines. Henry Porter, *The Pleasant History of the Two Angry Women of Abingdon* (London, 1599), sig. C3r; John Marston, *The Wonder of Women, or the Tragedie of Sophonisba as it Hath Beene Sundry Times Acted at the Black Friers* (London, 1606), sig. B1v.

56 In 3.1 of Marston's *The Dutch Courtesan* (*c.*1604), Tissefew asks Crispinella, 'Dost not weare high corke shooes: chopines?' to which she replies, 'Monstrous on[e]s.' John Marston, *The Dutch Courtezan. As It Was Playd in the Blacke-Friars, by the Children of her Majesties Revels* (London, 1605), sig. D4. See also Ben Jonson, *Cynthia's Revels, or The Fountain of Self-Love* (2.2.47–52).

57 In Marston's *Antonio and Mellida* (*c.*1599), the creaky, cork-soled shoes of the boy-actor are likened to his squeaky voice: 'thy voice sqeakes like a dry cork shoe.' John Marston, *The History of Antonio and Mellida. The First Part. As it Hath Beene Sundry Times Acted, by the Children of Paules* (London, 1602), sig. H4r.

58 Stubbes, *The Anatomie of Abuses*, sig. E4r.

59 According to Janet Arnold, 'In 1595 Peter Johnson made [Queen Elizabeth] the first shoes which are described as having high heels and arches . . . The Queen's high heels were probably made of wood.' Arnold, *Queen Elizabeth's Wardrobe Unlock'd*, 214.

60 Brome, *Court Begger*, sig. R1r.

61 Brome, *Court Begger*, sig., S2r. See also Albert Feuillerat, *Documents Relating to the Office of the Revels in the Time of Queen Elizabeth* (Louvain, 1908), 19, 35; see also 21, 24–6, 30, 32, 38, 40, 43–4, 92, 142, 159, 177, 201, 210, 217, 242, 262, 286–7, 349. One 'Shewemaker [i.e. shoemaker]' was paid to make 'xxxvij payre of Maskinge shewes' (92).

62 Cf. 'shorte buskyns for the Maske of Italyen wemen' made of 'velvett Carnacion' and 'longe buskyns for the hunters of Acteons Maske' made of 'velvett Orrenge'; 'their hose being verie Longe paned of rased velvet ground yealowe and rasing greene likewise Laid with silver Lace and drawne out with tincell sarcenett.' Feuillerat, *Documents*, 32, 287.

63 Shoes and buskins were frequently the end point of this process: as fabric pieces became smaller and smaller in the process of being translated, they were eventually used to make shoes. Thus, for example, 'Longe hanginge sleves . . . with collours of Clothe of Tissewe gold and redd velvett' used in a masque of 'Venetian Senators' were first 'translated into hed peces & undersleeves for Turkes and agayne from thence in to Shoes and now not Serviceable nor chargeable' and 'vj Turkye gownes of Crymesen rewed with golde threed' were 'translated in to buskyns' which likewise became 'not Serviceable nor Chargeable'. Feuillerat, *Documents*, 19, 21.

64 Bowsher and Miller, *The Rose and the Globe*, 144–5, 192. Any delicate shoes passed down as 'ffees' for court performances or acquired second hand would likely not have survived.

65 Bowsher and Miller, *The Rose and the Globe*, 196.

66 Bowsher and Miller, *The Rose and the Globe*, 196.

67 M[arie] Channing Linthicum, *Costume in the Drama of Shakespeare and his Contemporaries* (Oxford, 1936), 153–4; Janet Arnold, 'Decorative Features: Pinking, Snipping and Slashing', *Costume* 9 (1975), 22–6; Jane Ashelford, *The Art of*

Dress: Clothes and Society 1500–1914 (London, 1996), 28; Lucy Pratt and Linda Woolley, *Shoes* (London, 1999), 16.

68 Phillip Stubbes, *The Second Part of the Anatomie of Abuses. Conteining the Display of Corruptions, with a Perfect Description of Such Imperfections, Blemishes and Abuses, as Now Reigning in Everie Degree, Require Reformation for Feare of Gods Vengeance to be Powred upon the People and Countrie, without Speedie Repentance, and Conversion unto God* (London, 1583), sig. F4r.

69 Thomas Heywood, *The Foure Prentices of London With the Conquest of Jerusalem. As it Hath Bene Diverse Times Acted, at the Red Bull, by the Queenes Majesties Servants* (London, 1615), sig. B3v; Thomas Heywood, *The Rape of Lucrece. A True Roman Tragedie. With the Severall Songes in Their Apt Places, by Valerius, the Merrie Lord Amongst the Roman Peeres. Acted by Her Majesties Servants at the Red-Bull, Neere Clarken-well* (London, 1608), sig. F2r. See also William Goddard's Satire 6: 'Shee makes hir harte & heeles exceeding light, /. . . with lightest corke' in *A Mastif Whelp and Other Ruff-island-lik Currs Fetcht from Amongst the Antipedes Which Bite and Barke at the Fantasticall Humorists and Abusers of the Time* (Dordrecht, [1616?]), sig. H1r.

70 Bowsher and Miller, *The Rose and the Globe*, 199.

'Apparel oft Proclaims the Man': Dressing Othello on the English Renaissance Stage

1 The play throughout refers to items of clothing and dress from nightgowns, cloaks, coats, to accessories such as a handkerchief, jewels, gloves, purses, fans, materials like bombast and fustian, and to practices of dressing. William Shakespeare, *Othello*. E.A.J.Honigman, ed. Arden Shakespeare, Third series (London, 1996). All references are to this edition.

2 Two earlier ambassadorial visits occurred in 1589 and 1595. See Nabil Matar and Rudolph Stoeckel, 'Europe's Mediterranean

Frontier', in *Shakespeare and Renaissance Europe*, Andrew
Hadfield and Paul Hammond eds (London, 2004).

3 Nabil Matar, *Turks, Moors, and Englishmen in the Age of
Renaissance Discovery* (New York, 1999), 8. According to Emily
C. Bartels, the 'globally complex' Moors 'uniquely' represented
'the intersection of European and non-European cultures' and
were essential to any hopes England had for a global economy.
Speaking of the Moor: from Alcazar to Othello (Philadelphia,
PA, 2008), 5, 20.

4 See also *Antony and Cleopatra*, as well as Thomas Heywood,
Fair Maid of the West Part I (1600–3), and Ben Jonson,
The Masque of Blackness (1605). See also Elliot H. Tokson,
*The Popular Image of the Black Man in English Drama,
1550–1688* (Boston, 1982) for a list of plays; Anthony Gerard
Barthelemy, *Black Face, Maligned Race: The Representation of
Blacks in English Drama from Shakespeare to Southerne* (Baton
Rouge, LA, 1987); Emily Bartels, 'Making More of the Moor:
Aaron, Othello, and Renaissance Refashionings of Race',
Shakespeare Quarterly 41(4) (1990), Bartels, *Speaking of the
Moor*, as well as Jack D'Amico, *The Moor in English
Renaissance Drama* (Tampa, FL, 1991) and Virginia Mason
Vaughan, *Performing Blackness on English Stages* (Cambridge,
2005), for example.

5 William Harrison, *The Description of England* 1587, George
Edelsen ed. (Ithaca, NY, 1968), 146. Blackwork was a popular
decorative motif for sleeves, doublets, smocks and gowns
throughout the sixteenth and seventeenth centuries, having come
into Spain from the Moors of Northern Africa. See Jane
Ashelford, *Dress in the Age of Elizabeth I* (London, 1988) for a
number of examples, particularly portraits of Mary Cornwallis
by George Gower, 1580–5, Amy Gurdon, unknown artist, 1590,
and *Portrait of a Young Man* with a Blackwork Doublet, English
School, 1590.

6 I have chosen to use the portrait of Dudley because it is such
a clear rendition of the iconic English look, consistent
throughout the period. See, for example, portrait of Robert
Devereux by Marcus Gheeraerts, *c*.1596, and Robert Peake
the Elder's portrait of Henry, Prince of Wales, *c*.1610. While the
doublet and the hose were the essentials of masculine attire

throughout Europe, I will focus particularly on English male clothing.

7 For further reading on the subject of early modern masculinity see, for example, David Kuchta, *The Three-Piece Suit and Modern Masculinity: England, 1550–1850* (Berkeley, CA, 2001); Stephen Orgel, *Impersonations: The Performance of Gender in Shakespeare's England* (Cambridge, 1996); Bruce R. Smith, *Shakespeare and Masculinity* (Oxford, 2000); Mario di Gangi, *Sexual Types: Embodiment, Agency, and Dramatic Character from Shakespeare to Shirley* (Philadelphia, PA, 2011); *The Homoerotics of Early Modern Drama* (Cambridge, 1997); Will Fisher, *Materializing Gender in Early Modern English Literature and Culture* (Cambridge, 2006); Alexandra Shepard, *Meanings of Manhood in Early Modern England* (Oxford, 2006) as well as Christian Billings, *Masculinity, Corporeality and the English Stage: 1580–1635* (Burlington, VT, 2008).

8 See Michael Neill, ' "Mulattos", "Blacks", and "Indian Moors": Othello and Early Modern Constructions of Difference', in Michael Neill's *Putting History to the Question: Power, Politics, and Society in English Renaissance Drama* (New York, 2000), 269–84; Eldred D. Jones, *Othello's Countrymen: The African in English Renaissance Drama* (London, 1965), *The Elizabethan Image of Africa* (Charlottesville, VA, 1971).

9 See Barbara Fuchs, *Exotic Nation: Maurophilia and the Construction of Early Modern Spain* (Philadelphia, PA, 2009).

10 Andrew Borde, *The Fyrst Boke of the Introduction of Knowledge* (London, 1549), xxxvi.

11 See Natalie Zemon Davis, *Trickster Travels: a Sixteenth-century Muslim Between Worlds* (New York, 2006).

12 Leo Africanus, *The History and Description of Africa*, trans. John Pory, Robert Brown ed. (London, 1896), 290.

13 Fuchs, 13. María Judith Feliciano, 'Muslim Shrouds for Christian Kings: A Reassessment of Andalusi Textiles in Thirteenth-century Castilian Life and Ritual', in *Under the Influence: Questioning the Comparative in Medieval Castile*, Cynthia Robinson and Leyla Rouhi eds (Boston, 2005), 109.

14 Quoted in Fuchs, 22–3.

15 Quoted in Fuchs, 94–5.

16 Fray Damián Fonseca, *Relación de la expulsion de los moriscos del reino de Valencia* (Rome, 1612, 1878), 117–18. Quoted in Fuchs, 71–2, 71.

17 The *marlota* was often worn in the *cañas*, or equestrian games, popular in Spain, in which the participants always wore Moorish costume; Fuchs, 70.

18 Cesare Vecellio, *Habiti Antichi et Moderni* (1598), *The Clothing of the Renaissance World*, Margaret F. Rosenthal and Ann Rosalind Jones eds (London, 2008), 485. A 'fazzuolo' is like a large handkerchief; it is attached to the turban and goes under the chin.

19 Rosenthal and Jones, *The Clothing of the Renaissance World*, 537. I refer the reader to the painting, *Supper at Emmaus*, 1506, by the Venetian painter, Marco Marziale. Here the Moor is wearing a striped, brightly coloured robe, with a headdress and a white turban.

20 James Melville, *Memoirs of Sir James Melville of Halhill*, A. Francis Steuart ed. (London, 1929 [1683]), 95.

21 See, for example, Jonathan Gil Harris, *Foreign Bodies: Discourses of Social Pathology in Early Modern England* (Cambridge, 1998); Anne Rosalind Jones and Peter Stallybrass, *Renaissance Clothing and the Materials of Memory* (Cambridge, 2000); Roze Hentschell, *The Culture of Cloth in Early Modern England: Textual Constructions of a National Identity* (Burlington, VT, 2008); Hentschell, 'Treasonous Textiles: Foreign Cloth and the Construction of Englishness', *Journal of Medieval and Early Modern Studies*, 32(3) (Durham, NC, 2002), 543–70; Ulinka Rublack, *Dressing Up: Cultural Identity in Renaissance Europe* (Oxford, 2011).

22 Thomas Dekker, *The Gull's Hornbook*, R.McKerrow ed. (London, 1904), 35; grogram is a coarse fabric made of silk and wool.

23 Harrison, 146–7.

24 Philip Stubbes, *The Anatomie of Abuses*, Margaret Jane Kidnie ed. (Tempe, AZ, 2002 [1583]), 67, 103, 113, 67; *Much Ado*

About Nothing, Arthur Ralegh Humphreys ed. (London, 1981), 3.3.124. See also Vincent, *Dressing the Elite*, 127–31 for a discussion of deformity through clothing.

25 Baldesar Castiglione, *The Book of the Courtier*, trans. George Bull (London, 1967), 136.

26 *Book of the Courtier*, 30; The Italian is 'la bellezza estrinseca è vero segno della bontá intrinseca e nei corpi è impressa . . . per un carattere dell'anima'. Baldassar Castigione, *Il Libro del Cortegiano* (Milan, 2000), 320. Erika Rummel ed., The *Erasmus Reader* (Toronto, 1990), 108.

27 Harrison, 148.

28 Stubbes, *Anatomie*, 95.

29 Robert Greene, *Greenes Newes both from Heaven and Hell* (London, 1593), 7–12.

30 Charles William Eliot ed., *English Poetry I: from Chaucer to Gray* (New York, 1930), 190.

31 David Kuchta, 'The Semiotics of Masculinity in Renaissance England', in *Sexuality & Gender in Early Modern Europe*, James Grantham Turner ed. (Cambridge, 1993), 235, 234, 237.

32 See also the 1600 painting of *Procession of Queen Elizabeth I* with her courtiers all dressed in doublet and hose, attributed to Robert Peake the Elder. For a softer collar and an exaggerated doublet, see the portrait of Thomas Cavandish by an unknown artist from 1591; in the 1610 portrait of Henry Frederick, Prince of Wales, after Isaac Oliver the prince is wearing an enormous ruff at his collar, and a large doublet in the military motif; and even in the 1616 portrait by Isaac Oliver, Richard, Earl of Dorset wears a large rebato at his neck, with doublet and embroidered hose and armour nearby.

33 Trying to control her fear in Arden forest, Rosalind says: 'I could find in my heart to disgrace my man's apparel and cry like a woman; but I must comfort the weaker vessel, as doublet and hose ought to show itself courageous to petticoat' (2.4.4–7). Celia, upset with Rosalind's critiques of women, tells her: 'We must have your doublet and hose plucked over your head, and show the world what the bird hath done to her own nest' William Shakespeare, *As You Like It*, Juliet Dusinberre ed. (London, 2006) (4.1.189–91).

34 An examination of European attire reveals that the doublet and hose were ubiquitous throughout. See, for example, Vecellio, who portrays soldiers, such as a Venetian foot soldier and a bravo (a retained fighter) in doublet and hose (162, 165), as well as two young men (160, 161) wearing ruffs, and exaggerated doublets and hose; one carries a handkerchief. I am focusing on the particular English brand of this custom, but the two looks are very similar.

35 Ashelford, 46.

36 Anne Hollander, *Seeing Through Clothes* (New York, 1978), 231.

37 Ashelford, 46–7; Stubbes, 97.

38 Amanda Bailey, *Flaunting: Style and the Subversive Male Body in Renaissance England* (Toronto, 2007), 6; Thomas Middleton and Thomas Dekker, *The Roaring Girl* in *English Renaissance Drama*, David M. Bevington, Lars Engle, Katharine Eisaman Maus and Eric Rasmussen eds (New York, 2002), *Epistle*, lines 1–2. See also Robert Greene, *A Groats-Worth of Wit* (1592) (Oxford, 2007), 41 when referring to Shakespeare as an 'upstart crowe, beautified with our feathers, that with his *Tygers hart wrapt in a Players hyde* supposes he is as well able to bombast out a blank verse as the best of you'.

39 Susan Vincent, in *The Anatomy of Fashion: Dressing the Body from the Renaissance to Today* (London, 2009), writes that the doublet 'tight fitting and well wadded ... drew its influence from contemporary plate armour' (49). James Laver, *Costume and Fashion: A Concise History* (London, 1982), 88. See *Sir Philip Sidney*, English School, from *c.*1577 in the National Portrait Gallery.

40 Stubbes, 95.

41 See *The Procession Portrait*, 1601, attributed to Robert Peake the Elder, at Sherborne Castle.

42 See Ashelford, Laver and Vincent.

43 Castiglione, *The Courtier*, 60. See Natasha Korda's 'How to Do Things with Shoes' and Russsell Jackson's 'The Stylish Shepherd' for a further discussion of legs.

44 Vincent, *Anatomy of Fashion*, 97. See also Vincent's discussion of the role of the legs in dancing and other courtly duties, 98–9.

45 Robert Carey, *Memoirs of Robert Carey*, F.H.Meres ed. (Oxford, 1972), 20–1.

46 Hollander, *Seeing Through Clothes*, 3. See the portrait of George Villiers, Duke of Buckingham, attributed to William Larkin, *c*.1616, in which his ceremonial robes actually frame the vision of doublet and hose (National Portrait Gallery).

47 John Knox, *First Blast of the Trumpet Against the Monstrous Regiment of Women*, Edward Arber ed. (London, 1878 [1558]), 24.

48 John Florio, *Queen Anna's New World of Words, or Dictionarie of the Italian and English Tongue* (London, 1611), 322; Francis Bacon, *Of the Advancement of Learning*, 1605, G.Watts ed. (London, 1869), I.ii. 6.

49 John Williams, *A Sermon of Apparel, Preached before the Kings Majestie and the Prince his Highnesse at Theobalds, the 22 of February, 1619* (London, 1620), 24–5. Stubbes, 95–6. Richard Brathwaite, *The English Gentleman and Gentlewoman* (London, 1641), 278.

50 Philip Gawdy, *Letters of Philip Gawdy*, Isaac Herbert Jeayes ed. (London, 1906), 90–1.

51 James I, *The True Law of Free Monarchies and Basilikon Doron*, Daniel Fischlin and Mark Fortier eds (Toronto, 1996), 161, 163.

52 See Thomas Nagel, 'Concealment and Exposure', *Philosophy and Public Affairs* 27 (1998), 3–30. The rumour was that the ambassador, with the help of some of his followers, had 'poisoned their interpreter, being borne a Granado ... [and] their revernd aged pilgrim' who were part of the entourage. This occurred during sensitive discussions with Elizabeth who had requested that the King of Morocco send Morisco soldiers to help her fight the Spanish. Henry de Castries, *Les Sources inédites de l' histoire du Maroc par le Comte Henry de Castries, Première Série – Dynastie Saadienne, Archives et Bibliotèques d'Angleterre*, 3 vols (Paris, 1919–35), 2, 203, 209. See also Nabil

Matar and Rudolph Stoeckel, 'Europe's Mediterranean Frontier', 233–4.

53 Nabil Matar and Rudolph Stoeckel argue that in portraying Moors, Shakespeare has 'racialized and blackened them in such a way that they looked completely different from the Moors who had been visiting England for decades'. 'Europe's Mediterranean Frontier', 249.

54 'Enter Morochus a tawnie Moore all in white', Virginia Vaughan, *Performing Blackness on English Stages, 1500–1800* (Cambridge, 2003), 59.

55 See 'Black *Hamlet*: Battening on the Moor', Patricia Parker in *Shakespeare Studies* (2003), 31, 127–64 for a discussion of the contrast between black and white as well as a discussion of blackness in the play and its cultural significance.

56 Ian Smith, 'White Skin, Black Masks: Racial Cross-dressing on the Early Modern Stage' *Renaissance Drama*, 32 (2003), 36. In this insightful essay, Smith argues that such a covering of the skin, a 'staging' of blackness, also 'involved the attempts to produce blackness itself' as an 'approximation of physiognomic difference' (43).

57 Ben Jonson, *The Masque of Blackness*, David Lindley ed., *Court Masques: Jacobean and Caroline Entertainments 1605–1640* (Oxford, 1990), l. 140.

58 Smith, 43.

59 Jane Schlueter argues that the image is from the German play, *A Very Lamentable Tragedy of Titus Andronicus and the Haughty Empress* (published in 1620), perhaps inspired by Shakespeare's play or a lost play, *tittus & vespacia*, referred to in Henslowe's *Diary*. Jane Schlueter, 'Rereading the Peacham Drawing', *Shakespeare Quarterly* 50(2) (Summer 1999), 171–84.

60 Schlueter, 'Rereading the Peacham Drawing', 175–6. See Martin Holmes, *Shakespeare and his Players* (London, 1972), 150–3.

61 There are similar references to military dress in George Peele's 1595 *The Battle of Alcazar*, where the blood-stained clothing of Muly Hamet embodies his role as a warlike monster; he is referred to as the 'barbarous' and 'accursed Moore', described as wearing a 'shirt staind with a cloud of gore', 'sword in hand' and

accompanied with 'deuils coted in the shapes of men'. His uncle, Abdelmelec, who Muly Hamet later kills, says that Hamet 'clads himself in a coat of hammered steele' (lines 1.1.54, 1.2.34, 1.1.19–23, 3.1.902).

62 See Marcus Gheerhaerts's 1594 portrait of Captain Thomas Lee wearing a doublet but with bare legs and feet. See also Jones and Stallybrass, *Materials*, 52 for discussion of Lee's sartorial choice and how he distinguishes himself from Elizabeth's 'silken-hosed courtiers'.

63 Vecellio, *Clothing*, 106. See the illustrations for Venetian nobleman on 106, as well as young nobleman on 108 and discussion of the clothing underneath.

64 If Othello were dressed like the ambassador, would the fabric have been white, as is mentioned in the stage directions from the Folio edition of *Merchant*? See S.P.Cerasano, ' "Borrowed Robes", Costume Prices, and the Drawing of *Titus Andronicus*', *Shakespeare Studies* 22 (1994), 54.

65 See Robert Hornback, 'Emblems of Folly in the First *Othello*: Moor's Coat and "Muckender" ', *Comparative Drama* 35 (2001), 69–99; and Patricia Parker, 'Black *Hamlet*', 157, for discussion of Othello and the black-faced Morris dancer.

66 Castiglione, *The Courtier*, 134–5. Castiglione uses 'trasmutare', which means to change, replace or transform.

67 Rublack, 138; Ibn Khalûn, *The Muqadddimah: and Introduction to History*, trans. Franz Rosenthal, N.J.Dawood ed. (Princeton, NJ, 1967), 116.

68 Bronwen Wilson, *The World in Venice: Print, the City, and Early Modern History* (Toronto, 2005), 102.

The Stylish Shepherd, or, What to Wear in *As You Like It*'s Forest of Arden

1 Images from all the productions discussed can be found at http://internetshakespeare.uvic.ca and http://googleimages.com. Valuable and well-illustrated accounts of the play's production history can be found in: Robert Smallwood, *Shakespeare at*

Stratford: 'As You like It' (London, 2003); Penny Gay, *As She Likes It. Shakespeare's Unruly Women* (London and New York, 1994), ch. 2; and the introductions to the editions of the play edited by Alan Brissenden (Oxford, 1993), Michael Hattaway (Cambridge, 2000) and Juliet Dusinberre (London, 2006). References to the text in the present chapter are taken from the last of these.

2 Stephen Orgel, *Impersonations. The Performance of Gender in Shakespeare's England* (Cambridge, 1996), 108.

3 John Lyly, *Galatea, Midas*, George K. Hunter and David Bevington eds (Manchester, 2002), *Galatea*, 1.3.13–23.

4 Sir Philip Sidney, *The Old Arcadia*, Katherine Duncan-Jones ed. (Oxford, 1985), 24–5.

5 Sir Philip Sidney, *The Old Arcadia*, 34.

6 Barbara Hodgdon, 'Sexual Disguise and the Theatre of Gender', in *The Cambridge Companion to Shakespearean Comedy*, Alexander Leggatt ed. (Cambridge, 2002), 179–97, 183.

7 Lesley Wade Soule, 'Subverting Rosalind: Cocky Ros in the Forest of Arden', *New Theatre Quarterly* 7(26) (May 1991), 126–36, 127.

8 Juliet Dusinberre, *Shakespeare and the Nature of Women* (3rd ed.) (Basingstoke, 2003), 233.

9 Valerie Traub, 'Desire and the Differences it Makes', in *The Matter of Difference. Materialist Feminist Criticism of Shakespeare*, Valerie Wayne ed. (Hemel Hempstead, 1991), 81–114 (104–5).

10 Jean Howard, 'Cross-dressing, the Theatre, and Gender Struggle in Early Modern England', *Shakespeare Quarterly* 39(4) (Winter, 1981), 418–40, 434, 435.

11 The text cited is that of the one-volume Oxford Complete Works (2nd ed.) (Oxford, 2005).

12 On the Coombe performances, see John Stokes, *Resistible Theatres. Enterprise and Experiment in the Late Nineteenth Century* (London, 1972).

13 'As You Like It at Coombe House' (*Dramatic Review*, 6 June 1885), in *Reviews by Oscar Wilde*, Robert Ross ed. (London,

1908), 34–5. Wilde comments on the colour scheme of the costumes ('brown and green were the dominant colours, and yellow was most artistically used'), but not on the effect of the cross-dressing.

14 On Daly's Shakespeare productions, see Marvin Felheim, *The Theater of Augustin Daly. An Account of the Late Nineteenth-century American Stage* (Cambridge, MA, 1956), ch. 6; and Charles H. Shattuck, *Shakespeare on the American Stage. Volume 2: from Booth and Barrett to Sothern and Marlowe* (Washington, DC, 1987), ch. 2, 'Augustin Daly and the Shakespeare Comedies'.

15 *Saturday Review*, 6 July 1895: *Our Theatres in the Nineties* (London, 1932), I, 170–7, 175.

16 *Saturday Review*, 6 December 1896: *Our Theatres in the Nineties*, II, 264–71, 269.

17 Gordon Crosse, *Diaries* (21 vols, MS Birmingham Shakespeare Library), IV, 67. The diaries were the basis for Crosse's *Shakespearean Playgoing 1890–1952* (London, 1953), but contain many details not included there.

18 *Saturday Review*, 12 October 1907: Max Beerbohm, *Around Theatres* (London, 1953), 477–8, 480.

19 Quoted in Russell Jackson, 'Remembering Bergner's Rosalind', in *Shakespeare, Memory and Performance*, Peter Holland ed. (Cambridge, 2006), 237–55, 243.

20 Wolcott Gibbs, 'Miss Hepburn in Arden', *New Yorker*, 5 February 1950, 48–50, 48.

21 'Shakespeare in Stratford-upon-Avon: The Royal Shakespeare Company's "Half Season", April–September 1996', *Shakespeare Quarterly* 48(2) (Summer 1997), 208–15, 209.

22 Quoted by Smallwood, *Shakespeare at Stratford: 'As You Like It'*, 108.

23 Alan Brissenden ed., *As You Like It* (Oxford, 1993), 65.

24 Anne Hollander, *Sex and Suits. The Evolution of Modern Dress* (New York, 1994), 148, 150.

25 Roger Warren, 'Shakespeare in Britain, 1985', *Shakespeare Quarterly* 37(1) (Spring 1986), 114–20, 118. In *Players of Shakespeare 2*, Russell Jackson and Robert Smallwood eds

(Cambridge, 1988), 55–72, Shaw and Stevenson describe their work in the production.
26 Jan Kott, *Shakespeare our Contemporary*, trans. Boleslaw Taborski with a preface by Peter Brook (London, 1965), 190–236.
27 Laurence Senelick, *The Changing Room. Sex, Drag and Theatre* (London and New York, 2000), 148.
28 Peter Holland, *English Shakespeares. Shakespeare on the English Stage in the 1990s* (Cambridge, 1997), 91.
29 Senelick, *The Changing Room*, 149.
30 Holland, *English Shakespeares*, 94.
31 Holland, *English Shakespeares*, 94.
32 Dusinberre ed., *As You Like It*, 26.
33 *An Apology for the Life of Colley Cibber*, B.R.S.Fone ed. (Ann Arbor, MI, 1968), 72.
34 Simon Reade, *Cheek By Jowl. Ten Years of Celebration* (Bath, 1991), 95.

How Designers Helped Juliet's Nurse Reclaim Her Bawdy

1 *Saturday Review*, 28 September 1895, 19; for Shaw on Shakespeare's flaws, see his preface to *Man and Superman*.
2 Shakespeare *Romeo and Juliet* Forbes-Robertson prompt book, Victoria & Albert Museum.
3 An early reference to the Nurse's costume suggests that she could be dressed not only simply, but meanly. Oliver Goldsmith described his adventures as an actor, in 1760, touring with a penniless troupe of strolling players. In their ramshackle production of scenes from *Romeo and Juliet* the costumes for the wealthy Capulets and Montagues were very makeshift and unconvincing. 'In short there were but three figures among us that might be said to be dressed with any propriety; I mean the nurse, the starved apothecary and myself.' Gamini Salgado, *Eyewitnesses of Shakespeare:*

First Hand Accounts of Performances 1590–1890 (London, 1975), 192.

4 Shakespeare, *Romeo and Juliet* David Garrick edition, 1744. Victoria & Albert Museum.

5 See Jill Levenson, *Shakespeare in Performance Romeo and Juliet* (Manchester, 1987), ch. II; René Weiss, 'Introduction', *Romeo and Juliet*, The Arden Shakespeare (London, 2012), 52–94.

6 *Dramatic Magazine*, November 1829, 267, review praising Fanny Kemble's Juliet.

7 Leigh Hunt, *Dramatic Criticism 1808–1831*, Lawrence Huston Houtchens and Carolyn Washburn Houtchens eds (Oxford, 1950), 285.

8 See Janet Arnold, *Patterns of Fashion 1* (London, 1972), 60.

9 Davenport played the Nurse to Harriet Smithson's Juliet. The reviewer in *The Spectator* said the performance was 'unalloyed perfection'. The reviewer in the *Dramatic Magazine*, November 1829, praised her, saying that 'the Nurse was Mrs. Davenport, which needs no further comment'.

10 See Stuart Sillars, *The Illustrated Shakespeare 1709–1875* (Cambridge, 2008).

11 Robyn Asleson, 'She Was Tragedy Personified', *Sarah Siddons and Her Portraitists* (Los Angeles, CA, 1999), 89.

12 *Etiquette of Good Society* (London, 1889), 80.

13 *The Academy*, 15 November 1884, 664, 331–2.

14 Ellen Terry, *Memoirs*, Christopher St John ed. (New York, 1932; Westport, CT, 1970), 164.

15 Ellen Terry, *Memoirs*, 164.

16 Kate Terry Gielgud, *An Autobiography* (London, 1953), 207.

17 See Shakespeare clippings: *Romeo and Juliet*, the Library of Birmingham, Birmingham, UK.

18 These images are easily found on the internet.

19 *The Athenaeum*, 8 May 1909, Frank Benson's production of *King John* at Stratford-upon-Avon.

20 See Judith Buchanan, *Silent Shakespeare: An Excellent Dumb Discourse* (Cambridge, 2009), 127, n. 38.

21 Ellen Terry, *Four Lectures on Shakespeare*, intro. Christopher St John (London, 1912), 144.

22 Christopher St John, *Ellen Terry* (London, 1907), 177; see also Christopher St John, 'Preface and Notes', in *Memoirs*, Ellen Terry (New York, 1932; Westport, CT, 1970). See also Michael Holroyd, *A Strange Eventual History: The Dramatic Lives of Ellen Terry, Henry Irving, and their Remarkable Families* (London, 2008), 475–6.

23 John Gielgud, *Distinguished Company* (London, 1972), 15.

24 Ellen Terry, St John *Memoirs* (London, 1907), 280.

25 J.C.Trewin, *The English Theatre* (London 1948), 85.

26 J.C.Trewin, *Theatre*, 85.

27 George Bernard Shaw, *Shaw on Shakespeare*, Edwin Wilson ed. (London, 1961), 290.

28 John Gielgud in *Early Stages* (London, 1974), 50–1, describes the costume, gold-sprayed tights and jerkin, and the costume's problems: 'I was given white tights with soles attached to them underneath and no shoes. My feet looked enormous, and it was most uncomfortable to fight or run about.' He also objected to the black wig, orange make-up and a very low-necked doublet that made him look in photographs like 'a mixture of Rameses of Egypt and a Victorian matron'. The costumes, only half-finished by dress rehearsal, 'smelt abominably of the gold paint with which they were lavishly stencilled and fitted very badly'. This was the performance where one critic noted that 'Mr. Gielgud has the most meaningless legs imaginable'.

29 Paul Shelving, 'A Note Upon Stage Decoration', *The Beacon*, January 1923, reprinted in *Paul Shelving (1888–1968), Stage Designer: An Exhibition Held at Birmingham City Museum and Art Gallery, 7 June–27 July 1986*, Tessa Sidey ed. (Birmingham, 1986).

30 *Birmingham Weekly*, 24 May 1922.

31 John Gielgud, *Early Stages* (London, 1974), 51.

32 Sir Barry Jackson and Birmingham Repertory Theatre Archives, the Library of Birmingham, Birmingham, UK.

33 Claire Cochrane, *Shakespeare and the Birmingham Repertory Theatre 1913–1929* (London, 1993).

34 *Birmingham Post*, 29 May 1922. Ironically, the costume's wimple and coif are reminiscent of the ecclesiastical dress of a medieval abbess, as well as Chaucer's Wife of Bath, discussed on p. 183.

35 *Evening Dispatch*, 29 May 1922.

36 *Birmingham Mail*, 29 May 1922.

37 *Birmingham Mail*, 29 May 1922.

38 John Gielgud, *Early Stages* (London, 1974), 51.

39 See Ann Rosalind Jones and Margaret Rosenthal, *Habiti Antichi et Moderni, The Clothing of the Renaissance World* (London, 2008).

40 Herbert Farjeon, np, 31 May 1924.

41 *The Spectator*, 31 May 1924.

42 For OUDS see Humphrey Carpenter, *OUDS: A Centenary History of the Oxford University Dramatic Society, 1885–1985* (Oxford, 1985).

43 'Actress' is used throughout instead of 'actor' because that was the term in use during the periods under discussion.

44 In the 1935 production, several members of the OUDS cast returned, including George Devine, the OUDS president who had invited Gielgud to Oxford and cast himself as Mercutio. In London, Devine played the 'clown' Peter. See Humphrey Carpenter, *OUDS: A Centenary History of the Oxford University Dramatic Society 1885–1985* (Oxford, 1985).

45 John Gielgud, *Early Stages* (London, 1974), 126.

46 John Gielgud, *Early Stages*.

47 Michael Mullin, *Design by Motley* (Cranbury, NJ, 1996), 49–50.

48 See Michael Mullin, *Design by Motley*, for design chronology.

49 Because he was acting in a film, Gielgud played Mercutio and Olivier played Romeo during the first weeks of the production. When Gielgud's filming ended, they switched roles for the remainder of the run.

50 Mullin, *Design by Motley*, 49–50. Mullin reports that the Motley sketches for the Nurse (London production) 'make her look almost sinister' (50).

51 Motley's pattern for a wimple is a simple piece of cloth placed over the head with a hole for the face; 'the easiest material is fine jersey because this clings to the face'. Motley, *Designing & Making Stage Costumes* (New York, 1964), 98.

52 Within the early modern economy, servants were often paid or rewarded with gifts from their employer's own wardrobes. The under-skirt in Motley's costume suggests a gift that was too 'rich' to wear openly.

53 Leigh Hunt, *Dramatic Criticism 1808–1831*, Lawrence Huston Houtchens and Carolyn Washburn Houtchens eds (Oxford, 1950), 285.

54 W.A.Darlington, cited in Michael Billington, *Peggy Ashcroft 1907–1991* (London, 1991).

55 The only major cuts were the second chorus (2.1) and Peter and the musicians in 4.5. See René Weiss, 'Introduction', *Romeo and Juliet* (London, 2012), 45.

56 Stephen Williams, nd, np.

57 *Oxford Magazine*, 11 February 1932.

58 The clipping has no date or publication. Clippings in Box ADD MS 81539 in the Gielgud Papers, British Library, were generally cut out of the papers without keeping the date or name of publication. This is indicated in notes by nd, np.

59 E.A.Baughan, nd, np.

60 October 1935, np.

61 The cast included Orson Welles as Tybalt, Basil Rathbone as Romeo and Brian Aherne as Mercutio.

62 Brooks Atkinson, *New York Times*, 21 December 1934; John Mason Brown, *New York Post* and Edith J.R. Issacies, *Theater Arts Monthly*, cited in Samuel L. Leither *The Encyclopedia of the New York Stage 1930–1940* (New York, 1989), 687–8.

63 For a full production history see Russell Jackson, *Shakespeare Films in the Making* (Cambridge, 2007), 127–61.

64 For Messel's comments on the costumes, see William Shakespeare, *'Romeo and Juliet': A Motion Picture Edition. Illustrated with Photographs. Produced for*

Metro-Goldwyn-Meyer by Irving G. Thalberg. Directed by George Cukor. Arranged for Screen by Talbot Jennings (New York, 1936), 267–8; for drawings of the costumes, see William Shakespeare, *'Romeo and Juliet'. With Designs by Oliver Messel* (London, 1936); for an overview of his career see Thomas Messel, *Oliver Messel: In the Theatre of Design* (New York, 2012); *Oliver Messel: An Exhibition Held at the Theatre Museum, Victoria and Albert Museum 22 June–30 October 1983*, Roger Pinkham ed. (London, 1983).

65 For Adrian's comments on the costumes and Gibbons' on the sets, see William Shakespeare, *'Romeo and Juliet': A Motion Picture Edition*, 261–3.

66 For examples of the range of Gibbons' designs, see *The Philadelphia Story* for tasteful upper-class American decor and MGM's *Marie Antoinette* for his flair for historical excess.

67 See Howard Gutner, *Gowns by Adrian: the MGM Years, 1928–41* (New York, 2001).

68 *Variety*, 26 August 1936, 120.

69 Russell Jackson, *Shakespeare Films in the Making* (Cambridge 2007), 128.

70 Adrian, somewhat excluded in the *Romeo and Juliet* publicity, would have his own research trip to France three years later in preparation for *Marie Antoinette* (1938), starring Norma Shearer.

71 Choreography Marius Petipa, additional choreography Ninette de Valois/Frederic Ashton. Sadler's Wells Ballet Royal Opera House, London, 20 February 1946.

72 William Shakespeare, *'Romeo and Juliet': A Motion Picture Edition*, 154, 179 .

73 J.C.Trewin, *Edith Evans*, Theatre World Monograph No. 2 (London, 1954); see also Michael Billington's obituary of Dame Edith Evans, DBE, *Guardian*, 15 October 1976.

74 *TCM Tribute to Edna May Oliver*, http://www.youtube.com (viewed May 2014).

75 William Shakespeare, *'Romeo and Juliet': A Motion Picture Edition*, 214.

76 Frank Nugent, 'The Bard Passes His Screen Test', *New York Times*, 30 August 1936.

77 William Shakespeare, *'Romeo and Juliet': A Motion Picture Edition*, 156.

78 William Shakespeare, *'Romeo and Juliet': A Motion Picture Edition*, 179.

79 Hubbard Keavy, 'A Visit to "Romeo" Set in Hollywood', *The Hartford Courant*, 12 April 1936. It was well known that Barrymore was drinking heavily during the filming, so the subtext is probably a rather drunken Mercutio.

80 Earlier in the scene when Mercutio flirts with the women, it is clear he is a well-known favourite.

81 Their work corresponds to Erving Goffman's theory in *The Presentation of Self in Everyday Life* (New York, 1959) that an individual's decision to dress in a certain style is a performance. Goffman contends that individuals dress themselves for the outside world as though going on stage.

82 Juliet (Margot Fonteyn) leaps through the air and lands with legs curled under on the Nurse's lap in *Romeo and Juliet*, choreographed by Kenneth MacMillan for the Royal Ballet (Covent Garden, 1964); Rudolf Nureyev was Romeo; design was by Nicholas Georgiadis.

83 Geoffrey Chaucer, *The Canterbury Tales*, David Wright ed. (Oxford, 1986), 14.

84 See, for example, Russell Jackson, *Romeo and Juliet*, Shakespeare in Stratford Series (London, 2003); Jill Levenson, *Shakespeare in Performance Romeo and Juliet* (Manchester, 1987).

85 *Vogue* magazine ran a series of *Romeo and Juliet* photos by Annie Liebowitz; the full-page picture of Estelle Parson wearing an elaborate white coif is immediately recognizable as the Nurse – although now the black, long-sleeved, floor-length, full-skirted garment she wears is a block-printed faille dress by fashion designer Proenza Schouler. Gia Kourlas, 'Love of a Lifetime', *Vogue*, December 2008.

Shakespeare Stripped: Costuming Prisoner-of-war Entertainments and Cabaret

1 From Jonson's dedication in the First Folio 1623.

2 Sir David Piper, later Director of the National Portrait Gallery and the Fitzwilliam and Ashmolean museums, describes wearing a pair of briefs made from flour sacking during his time as a PoW in Shirakawa camp, Taiwan. 'Looking Back 1965' in the posthumously published *I Am Well, Who Are You?*, David Piper (Exeter, 1998), 11. The Imperial War Museum has several examples, including these: http://www.iwm.org.uk/collections/item/object/30088810.

3 Ronald Searle, *To the Kwai and Back, War Drawings 1939–45* (London, 2006), 7.

4 Ronald Searle, *To the Kwai and Back, War Drawings 1939–45* (London, 2006), 9.

5 Michael Dobson, *Shakespeare and Amateur Performance: A Cultural History*, and Richard Fawkes, *Fighting for A Laugh. Entertaining the British and American Armed Forces 1939–1946* (London, 1978).

6 Theatrical entertainment was by no means the only distraction at Changi or in other PoW camps. Changi, for instance, had a 'university' where men gave lectures, a library (common in many camps), a literary society and a choir.

7 *Wirebound World*, a remarkable document detailing the PoW theatre in Stalag Luft III, lists the repertoire of the theatre company there. It includes plays by G.B.Shaw, Oscar Wilde, J.B.Priestley and Ben Travers. H.P.Clark, *Wirebound World. Stalag Luft III* (London, 1946).

8 See Michael Dobson, *Shakespeare and Amateur Performance: A Cultural History* (Cambridge, 2011), 135–48 and also Laurence Senelick's *The Changing Room: Sex, Drag and Theatre* (London, 2000), 364. 'Approximately 70,000 Americans, a number of them professional actors, were confined in seventy German Stalags; as it had in the earlier conflict [World War I], the YMCA sent shipments of curtains, draperies, lighting equipment, make-up, costumes,

musical instruments and lumber, which the prisoners were sworn to use only for theatrical purposes and not for escapes'.

9 W.J.Beckerley to Jennifer Aylmer, 4.28.74 V&A Registered File Number: RP/1975/1070. Sime Road Camp had been the combined headquarters of the British Army and Royal Air Force until the capitulation; the Japanese initially used it as an intern camp for civilians but added military prisoners in 1944.

10 Guide to the Concert and Theatre Programs Collection, Second World War 1939–45. http://www.awm.gov.au/findingaids/special/Souvenirs/ww2ctp.xml.

11 The costume is in the IWM: http://www.iwm.org.uk/collections/item/object/30081382.

12 See, for example, an article in the *Daily Telegraph* (2005) about a rubber factory operating in the camp which manufactured shoes, prosthetics and cricket ball covers: http://www.telegraph.co.uk/news/worldnews/asia/singapore/1499224/How-resilient-Changi-Industries-shod-and-clothed-British-PoWs.html. Also, J.G.Clementson, *Changi Industries Incorporated: Don't Ever Say Again 'It Can't Be Done'* (Singapore, 2005).

13 Ronald Searle, Sketchbook: Theatre Notes and Stage Designs, The Barn Theatre, Spring Season 1944, Sime Road Prison Camp. Catalogue number Art IWM ART 15748, 2 (page references allude to the digitized version on IWM website rather than the physical numbers Searle sometimes gives to pages).

14 Ronald Searle, Sketchbook: Theatre Notes and Stage Designs, The Barn Theatre, Spring Season 1944, Sime Road Prison Camp. Catalogue number Art IWM ART 15748, 12, V&A S.408: 1–1978, Programme from Rag Bag Revue by Ronald Searle.

15 Ronald Searle, Sketchbook: Theatre Notes and Stage Designs, The Barn Theatre, Spring Season 1944, Sime Road Prison Camp. Catalogue number Art IWM ART 15748, 24.

16 Many thanks to my colleague Dr Beverley Hart for her observations on this matter.

17 Ronald Searle, *To the Kwai and Back, War Drawings 1939–45* (London, 2006), 158.

18 David Piper, *I Am Well, Who Are You?* (Exeter, 1998).

19 Scottish costume comes up again in Searle's IWM sketchbook when he is designing for 'Scotch Variety'; Ronald Searle, Sketchbook: Theatre Notes and Stage Designs, The Barn Theatre, Spring Season 1944, Sime Road Prison Camp. Catalogue number Art IWM ART 15748, 11.

20 V&A s.416-1978 design for *Hamlet Goes Hollywood* by Ronald Searle.

21 Judith Walkowitz, *Nights Out: Life in Cosmopolitan London* (London and New Haven, CT, 2012), 255 and 284.

22 See Frank Mort, 'Striptease: The Erotic Female Body and Live Sexual Entertainment in Mid-Twentieth Century London', *Social History* 32, 32(1) (2007), 27–53.

23 Letter from Helen O'Brien, 4.27.1992 V&A Registered File Number 1992/544.

24 Eve Club brochure 1962, V&A Building File: Eve Club.

25 Cited in Frank Mort, 'Striptease: The Erotic Female Body and Live Sexual Entertainment in Mid-Twentieth Century London', *Social History* 32, 32(1) (2007), 43.

26 Helen O'Brien obituary, *Telegraph*, 20 September 2005.

27 Helen O'Brien obituary, *Guardian*, 29 September 2005.

28 Yes, they still exist.

29 Eve Club brochure 1962, V&A Building File: Eve Club.

30 'The girls' poses recall the regular play of the pistons. They are not so much of military precision as they correspond in some other way to the ideal of the machine. A button is pressed and the girl contraption cranks into motion, performing impressively at thirty-two horsepower.' Siegfried Kracauer, 'Girls and Crisis', 1931. Reproduced in *The Weimar Sourcebook*, Anton Kaes, Martin Jay and Edward Dimendberg eds (Berkeley, CA, 1994), 565–6.

The Designers

1 Draper – in a costume design studio, the draper creates garments or patterns by draping the fabric on a dress form.

2 The bottle-top school of design means creating a look of luxury in costumes while using inexpensive materials.

INDEX

Aaron, 108, 120, 121, 122
ACT. *See* American Conservatory Theater
Africanus, Johannes Leo: *A Geographical History of Africa*, 108–9, 10
Aguecheek, Andrew, 16
Aickin, Elinor: *Romeo and Juliet*, 163–64, 169
Alfred Jackson Girls, 202
Aliena, 137, 148
Alleyn, Edward, 32, 253n43
All's Well That Ends Well, 17
American Conservatory Theater (ACT), 216, 217
American Shakespeare Festival Theatre, 211, 212
Anderson, Mary: *Romeo and Juliet*, 158, 161, 163
Anne of Denmark, 25, 40, 42
Antonio, 59
Antony, 34
Antony and Cleopatra, 13, 31, 186, 200, 201, 218, 223
Archer, Helen, 195–96, 197, 198
Arnold, Janet, 210, 255n59
Arnold, John, 41
Asche, Oscar: *As You Like It*, 142
Ashcroft, Peggy: *As You Like It*, 147–49; *Romeo and Juliet*, 171, 172–73

As You Like It, 13, 15, 131–56; Declan Donellan, 153–54; Edith Evans, 150–52; Elisabeth Bergner in Paul Czinner's film, 143–45; Juliet Stevenson, 150–52; Katharine Hepburn, 145–47; New York Shakespeare Festival, 211; Nigel Playfair, 17; Adrian Noble, 150, 151; Oscar Asche, 142; Peggy Ashcroft, Vanessa Redgrave at Stratford-upon-Avon, 147–49; all-male productions 152–55; Stratford-upon-Avon 1957, 1961 and 1980, 147–49; Stratford-upon-Avon 1985, 150–52; Stratford-upon-Avon 1996, 145–47
Atkins, Eileen: *As You Like It*, 149
Atkinson, Brooks, 146
Ayliff, H.K., 11; *Romeo and Juliet*, 166, 167, 184

Bacon, Francis, 117
Bailey, Amanda: *Flaunting*, 242n16
Bailey, James: *As You Like It*, 146

Bakst, Leon: *Ballets Russes*, 17, 169–70
Ball, Bill: *Cyrano de Bergerac*, 216; *Taming of the Shrew*, 216
Bannen, Ian: *As You Like It*, 148
Barker, Harley Granville, 228n17; *A Midsummer Night's Dream*, 16, 19; *Twelfth Night*, 16; *The Winter's Tale*, 16
Barn Theatre, 188, 190, 194
Barrymore, John: *Romeo and Juliet*, 176, 181, 273n79
Bartels, Emily C., 108, 257n3
Barthes, Roland, 11
Barton, John: *Measure for Measure*, 220
Bassanio, 5, 47, 51, 52, 53–54, 57–58, 242n16
beards, 56, 243n24
Beatrice, 116
Beckerley, John, 189, 190
Beerbohm, Max, 142
Belch, Sir Toby, 16
Benois, Alexander: *Ballets Russes*, 17
Benson, Frank: *Romeo and Juliet*, 163
Bentley, Thomas: *The Monument of Matrons*, 78
Bergner, Elisabeth: *As You Like It* (film), 143–45
Berry, Cecily, 220
Bibbiena, Bernardo: *The Courtier*, 116
Billington, Michael, 146, 149, 151
Birmingham Repertory Company, 165–70, 172, 184; 'Hamlet in plus-four', 11

Blackman, Bob, 216
Blackwork, 106, 257n5
Blakemore, Michael: *Next Season*, 2
Boleyn, Anne, 37, 39, 234n60
Borachio, 111
Borde, Andrew, 108
bottle-top school of design, 276n2
Boyarin, Adrienne Williams, 55
Brabantio, 123, 125
Braithwaite, Richard, 118
Branagh, Kenneth: *Love's Labour's Lost*, 12
Braster, Margaret, 81
Brayton, Lily: *As You Like It*, 142
Brecht, Bertolt, 10–11, 18
Brickland, John, 70
Bridge On the River Kwai, 187
Briggs, Henry Perronet, 160
Brome, Richard: *The Court Begger*, 88, 100
Brook, 65, 67, 69, 79
Brook, Peter: *A Midsummer Night's Dream*, 19; *Prince Genji*, 208
Brown, Allen, 72
Brown, Ivor, 151–52
Buckley, Kate: *Antony and Cleopatra*, 218
Burbage, Richard, 251n25
Burghley, Lord, 41
Burton, Richard, 212
Bury, John: *The Wars of the Roses*, 18
Busino, Orazio, 29
Byrde, Thomas, 73

Caius, 245n3
Calhoun, Eleanor, 140

Calvert, Samuel, 43
Campbell, Lady Archibald, 140
Campbell, Mrs Patrick: *Romeo and Juliet*, 161
Capon, William, 14
Carey, Robert, 116
Carpaccio, 166, 168, 172, 173, 182, 210
Carpenter, Sarah, 58
Cassio, 112, 113, 119–20, 124, 125
Castellani, Renato: *Giulietta e Romeo*, 182
Castiglione, Baldessare: *The Courtier*, 91, 111, 116, 126
Cavandish, Thomas, 260n32
Celia, 147–48, 149, 150, 155, 211, 260n33
Chakravarty, Urvashi, 242n16, 242n18, 244n28
Chamberlain, Lord, 42, 94, 118
Chamberlain, Neville, 187
Changi Concert Party, 189
Changi Jail, 187, 189, 193, 274n6
Changi Theatre group, 189
Charlemagne, 126, 127
Chaucer, 166, 183, 270n34; The Miller's Tale, 57
Cheek by Jowl: *As You Like It*, 153–54; *A Midsummer's Night Dream*, 202
Chettle, Henry: *Kindharts Dreame*, 93
Chichester Theatre, 209
Church, Esmé: *As You Like It*, 151
Churchyard, Thomas, 237n81
Cibber, Colley, 156
Claudius, 12, 194

Cleopatra, 15, 31, 33, 38, 200, 218, 236n70. See also Antony and Cleopatra
Cleveley, William, 74, 246n18
clothes as security for loans, 43, 237n88
Cobb, Ronald, 7, 186–87, 195, 196,198, 202
Cobham, Eleanor, 39, 236n73
Cochran, C.B., 176
Cochrane, Claire, 167
Cochrane, Jeanetta, 208
Colorado Shakespeare Festival, 216
Cooke, George Frederick, 14
Coombe Woods, 140, 265n12
Coriolanus, 16, 223
Cornell, Katharine: *Romeo and Juliet*, 174
Cort Theatre, 145
Costume, 19
Coward, Noël, 189, 213
Cowley, Richard: *The Seven Deadly Sins, Part Two*, 240n10
cross-dressing, 2, 59, 141, 153, 155, 242n19, 244n30, 265n13
Crosse, Gordon, 142; *Shakespearean Playgoing 1890–1952*, 266n17
Croxton: *Play of the Sacrament*, 240n10
Cukor, George: *Romeo and Juliet*, 175, 184
Cunningham, Bill, 211
Cusack, Niamh: *As You Like It*, 146–47
Cymbeline, 11, 12, 13, 166

Czinner, Paul: *As You Like It* (film), 143

Dainty, 88, 91, 100
Daly, Augustin, 266n14; *Twelfth Night*, 141; *The Two Gentleman of Verona*, 141
Daly, Mrs W.: *Romeo and Juliet*, 160
Davenport, Mrs: *Romeo and Juliet*, 158, 160, 268n9
David, John: *As You Like It*, 149
Davies, Mandy Rice, 197
Dekker, Thomas, 23, 97, 115, 126, 127; *The Guls Horne-booke/Gull's Hornbook*, 92–93, 110; *Lust's Dominion, or the Lascivious Queen*, 106; *The Shoemaker's Holiday*, 98; *Westward Ho*, 99
de Lalaing, Antoine, 109
Desdemona, 124, 127
designers, contemporary, 7, 207–24
Dessen, Alan C., 88: *Dictionary of Stage Directions in English Drama, 1580–1642*, 88, 249n8, 250n14
Devine, George, 270n44; *Romeo and Juliet*, 170
Diaghilev, Sergei: *Ballets Russes*, 9–10, 17, 169
Diffen, Ray: *The Importance of Being Earnest*, 209; *Much Ado About Nothing*, 211
disguisings, 40–45
Dobson, Michael, 188

Dodd, Ian, 154
Donellan, Declan: *As You Like It*, 153–54, 155
Donne, John, 233n48
Dorney, Kate, 7, 185–203
Douglas, 44
Dowling, Joe: *Othello*, 210
Downton, Thomas, 95
Drakakis, John, 242n19, 244n28
draper, 209, 276n1
Drummond, Dolores: *Romeo and Juliet*, 158, 161
Drury Lane, 13, 15, 159
Dudley, Robert, 107, 113, 114, 115, 119, 257n6
Duke of Alençon, 36
Dusinberre, Juliet, 136, 156
Dyer, Elizabeth, 81

Edgar, David, 10–11
Edward, the Black Prince, 14
Edwards, Ben: *The Ballad of a Sad Café*, 209; *Hamlet*, 209, 213
Edwards, Jack: *Hamlet*, 214
Elam, Keir, 10
el-Ouahed, Abd, 106, 107, 108, 116–17, 119, 123
Elizabeth I (queen), 5, 23–46, 96, 99, 106, 110, 115, 117, 236n70, 255n59, 262n52
Elizabeth I with the Cardinal and Theological Virtues, 232n40
Elizabethan Stage Society, 16
Ellen Terry Memorial Museum, 164
Elliott, Michael: *As You Like It*, 148

Emilia, 126
English anxiety, 244n30
English Stage Company, 18
Entertainments National Service Association (ENSA), 198
Etiquette of Good Society, 161
Evans, Edith: *As You Like It*, 151, 152, 158; *Romeo and Juliet*, 171, 173–75, 179, 180, 183, 188
Every Man in his Humour, 13–14

Falstaff, 46, 63, 65, 66, 67, 68–69, 74, 75, 76–77, 78, 79, 80, 81, 84
Farjeon, Herbert, 170
Faucit, Helen: *Romeo and Juliet*, 160
Fawkes, Richard, 188
Fazzula, 259n18
fazzuolo, 110, 259n19
Fernando, King, 109
Festival Theatre, 17
Ffrangcon-Davies, Gwen: *Romeo and Juliet*, 167
Fiennes, Ralph: *Coriolanus*, 223
First World War, 17, 187, 274n8
Fitzdottrel, 98–99
Fitzgeffrey, Henry: 'Play-house Observation', 93
Fletcher, Bob, 216
Florio, John, 117, 242n19
Flugle, J.C.: *The Psychology of Clothing*, 182
footing, 88, 91
Forbes-Robertson, Johnston: *Romeo and Juliet*, 158
Ford, Master, 64, 65–66, 67, 68, 69, 76, 79–81, 82, 245n3

Ford, Mistress, 64, 65–66, 73, 75, 76–77, 79–80
Fortescue, John: *The Governance of England*, 230n22
fortune, 53, 243n20
Frank, David, 218
Fraser, Claud Lovat: *As You Like It*, 17
Frederick, Henry, 260n32
Fuerst, Walter René: *Twentieth Century Stage Decoration*, 10
Funicello, Ralph, 216; *Dr Faustus*, 217
Furse, Roger: *Hamlet*, 18; *Henry V*, 18; *Richard III*, 18

Ganymede, 6, 135, 137, 138–39, 142, 143, 144, 145–47, 148–49, 151, 153, 154; boots, 8
Garbo, Greta: *Queen Christina*, 143
Garrick, David, 227n13; *Antony and Cleopatra*, 13; *Hamlet*, 13; *Macbeth*, 13; *Richard III*, 14; *Romeo and Juliet*, 158–59
Gawdy, Philip, 118
George a Greene, 49, 240n9
George a Greene, the Pinner of Wakefield, 48, 49, 51, 59
Gertrude, 2, 194, 213
A Gest of Robyn Hode, 55, 240n8
Gheerhaerts, Marcus, 264n62
Gibbons, Cedric: *Romeo and Juliet*, 177, 272nn65–66
Gibbs, Mrs: *Romeo and Juliet*, 159

Gibbs, Wolcott, 146
Gielgud, John, 158; *Beckett*, 212; *Early Stages*, 269n28; *Hamlet*, 209, 212–14; *Romeo and Juliet*, 165, 166, 169, 170–75, 180, 183, 184, 270n44, 270n49
Gielgud, Kate Terry, 163
Gilbert, Sir John, 160
Giles, Thomas, 41
Gill, Peter: *Much Ado About Nothing,* 211
Globe Theatre, 8, 19, 43, 101, 171, 210
Glyn, Isabella, 15
Godwin, Edward William: *Romeo and Juliet*, 140
Goffman, Erving: *The Presentation of Self in Everyday Life*, 273n81
Gold, Margaret, 246n17
Goldsmith, Oliver, 267n3
Goneril, 39, 40, 233n45
Goodbody, Buzz: *As You Like It*, 149
Gorges, Ferdinando, 116
Goscome, Joanna, 71
Goscome, John, 70–71
Goscome, Thomas, 70–71
Gosson, Stephen, 5, 23, 24, 40, 41, 44, 46, 94, 98; *Plays Confuted in Five Actions*, 92
Gott, Barbara: *Romeo and Juliet*, 170
Gray, Terence, 17
Great Chronicle, 29
Greek theatre, ancient 2, 94
Greene, Graham: *The End of the Affair*, 12

Greene, Robert: *Newes both from Heaven and Hell*, 111; *A Quip for an Upstart Courtier*, 97
Greenwood, Jane, 7, 208–16; advice to aspiring designers, 215–16; *Arthur*, 209; *As You Like It*, 211; *The Ballad of a Sad Café*, 209; beginnings, 208–10; *Can't Stop the Music*, 209; early influences, 210; *The Four Seasons*, 209; *Glengarry Glen Ross*, 209–10; *Hamlet*, 209, 212–14; *The Importance of Being Earnest*, 209; influences in using historical periods in Shakespeare productions, 210–12; input from actors on design, 215; *Love's Labour's Lost*, 212; *The Merry Wives of Windsor*, 212; modern-dress Hamlet, 212–14; *Much Ado About Nothing,* 211; *Othello*, 210
grogram, 110, 259n22
Gurr, Andrew, 241n14, 244n31
Guthrie, Tyrone, 17, 209
Guthrie Theater, 209, 217

Hakluyt, Richard: *The Principall Navigations, Voiages and Discoveries of the English Nation*, 51
Hal, Prince, 29, 34, 38, 46, 141
Hamet, Muly, 106, 263n61
Hamlet, 8, 12, 18, 35, 36, 111, 185, 200, 209, 212, 217
Hamlet, 13, 14, 15, 35, 91–92, 98, 102, 122, 200, 212–14

Hands, Terry: *As You Like It*, 136
Harris, Margaret, 18, 171; *Romeo and Juliet*, 157. *See also* Motley
Harris, Sophia, 18, 171; *Romeo and Juliet*, 157. *See also* Motley
Harrison, William: *Description of England*, 106, 110–11, 127
Hauser, Frank, 208
Hayward, Maria, 5, 23–46
Heeley, Desmond, 18, 208, 216; *The Matchmaker*, 217; *Measure for Measure*, 217; *Prince Genji*, 208; *Romeo and Juliet*, 175; *The Winter's Tale*, 217
Henry, Prince, 25, 38
Henry VIII (king), 27, 28, 39, 51. *See also King Henry VIII*
Henslowe, Philip: *Diary*, 5, 24, 28, 29, 35, 36, 38, 43, 49, 50, 94, 95, 97, 101, 253n45, 263n59
Hentzner, Paul, 27
Hepburn, Katharine: *As You Like It*, 145–47
Herbert, Jocelyn, 18
Her Majesty's Theatre, 17
Heywood, Thomas: *An Apology for Actors*, 94; *The Foure Prentices of London*, 102; *The Rape of Lucrece*, 102
Hill, Robert, 70
History plays, 19, 24, 37
Hodgdon, Barbara, 3, 134–35
Hogarth, William, 14, 227n13
Holbein, Hans, 14, 82

Holland, Peter, 154, 155
Hollander, Anne, 114, 117; *Sex and Suits*, 149
'honest clothes', 63–84
Howard, Jean E., 137
Howard, Leslie, 176; *The Scarlet Pimpernel*, 177
Howes, Edmund, 96, 253n46
Howme, Alexander, 26
Hume, Samuel J.: *Twentieth Century Stage Decoration*, 10
Hunt, Leigh 159, 173
Hurry, Leslie, 18

Iago, 105, 112, 113, 115, 119–20, 122–23, 124–25, 128, 210
ibn Khaldûn, Muhammad, 126–27
Ingland, Thomas, 81
Ingold, Tim, 86–87
Irving, Henry, 14–15; *Macbeth*, 16; *Othello*, 164; *Romeo and Juliet*, 158, 161

Jackson, Alfred: Girls, 202
Jackson, Barry, 166
Jackson, Nagel: *The Taming of the Shrew*, 220
Jackson, Russell, 4, 6–7, 9–20, 131–56, 177; *Love's Labour's Lost*, 12
Jacques, 136, 142, 154
James I (king), 5, 23–46, 117, 118, 124; *Basilikon Doron*, 118–19
James VI (king). *See* James I (king)
Jenkin, 48, 49, 240n9
Jenkins, 70

Jennings, Talbot: *Romeo and Juliet*, 180
Jennings, William, 38
Jessica, 58, 59
Jewell, Simon, 229
John of Gaunt, 45
Johnson, Peter, 255n59
Johnson, Richard: *As You Like It*, 147
Johnston, Alexandra, 49
Jones, Ann Rosalind: *Habiti Antichi et Moderni, The Clothing of the Renaissance*, 4; *Renaissance Clothing in the Materials of Memory*, 3–4, 49, 241n14
Jones, Inigo, 13
Jones, William, 26
Jonson, Ben, 14, 185, 248n3; *Epicene*, 90; *The Devil is an Ass*, 98; *Masque of Blackness*, 120; *The Staple of News*, 253n50
Jordan, Neil: *The End of the Affair*, 12
Juan, Prince, 109
Julia, 134
Julia, Raul: *Othello*, 210
Julius Caesar, 34, 250n11
Julius Caesar, 36, 233n53

Kahn, Michael: *Love's Labour's Lost*, 212; *The Merry Wives of Windsor*, 212
Katherine of Aragon, 39
Kean, Charles, 15
Kean, Edmund, 14
Keane, Doris: *Romeo and Juliet*, 164, 165
Keeler, Christine, 197

Kemble, Charles, 14
Kemble, Fanny: *Romeo and Juliet*, 160
Kemble, Philip, 14
Kempe, William, 93; *Nine Daies Wonder*, 94
King Henry IV, 24, 28, 34, 36, 44, 90, 141
King Henry VI, 37, 39
King Henry VIII, 39, 43; christening of Princess Elizabeth, 37, 234n60
King John, 14, 15, 33, 44, 163–64
King Lear, 33, 36, 39, 233n45; need, 234n57
King Richard II, 33, 37
King Richard III, 37, 38, 43
King Richard III, 43, 44
Knight, Stephen, 243n21
Komisarjevsky, Theodore, 17
Korda, Natasha, 6, 85–103; *Labor's Lost: Women's Work and the Early Modern English Stage*, 4
Kott, Jan: 'Shakespeare's bitter Arcadia', 153
Kynaston, Edward: *As You Like It*, 156

Laertes, 111
Lambert, J.W., 148
Langham, Michael: *The Matchmaker*, 217; *Measure for Measure*, 217; *The Winter's Tale*, 217
Lancelot, 47, 51–54, 56–57, 58, 59, 242n16, 242n19
Lee, Thomas, 264n62

Lefton, Sue, 156
Lennox, Patricia, 1–8, 157–84
Lennox-Boyd, Christopher, 227n13
Leo X (pope), 109
Lessing Theater, 144
Lester, Adrian: *As You Like It*, 154–55, 156
Levin, Bernard, 148
Lin, Erika T., 5, 47–61
Linthicum, M. Channing: *Costume in the Drama of Shakespeare and his Contemporaries*, 3, 231n26
Little Theatre movement 188
livery, 5, 47–61, 239n2, 239n5, 240n9, 241n13, 242n16
Lodovico, 124, 127, 128
Lopez, Antonio: *Much Ado About Nothing*, 211
Lorenzo, 58
Love's Labour's Lost, 12, 13, 137, 212, 223
Lyceum Theatre, 14, 16, 161, 163
Lyric Theatre, 154, 164
Lyly, John, 135, 137; *Galatea*, 132

Macbeth, 16, 37, 186, 198
Macbeth, 13, 15, 194, 198
Macbeth, Lady, 16
MacIntyre, Jean: *Costumes and Scripts in the Elizabethan Theaters*, 3, 227n9
Macklin, Charles, 13, 14, 227n11; *Macbeth*, 186
Macmillan, Harold, 197
MacMillan, Kenneth: *Romeo and Juliet*, 273n82

Macready, William Charles: *As You Like It*, 15; *King John*, 15
Maid Marian, 57, 59
Malvolio, 16, 97; stockings, 254n51
Mamoulian, Rouben: *Queen Christina*, 143
Manhattan Theatre Club, 211
Marcus, 33
Margaret of Austria, Princess, 109
Margaret, Queen, 39
marlota, 109, 259n17
Marston, John: *Antonio and Mellida*, 254n57
Martin, Nicky, 222
Mary Queen of Scots, 42, 44
Matar, Nabil, 106, 108, 263n53
McClintic, Guthrie: *Romeo and Juliet*, 174
McRae, Hilton: *As You Like It*, 150
Melibeus, 132
Melville, James, 110
The Merchant of Venice, 5, 47–61, 90, 106, 120, 199, 220, 230n21
The Merchant's Surety, 55
The Merry Wives of Windsor, 5–6, 15, 63–84, 212, 245n2
Messel, Oliver, 18; *The Miracle*, 176–77; *The Private Life of Don Juan*, 177; *Romeo and Juliet*, 157, 175–78, 181, 183, 184, 271n64; *The Scarlet Pimpernel*, 177
MGM, 143, 175, 177, 178, 271n64, 272nn65–67

A Midsummer Night's Dream, 13, 16, 17, 19, 98, 201, 218, 223, 224, 229n3
Mirabella, Bella, 6, 105–28
modern dress, 11, 139, 149, 166, 218, 220; Hamlet, 212–14
Moiseiwitsch, Tanya, 18, 228n20; Prince Genji, 209
MoLA. *See* Museum of London Archaeology
Monks, Aiofe, 1, 3
Montague, Alice, 96
Montgomery, Elizabeth, 18, 171; *Romeo and Juliet*, 157. *See also* Motley
Moore, Ben, 216
moral valence, 246n17
Morgan, Robert 216–24; ACT, 216, 217; American Players Theater, 218; *Antony and Cleopatra*, 218, 223; beginnings, 216–18; designing for historical periods, 222–23; design process for a Shakespeare play versus other plays, 221–22; *Dr Faustus*, 217; *Measure for Measure*, 220, 223; *Midsummer's Nights Dream*, 218, 223, 224; Oregon Shakespeare Festival, 217; special challenges in designing Shakespeare productions, 218; *Winter's Tale*, 223; working with the director and/or production designer, 221
Morisco attire, 106, 109, 126

Motley, 18, 147, 171–72, 173, 210; *Romeo and Juliet*, 157, 174–75, 179, 181, 183, 184, 270n50, 271nn51–52. *See also* Harris, Margaret; Harris, Sophia; Montgomery, Elizabeth
Much Ado About Nothing, 111, 116, 211, 224
Mullin, Michael, 172, 270n50
Museum of London Archaeology (MoLA), 85, 102, 248n1

National Theatre, 152, 209
Negri, Richard: *As You Like It*, 148
Neil, Michael, 108
Neilson, Adelaide, 141
Nerissa, 244n30
New Theatre, 151, 170
New York Shakespeare Festival: *As You Like It*, 211
Noble, Adrian: *As You Like It*, 150, 151
North, Mary, 73–74

Oberon, 13, 19
O'Brien, Jack: *As You Like It*, 220; *Hamlet*, 217; *A Midsummer Night's Dream*, 224
O'Brien, Jimmy, 195, 196, 197, 198
Ohlgren, Thomas, 243n21
Old Globe, 207, 217
Old Gobbo, 53, 56, 57, 58
Old Vic, 17, 151, 152, 172
Oliver, 138, 147, 148

Oliver, Edna May: *David Copperfield*, 180; *Little Women*, 180; *Romeo and Juliet*, 158, 176, 179, 180–81, 183; *A Tale of Two Cities*, 180
Oliver, Isaac, 260n32
Olivier, Laurence: *As You Like It*, 143; *Romeo and Juliet*, 172, 270n49
Orgel, Stephen: *Impersonations*, 132
Orkin, Martin, 108
Orlando, 135, 137, 138, 139, 144, 147, 148, 149, 150, 151, 152, 153, 154; female, 140–43
Ormerod, Nick: *As You Like It*, 153–54, 202
Orsino, 16, 135, 136
Othello, 105–28, 210
Othello, 6, 105–28, 164, 264nn64–65
OUDS. *See* Oxford University Drama Society
Oxford Playhouse, 208
Oxford University Drama Society (OUDS), 170–71, 174, 270n44

Page, Anne, 67
Page, Master, 65, 69
Page, Mistress, 64, 66, 73, 76, 77, 78, 79, 83
Parson, Estelle: *Romeo and Juliet*, 273n85
Peacham, Henry, 5, 186–87; *Titus Andronicus*, 12, 108, 121, 238n95

Peele, George: *The Battle of Alcazar*, 106, 263n61
Percy, Lady, 90
Phebe, 137, 138, 147, 211
Philip the Fair, 109
Phillida, 132–33, 135
Pickering, Morris, 38
Piper, David, 193, 274n2
Pistol, 66, 69
Planché, James Robinson: *King John*, 14
Platter, Thomas, 43, 250n11
Playfair, Nigel: *As You Like It*, 17
Poel, William: *Coriolanus*, 16
Polonius, 111, 214
Portia, 56, 59, 90, 199, 244n30
Pory, John: *A Geographical History of Africa*, 108–9
post-play jigs, 93, 250n11
Potter, Sally: *Orlando*, 138
Princess's Theatre, 15
prisoner-of-war entertainments and cabaret, 185–203
Public Theater, 210; New York Shakespeare Festival, 207
Puck, 13, 19

Quickly, Mistress, 63, 65, 68
Quince, Peter, 15

Rabb, Ellis: *The Merchant of Venice*, 220
Rabb, Lily, 215
Radio City Music Hall, 146
Rag Bag Revue: *Hamlet Goes Hollywood*, 191
Ralegh, Walter, 107, 113, 115, 119

Rathbone, Basil: *Romeo and Juliet*, 176, 271n61
Raymond's Revuebar, 196, 197
Redgrave, Vanessa: *As You Like It*, 148–49
Regan, 39, 40, 233n45
Rehan, Ada: *As You Like It*, 144; *Henry IV*, 141; *Twelfth Night*, 141; *The Two Gentlemen of Verona*, 141
Reinhardt, Max, 227n2; *The Miracle*, 177
Rich, Barnabe, 93
Richard II, 33, 45
Richard III, 14, 36
Richard III, 18
Richards, Judith, 38–39
Richardson, Catherine, 5–6, 63–84, 228; *Shakespeare and Material Culture*, 4
Robin Hood, 48–50, 55, 57, 59, 239n7, 243n22
Romeo, 97, 157–84, 200, 270n49, 271n61
Romeo and Juliet, 7, 97, 157–84, 200, 267n3, 273n82, 273n85. *See also Romeo and Juliet*'s Nurse
Romeo and Juliet's Nurse, 7, 97, 116, 157–84, 267n3, 268n9, 270n50, 273n82; Gielgud and Motley 1932 and 1935, 170–75; MGM, Hollywood, Oliver Messel and Adrian 1936, 175–81; Paul Shelving and the Birmingham Repertory Company 1922 and 1924, 165–70; Shelving, Motley and Messel, 181–84.

Rosalind 113, 136, 137, 138, 139, 140, 141, 142, 143–45, 147, 148, 150, 151, 156, 215, 260n33; two all-male productions, 152–55. *See also* Bergner, Elisabeth; Redgrave, Vanessa; Rehan, Ada
Rose Theatre, 48, 85, 101, 102
Rosenthal, Margaret F.: *Habiti Antichi et Moderni, The Clothing of the Renaissance*, 4
Roth, Ann, 216
Rowlands, Samuel, 93
royal clothing at court and in the plays of Shakespeare, 1598–1613, 23–46; conspicuous consumption, 24–27; disguisings and disguise, 40–45; kingship and female rule, 37–40; magnificence, 27–30; symbols of power, 30–36
Royal Court Theatre, 18
Royal Shakespeare Company (RSC), 2, 19, 136, 146, 149, 150, 175, 220
Roydon, John, 81
RSC. *See* Royal Shakespeare Company
Rylance, Mark, 19

Sargent, John Singer, 16
sartorial signifiers, 53, 56, 244n26
Sateren, Terry: *Measure for Measure*, 217
Savoy Theatre, 16
Schlueter, Jane, 121, 263n59
Schuler, Duane, 217

Searle, Ronald, 276n19; *Cinderella*, 190, 194; *Hamlet Goes Hollywood*, 7, 186, 187–88, 191, 192–94, 203; *Man of Destiny*, 194; *Molesworth*, 187; *To the Kwai and Back*, 187, 188, 189, 190
Sebastian, 16
Second World War, 186, 187, 188, 198
Shaw, Fiona, 266n25; *As You Like It*, 150
Shaw, George Bernard, 141, 142, 158, 165, 175, 189, 274n7
Shaw, Glen Byam: *As You Like It*, 147
Shaw Theatre, 149
Shearer, Norma: *Marie Antoinette*, 272n70; *Romeo and Juliet*, 176, 177, 180
Shelving, Paul, 11; *Romeo and Juliet*, 157, 165–70, 172, 173, 181, 182, 183, 184
Shepherd, 230n19
Shepperton Studios, 12
shoes, 6, 85–103, 140, 254n54, 255n59, 255nn63–64, 275n12
Shylock, 5, 47, 52–55, 172, 199, 242n16
Siddons, Sarah, 160
Sidney, Basil: *Romeo and Juliet*, 164
Sidney, Sir Philip, 45, 135; *The Old Arcadia*, 133
Silvius, 138, 147
Sincler, John: *The Seven Deadly Sins, Part Two*, 240n10

Smith, Henry, 72
Smith, Ian: 'White Skin, Black Masks: Racial Cross-dressing on the Early Modern Stage', 263n56
Smith, Jane, 73–74
Smith, Lance, 73
Smithson, Harriet: *Romeo and Juliet*, 160, 268n9
Soule, Lesley Wade, 136
stage history of Shakespeare and costume: brief overview, 9–20
stage makeup, 243n23
Stallybrass, Peter: *Renaissance Clothing in the Materials of Memory*, 3–4, 49, 241n14
Staunton, Howard, 160
Stephen (king), 112, 120
St James's Theatre, 141
St John, Christopher, 164
stockings, 15, 30, 92, 95–96, 97, 101, 253n45, 253n46, 254n51
Stoeckel, Rudolph, 263n53
Stone, Elizabeth, 70, 71
Stow, John: *Annales*, 96, 253n46
Stoyle, Mark, 228
Strowde, Jane, 73
Strowde, Thomas, 73
Stubbes, Philip, 50, 59, 99, 111, 114–15, 118, 120, 127; *The Anatomie of Abuses*, 96–97, 241n11; *The Second Part of the Anatomie of Abuses*, 101–2
The Studio, 10
Styan, J.L., 17

sumptuary legislation, 27–28, 231n25

The Taming of the Shrew, 90, 216, 220
Tarlton, Richard, 93, 250n11
The Tempest, 13
Terry, Ellen: *Macbeth*, 16; *Romeo and Juliet*, 161–3, 164–65, 183
Thalberg, Irving: *Romeo and Juliet*, 177
Theatre Guild, 145
Theatre Royal, 18, 159
Thomas, John, 73
Thomson, Leslie: *Dictionary of Stage Directions in English Drama, 1580–1642*, 88, 249n8, 250n14
Thomson, Peter, 93–94
Thornton, Isabel: *Romeo and Juliet*, 167, 168, 170, 182–83
Tiramani, Jenny, 3, 19, 210
Titus Andronicus, 12, 33, 106, 108, 120, 121, 186, 238n95
Touchstone, 148, 211
Tower of London, 27, 38
Traub, Valerie, 136–37
Travers, Ben, 189, 274n7
Tree, Herbert Beerbohm, 202; *A Midsummer Night's Dream*, 17
Trewin, J.C., 148, 152
Troilus and Cressida, 12, 17, 224
Twelfth Night, 16, 97, 135, 141

The Two Gentlemen of Verona, 97, 134, 141
Twycross, Meg, 58

Vecellio, Cesare, 123, 261n34; *Habiti Antichi et Moderni, The Clothing of the Renaissance World*, 4, 109–10
Verheyen, Maryann, 222
Vicecomitis, Hieronimi, 109
Victoria & Albert Museum, 7, 186
Vincent, Susan: *Dressing the Elite*, 4, 116, 262n44
Viola, 16, 20, 136
Virgilia, 16

Walken, Christopher: *Othello*, 210
Wardle, Irving, 151, 153
Warren, Roger, 150
Waugh, Norah: *Corsets and Crinolines*, 208; *The Cut of Men's Clothes*, 208; *The Cut of Women's Clothes*, 208
Webster: *Westward Ho*, 99
Widdoes, Kathleen: *Rehearsing Hamlet*, 2
Wilde, Oscar, 16, 140, 141, 265n13, 274n7
Williams, Clifford: *As You Like It*, 152, 153
Williams, Gary Jay: *Our Moonlight Revels*, 228n21
Williams, John, 117–18
Wilson, Bronwen, 128

Windmill Theatre, 197, 202; *Revuedeville*, 195
Winter, Frank: *Aladdin*, 208
The Winter's Tale, 16, 17, 217, 223, 230n19
Withington, Phil, 83, 247n32
Woodward, Margaret, 208
Wotton, Sir Henry, 43

Woolf, Virginia: *Orlando*, 131, 138, 145

Zeffirelli, Franco: *Romeo and Juliet*, 182
Ziegfield Follies, 202
Zinkeisen, Doris: *Designing for the Stage*, 10, 19